# Transference and Countertransference in Non-Analytic Therapy

*Double-Edged Swords*

Judith A. Schaeffer

University Press of America,® Inc.
Lanham · Boulder · New York · Toronto · Plymouth, UK

4501 Forbes Boulevard
Suite 200
Lanham, Maryland 20706
UPA Acquisitions Department (301) 459-3366

Estover Road
Plymouth PL6 7PY
United Kingdom


Printed in the United States of America
British Library Cataloging in Publication Information Available

Library of Congress Control Number: 2006933350
ISBN-13: 978-0-7618-3631-5 (paperback : alk. paper)
ISBN-10: 0-7618-3631-4 (paperback : alk. paper)

**Dedicated to my sister**

*Helen Giometti*

**whose support of me as an author
never wavered**

# CONTENTS

# FOREWORD

Hidden in plain sight in many of the failed or conflicted psychotherapy or counseling sessions of our time is the powerful reality of the transference/countertransference dynamic. These feelings are a living part of ourselves and yet, in the modern rush to democratize therapy and to make it more cost-efficient, they have been ignored or managed in ways that do not recognize the influence that, acknowledged or not, they have on the course of treatment and, indeed, on the nature and destiny of every human relationship.

Dynamic psychotherapy is treatment that understands that our human experience is not dead cargo lashed securely in the hold of memory or tossed long ago over the rail into the wake of our storm tossed passage through life. Our emotional experience is, as we might say, alive within us and influencing us, whether we are aware of it or not, at every moment of our existence and in every one of our relationships not only with other persons but with institutions and places through which we journey and with the flags and symbols strung along the route of our existence.

If Diogenes carried a lamp in search of honesty, Sigmund Freud bore a glittering torch into the deepest caverns of personality in search of the truth. These passages have been sealed up in recent generations for classic American reasons. Americans want things fast, simple, cheap, and readily available to everybody. If a summary of *War and Peace* is enough to pass the test why bother making the arduous, involving, and time-consuming journey through the invisible but powerful outpouring of Tolstoy's imagination? People don't want to examine the reasoning or the calculation when the *Bottom Line* will do. They do not want to make the long day's journey into night when someone can tell them how everything came out *At the End of the Day.*

True professionals are the trained individuals whose schooling and licensing are evidence of their competence and a support when they "profess" to know more than others about a specific subject, such as brain surgery or rocket science. The latter are now reduced to the status of ironic exemption in the average person's claim to take on any prospective challenge. That is why so many obituaries about the totally unskilled but supremely confident include the information that the deceased "had never climbed a mountain before" or "had never sailed alone before," sad testimony, such notices, to the national assumption that everything is within reach in a democracy and that experts, or people who know something about a subject, are overrated and merely want to keep control of their field for themselves.

No field was more ripe in 20th century America for this amateur's harvest than that of counseling and psychotherapy. At mid-century the work of psychologist Carl Rogers (*Client-Centered Therapy)* had made the patient the source of all relevant knowledge and the processor of all solutions in counseling. Rogers was a popular teacher and a dynamic presence who slowly dismantled all professional criteria from the therapist, advocating, for example, that psychologists not even apply for the professional licenses for which their training qualified them.

When I visited him at the Center for the Studies of the Person in LaJolla, California, in 1973, there was, on principle, nobody in charge and a revolving reception chore fell that day to an individual described as a "Beach Person." They had celebrated the night before, Rogers explained to me, because a young man had completed his doctoral dissertation and decided *not* to submit it to his university as a requirement for his doctorate.

Rogers was a major influence in diminishing the role of the therapist and in obscuring the whole concept of transference. He told counselors that they should treat transference feelings, that is, unconscious attitudes toward other influential figures that are directed toward the therapist, as they would any other feeling. The appropriate response according to Rogers was to reflect the feeling back to the person without judgment or interpretation.

Rogers was only the most prominent of anti-professional psychologists who operationally dismissed the significance and the impact of transference feelings, in which the patient projects attitudes toward a father, for example, onto the therapist, and of countertransference feelings, the unconscious response, really appropriate for figures in the early life of the therapist, back toward the patient.

As an appreciation of any dynamic theory of personality or of psychotherapy shriveled under the impact of anti-professional advocates such as Rogers, government reimbursement for mental health treatment also shrank and a premium was placed on short term therapies that avoided any exploration of the unconscious dynamics of the person seeking help. The use of medication to treat emotional problems became so extensive that America was termed, in a book on the phenomenon, *Prozac Nation.* Training programs in psychodynamic theory and technique were victims of budget cutting and a search for more cost-effective treatment programs led to the neglect of the unconscious as a determining factor in life and in psychotherapy.

Although therapists may not have been trained to recognize or manage it, transference/countertransference feelings remained present and influential beneath the straight line radar of modernized therapy. Acknowledge it or not, patients still displaced feelings from figures from their past onto therapists in their present. And, whether aware of it or not, counselors still responded to patients with feelings whose real objects were figures in their own formative years of development.

This has led to many stalled or becalmed treatments as well as to situations in which dangerous situations arise because therapists, treating transference as if it were any other feeling, do not recognize its special powerful significance and the need to manage it skillfully if the therapy is to succeed. This inability to discern the ongoing role of transference and countertransference can lead to tangled and painful emotional involvements that negate the value of therapy and can seriously harm both parties in the relationship.

Dr. Schaeffer arrives at a critical moment with a lucid and inclusive treatment of these subjects that can only benefit both therapists and patients as they work through the issues of psychotherapy. This is a calm, professional examination of these dynamic realities that enables persons unacquainted with them to learn about their nature and management in the non-threatening and freeing atmosphere that is created by all good teachers. Those who already understand transference and countertransference will find reading this book like a wonderfully refreshing sabbatical from the intense demands of psychotherapy. Those aspiring to be professional counselors and therapists will find this an invaluable guide for their present study and for the journeys they have yet to make in helping other people.

While I have stressed how professional therapists will profit from this book, I cannot omit the ranks of general physicians, lawyers, teachers, and even business managers who would be enriched by reading this volume. I envy those about to read it for the first time. It will not be the last time that you take it down from your shelf to learn from the light that Dr. Schaeffer raises, as truly as Diogenes and Freud, to illuminate our search for honesty and truth about ourselves.

Eugene C. Kennedy, Ph.D.
Emeritus Professor of Psychology
Loyola University of Chicago

Chicago, Illinois
June, 2006

# PREFACE

Writing this book has been for me, a non-analytic clinician, both arduous and fulfilling. The subjects of transference and countertransference were hardly mentioned in my cognitive-behavioral doctoral program, yet they loomed large once I began to practice. For example, once, during the middle of the night, a client screamed at me on the phone, "It's the worst thing in the world when you can't talk to your mother when you need to!"

I turned to the literature, both psychoanalytic and psychodynamic, to get a handle on the phenomenon I was witnessing. Some concepts and processes I understood; some, I thought I understood but could not clearly explain to colleagues; some , I simply had to put in the category of "Yes, this is it, but what on earth is it!"

Hence I educated myself as I hope this book educates its readers. I read at least 350 psychoanalytic and psychodynamic books and articles. I compared the ideas they put forth, sifted the "wheat" from the "chaff," and held on to what was relatively concrete and what I could put in non-analytic language.

As a result, I believe this book is as devoid of psychoanalytic and psychodynamic terminology as possible while the magnificent ideas of Freud, Jung, Gill, Bollas, Gabbard, Meissner, Casement, and many others inform the explanations, conclusions, and concrete examples I offer. For there is no question that *all* therapists and clients transfer functions and roles they or others played in the past to each other. There is no question that *non-analytic* therapists must identify transference and countertransference as soon as possible. There is no question that they must diagnosis them accurately and give serious consideration to interpreting them to appropriate clients so that, rather than be controlled by them, they can control them and benefit from the major contribution they can make to variables responsible for positive outcome.

Otherwise, the double-edged swords of transference and countertransference will cut their way through what is working and enable variables responsible for negative outcome to gain a stronghold.

In trying to share the fruits of my learning with other non-analytic clinicians and students, I endeavored to find examples in my practice and those of my colleagues of both our failure to deal effectively with transference and countertransference and our success in this effort. I wished to help non-analytic clinicians and students make the greatest use possible of these powerful unconscious forces. I still wish to inspire them to contribute to the impressive but limited research already in print related to displaced material in non-analytic therapy.

In writing this book, my first concern was to make its message clear and relatively simple yet be true to the psychoanalytic and psychodynamic tradition, especially to generally accepted definitions of the highly abstract constructs of transference and countertransference. Not everyone will agree with all my explanations or conclusions, but I believe that the majority of theorists will agree that I have not strayed far from the main path of psychoanalytic and psychodynamic theory. At the same time, they will appreciate how I honor the educational and clinical background most of my readers and the language they need to use to unpack what happens in therapy.

Judith A. Schaeffer

Colorado Springs, Colorado
June, 2006

# ACKNOWLEDGMENTS

Many individuals have contributed to the writing of this book although I am the sole author. First and foremost are the psychoanalytic and psychodynamic theorists and clinicians whose ideas have made my thinking possible and the clients who have provided me with enlightening clinical experience.

Then there are those who read my drafts and made suggestions regarding their revision: Eugene Kennedy, Carol Schroeder, Charles Knoeckel, Erika Kaiser, Lisa Meeks, and Sharon Stewart. In addition, there are those who proofread and assisted me with formatting: Sister Ethel Widhalm, Sister Carlene Yonkers, and Sister Agnes Marie Regan. I am deeply indebted to each of them. I am also most grateful to the family members who stood by me with hope and encouragement as I labored: my sisters Mary Schaeffer Conroy and Helen Giometti; my brother Anthony J. Schaeffer: my brothers-in-law Tom Conroy and Dave Giometti; my sister-in-law Kathy Schaeffer; all my nieces and nephews but especially Michael Giometti, Liz Giometti, and Anne Schaeffer Durlinger, Alongside these family members are friends who showed keen interest, supported me with their prayers, and asked how I was doing month after month: Sister Martha Ann Reich, Kotik Lee, and Marge Leek.

I am also indebted to my sisters, the Sisters of St. Francis of Perpetual Adoration (Colorado Springs), for their interest, moral support, and prayers. Because there are too may to name individually, I thank them as a group.

To conclude, I owe my gratitude to my editors at University Press of America.

# INTRODUCTION

This is a book about *transference* and *countertransference,* double-edged swords whereby we transfer past conflicts to present interactions. It is about their often overlooked potential to make significant contributions to the outcome of non-analytic therapy. Especially in its focus on collaboration between therapists and clients to interpret transferred phenomena, this book makes practical application of clinically supported theory and noteworthy research.

Residing deep within the unconscious mind where there is no time (Freud, 1917), transference and countertransference become activated in the presence of similar situational clues. Already encoded in well-trodden subcortical neural pathways, material from the unconscious mind is propelled into the conscious efforts we make to deal with psychological pain. With the "help" of biochemical changes in the brain, we unconsciously re-stage conflict as if the past were the present. We displace thoughts and feelings about people in our past to those who resemble them in the present, assign them roles once played by others, take on old roles ourselves, and assume that by this re-staging, conflict will be resolved. While acting like children, for example, we assign the role of parent to spouse and therapist and then sit back to watch them perform better than their predecessors. In the end, however, they fail to do so, and we cannot replace our pain with a sense of well-being.

Unfortunately, time and time again we manage to forget what psychoanalytic theorists have told us for almost a century: in order to resolve conflict, we must face it squarely, experience and process the pain that it carries, and learn ways of ensuring that it does not happen again. By *not* identifying and reckoning with the forces that perpetuate our compulsion simply to repeat the past, namely transference and countertransference, we only make matters worse.

Hence, this book:

- a resource for non-analytic professionals whose work is being impacted by transferred material even though their primary intent is to correct thinking and support new behavior rather than process unconscious material;

- a text that exposes the dangers of presuming that old schemas fit new experiences simply because of similarities;
- a manual for practicing clinicians who might otherwise unwittingly allow displaced material to run rampant during the course of therapy, especially with clients of another culture, and consequently provide ineffective treatment or even get themselves in trouble;
- a guide for academicians and students to explore the tremendous benefit of identifying conflict, understanding its dynamics, embracing the pain inherent in it, mourning what should never have happened, and moving on.

# Overview of This Book

PART I begins with descriptions of transference and countertransference, psychoanalytic explanations for their existence, and definitions used in this book (Chapters One and Two). It then provides representative data from recent neuroscientific and cognitive research pertaining to brain mechanisms and biochemical changes that account for transferential and countertransferential processes. It also explains these processes from an information processing perspective (Chapter Three).

PART II examines how and why transference and countertransference are ubiquitous though subject to the values, beliefs, and behavioral patterns of distinctive cultures (Chapter Four). It describes forms in which transference and countertransference are most likely to manifest themselves as they interface with various cultures (Chapter Five).

Part III begins with an examination of three approaches to diagnosing transference and countertransference and weighs empirical evidence that supports diagnostic efforts (Chapter Six). It then presents a fourth approach: interpreting transference and countertransference to clients as a means of inviting their collaboration in managing them (Chapter Seven).

PART IV describes the attitude with which non-analytic clinicians should approach their interpretive work and presents specific guidelines for wording transference and countertransference interpretations (Chapter Eight). It then breaks complex tasks of diagnosing and interpreting transference and countertransference into manageable subtasks (Chapter Nine) and answers key questions regarding appropriate clients, frequency, and timing of interpretations (Chapter Ten). Finally, it explores how interpreting transference and countertransference to clients can help therapists perform their therapeutic roles during the three major phases of therapy (Chapter Eleven).

PART V describes transference love and countertransference love as they are likely to arise in therapy. It outlines ways of dealing with these potentially dangerous or beneficial aspects of being human and interacting in the intimate setting of therapy (Chapter Twelve).

# Contemporary Environments and Neuroscientific Advances

This book was written for four reasons that reflect today's academic and clinical environments and recent cognitive and neuroscientific research. First, as a general rule contemporary non-analytic graduate programs do not adequately treat the subject of transference and countertransference, leaving students and graduates unprepared for their activity in actual clinical work. Thus many non-analytic clinicians lack the art and skill of identifying and managing the transferential and countertransferential forces responsible for clients' and their own re-enactment of personal and interpersonal conflict. Even when they suspect transference and countertransference, they cannot diagnose them expeditiously or incorporate them into processes that bring clinical work to a successful conclusion. Even when transference and countertransference become noticeably problematic, they fail to seek supervision or consult colleagues. As a consequence, burdened with the weight of the past, clients end their therapy only to return with new issues, for once again they have unconsciously re-staged what has never worked. Furthermore, therapists who fail to change their own unwholesome, past-dependent relational patterns are minimally productive and unnecessarily stressful at best. At worst, they make serious mistakes.

Second, managed care has had a significant impact on the work of 2 century therapists. They no longer have the option of open-ended treatment even for dealing with serious problems. Regardless of their theoretical orientation they must achieve a positive outcome more quickly than earlier clinicians. They must manage transferred phenomena as soon as they arise in order that clients finish their work within their allotted sessions.

Due to a related restriction imposed by managed care, therapists can no longer define a positive outcome as clients acquiring insight and rebuilding their ego. Rather, they must translate outcomes into observable, measurable correlates and thereby demonstrate to insurance companies that clients have attained perceptible goals, such as acquiring new behaviors and reducing, if not eliminating, symptoms. Practitioners must also define whatever they do by functions that measure change. As a consequence, they must be aware of *all* variables that determine—or contribute to determining—whether clients make desired changes. They must be well versed in how transference and countertransference affect insight and impact the therapeutic alliance and goal attainment. They must detect and decode transferred material and manage it in decisive, though sensitive and respectful, ways.

Third, clients and their families, who as consumers expect timely, ethical, and efficacious treatment, belong to a litigious society eager to right wrongs. Though serious mistakes may be rare, unaddressed transferential and countertransferential material can cause professionals to make errors which clients or their relatives will then bring to the attention of Grievance Boards or lawyers. Should therapists give sexual expression to countertransferential love, for example, clients will hold them responsible for boundary violations. Should clients complete suicide, their families will presume that professionals who treated them deliberately chose not to address transferential signs of that possibility. Even if therapists successfully defend themselves before judges and juries, their reputations can be seriously damaged; their financial situation, greatly worsened; and their morale, dramatically lowered.

Fourth, recent cognitive and neuroscientific research findings have made it more and more compelling to recognize and manage phenomena previous thought to be "merely" psychoanalytic theory. It has become increasingly unwise to overlook phenomena actually instantiated in the brain.

## Clients' Unrealistic Attitudes

As if these four reasons were not enough, rare is the client that does not hold unrealistic, though rarely articulated, attitudes that have been formed by past conflictual experiences resultant from insufficiently, overly, or inappropriately met developmental needs.

- The first attitude is that therapy is a kind of magic. Unconsciously reenacting an early developmental stage in which others promptly attended to their needs, clients believe that their therapist will listen intently as they reveal their problems. Then their highly educated and experienced therapist will give advice, and they will feel better about their situation because they intend—on a conscious level—to follow that advice.
- The second attitude is that one's problems lie in the attitudes and behavior of others rather than oneself. Clients unconsciously relive a developmental stage in which they were "the center of the universe" and others were meant to "revolve" around them. They believe that they will figure out—with the help of their therapist—how to make *others* act differently. They themselves will have to make only minor adjustments.
- The third attitude is that therapeutic progress should be made sooner rather than later and, preferably, with limited effort as was physical and sexual development during adolescence. In addition, as consumers in a fast-paced, highly mechanized first world society, clients are primed to get what they need—or just want—quickly as well as effortlessly. No matter how chronic or serious their problems, they will to find workable solutions within a short time. If not, they will have grounds for being dissatisfied.

## Enduring Realities

As a consequence of these unrealistic attitudes, realistic 21st century therapists work quickly and diligently to help their clients accept three age-old, transference-and-countertransference-based realities relevant to successful therapeutic work.

- First, effective therapy is primarily interactive (Little, 1951) and relational. It is not a set of monologues during which clients present problems and therapists listen and find solutions. Rather, it is a highly complex and dynamic "drama" during the course of which clients and therapists not only weave verbal and non-verbal messages but also ask each other to play various roles on the "stage" of their collaborative, and in time conflictual, encounter. Therapy is none other than a relationship between two persons with personal and interpersonal histories whose experiences of feelings, expressions of feelings, and use of feelings in the clinical setting become interdependent (Heimann, 1950) as they work toward achieving mutually acceptable goals. Though therapy may have its magic-like aspects, it is by no means magic.
- Second, though most problems are personal on one level, they are interpersonal on another and therefore require solutions that are effective on both levels. Clients must address what they themselves do, *and most likely have done repeatedly in the past,* even as they define the contributions of others.
- Third, even relatively minor change is neither quick nor effortless. It requires painful honesty, steadfast attention, critical insight, sustained energy, and repeated practice. It demands the hard personal work without which new relational habits cannot replace old ones, and the future simply repeats a failed past.

Thus in order to empower their clients with appropriate motivation, insight, and skills, realistic non-analytic therapists become experts in dealing with transference, countertransference, and the interpersonal processes that mediate them.

# Double-edged Swords

It cannot be emphasized enough that transference and countertransference propel conflictual unconscious material into the dynamics of *both* analytic and non-analytic therapy. If existential, cognitive-behavioral, or any other non-analytically oriented therapists fail to notice these displaced phenomena at work in their sessions, they are limited in their ability to help their clients move beyond their one-sided accounts of problematic relationships and events outside of therapy. If, however, these therapists identify and decode displaced material that manifests itself during their sessions, their perception of what is going on relationally in therapy can complement and correct clients' accounts. Then, as therapists sensitively share their insight and invite corroboration or correction, clients can begin to realize that what is in fact transpiring in therapy is very similar, if not identical, to the unresolved conflicts at the core of their presenting problems. With this balanced, integrated insight, they can resolve their conflicts. They can heal themselves from within and so change their relationships with others that they transform their lives.

Simultaneously, therapists can realize how, through countertransference, they are also acting out old, conflictual interpersonal issues in their work with clients. Then they, too, can choose resolution over mindless repetition.

Even a cursory history of this century and the last reveals transference and countertransference as double-edged swords operating outside therapy no less than in it. We post-modern citizens staunchly support a Peace Corps and rush to rebuild our enemies' nations in large part because we unconsciously recall the calm before and after our two horrific world wars. At the same time, we unknowingly carry countless unresolved conflicts and the grievances they spawn from the past into the present as we engage in profiling, rape, child abuse, hate crimes, human trafficking, wars of ethnic cleansing, and even wars of liberation. We may even unconsciously re-elect to office those who responded decisively to crises years before or unintentionally minimize clergy sexual abuse and its cover-up because we transfer to those involved in them an aura of divinity and macho fatherhood.

In sum, as individuals, families, nations, and members of various ethnic, religious, and socio-economic groups, we have not adequately dealt with layer upon layer of individual and collective memory that unconsciously motivates us to re-stage the atrocities that were done to us or we did to others. As Brenner (1976) notes, transference and countertransference are ubiquitous. They should be the subject of many books intended for the population at large.

This book, by contrast, is written for non-analytical students and professionals in mental health fields who have not sufficiently studied the unconscious dynamics and power of transference and countertransference. It focuses on displaced phenomena that can and do undermine their otherwise excellent collaborative work with clients and thus the critical need for both therapist and client to identify and manage these two-edged swords even as they arise. It heads the prophetic words of Marmor (1989):

"The future of psychotherapy . . . lies with the further development of short-term therapeutic techniques" (Marmor, 1989, 259). Without them, regardless of orientation, therapists cannot withstand the pressures of health care reform to reduce therapeutic time. Without them, therapists cannot deal "economically and effectively with the deluge of emotional and behavioral problems" our disturbed society has spawned (259)

## Language, Cultural Diversity, and Context

In this book, pains are taken to change jargon into commonly used terms so that readers not versed in psychoanalytic "language" can read with comparative ease. Moreover, though the impact that cultural diversity has on transference and countertransference is short-changed because of space limitations, efforts are made to identify at least some of the unique cultural-based expectancies therapists and clients unconsciously bring to their interactions. Finally, though efforts are made to place constructs in the context of their original theories, no attempt is made to use those theories in their entirety. Rather, select aspects of analytic theories are placed within the context of non-analytic theories without sacrificing the essence of either, again so that readers can more easily interweave new material with the professional knowledge they already possess.

# PART I

## PSYCHOANALYTIC AND SCIENTIFIC BASES OF TRANSFERENCE AND COUNTERTRANSFERENCE

# CHAPTER ONE

# THE PHENOMENON CALLED TRANSFERENCE

## Introduction

We all engage in transference. It is a pervasive and ubiquitous phenomenon that takes place in many situations in life (Brenner, 1982). We reexperience the past in the present in a way that is inappropriate for the present (Greenson, 1969). We misperceive or misinterpret the present in terms of the past. We project or unconsciously send "messages" to select persons in our present life that they have become indistinguishable from significant others in our past. We unknowingly impose what has taken place in one setting on what is taking place in another, usually because the first event involved unresolved conflict. We unconsciously displace what still warrants our attention, usually because it bothers us.

This book focuses on just one of countless situations in life in which transference occurs naturally: psychotherapy. In fact, empirical data support the theory that psychoanalytic and non-psychoanalytic therapists alike deal with transference in their efforts to achieve positive therapeutic outcomes (Gelso & Hayes, 1998). Moreover, within psychotherapy, transference is usually concentrated; it is gathered, pronounced, and intense (Wilson & Weinstein, 1996).

Yet it is difficult to define *transference* in even this restricted setting because, since Freud first used the term in 1907, it has been used inconsistently and ambiguously. There has been no real agreement on its meaning, which has made it difficult, especially for non-psychoanalytic practitioners, to understand transference literature and apply empirical findings to clinical practice. The intent of this chapter is to explore key aspects of transference that have been described in representative literature and to create a definition which distills the essence of the phenomenon while not losing sight of its complexity. This chapter explores both classical and totalistic definitions of transference in the context of the clinical setting before presenting an operational definition for use in the rest of the book.

## Transference: Classical Definition

Freud's description of transference serves as a prototypic classical definition. *Transference is clients' unconscious displacement of feelings, attitudes, sensations, and thoughts about or toward persons in the clients' early life to their therapist, usually because of unresolved conflicts related to those early persons* (Freud, 1912). Clients' unconscious displacement of phenomena that have been repressed or buried in the unconscious mind serves the purpose of giving clients "new editions of old conflicts" (Freud, 1917, 454). Put in a neuroscientific context, transference is the reappearance, in the therapeutic setting and in the unconscious mind of the client, of an early-life event from which the client had to dissociate because of its overwhelming emotional impact (Schore, 2003a). Transference is an unconscious movement of conflictual desire and/or belief across space and time from one person in the past to another in the present (Lear, 1993).

Transference involves a resistance to facing psychic pain long enough and well enough to resolve the conflict causing the pain (Freud, 1917). Though the conscious mind knows that past conflicts need to be resolved, the unconscious mind uses transference as a means of avoiding conflict resolution. By simply repeating in their unconscious mind events that occurred when they were young, clients do not work within their conscious mind to resolve the conflictual elements of the events. For example, they do not reconcile their wish for an unconditionally accepting mother with their mother's frequent criticism of them. They do not give up their wish for this kind of a mother and accept the fact that with her limitations their mother did not fulfill their wish. They do not make plans to fulfill that wish themselves as best they can and/or reduce the scope of the wish so that others can begin to fulfill it.

Transference can also be thought of as a construct: clients' displaced, early-life, unresolved conflictual feelings and attitudes that surface in response to experiencing their therapist. Transference is a matter of displaced memories of affective and somatic states related to early-life significant others. It is a matter of memories recalled by clients in therapy in such a way that they are indistinguishable from actually occurring events. "Transference is...the manifestation of unconscious...memory as it intrudes upon the larger consciousness of self, breaking it up, stunting it, and even at times, taking it over entirely" (Meares et al., 2005, 290). More often than not, due to its conflictual elements, transference is accompanied by negative emotions and/or distressful physical symptoms.

## Transference as Involving Projection and Introjection

Transference, which is the displacement of the past to the present, involves the projection of some aspects of a figure in the client's past onto the therapist. For example, as clients displace their fear of their critical mother to their therapist, they attribute to their therapist their mother's habit of criticizing them. "You are like my mother," the client unconsciously senses, "and, like my mother, you will criticize what I do."

As clients engage in projection, therapists engage in introjection. They unconsciously receive what clients send. "You perceive me as your critical mother and believe I will criticize you," the therapist, as recipient of the previous projection, comes to sense on an unconscious level.

However, it is important to note that therapists engaging in introjection receive projections without identifying with them or owning them and the feelings connected with them (Stamm, 1995). They "accept" projections without necessarily confirming the perceptions inherent in them (Schafer, 1968). Rather, confirmation of a projection depends primarily on the therapists' countertransference: their own unresolved conflicts (Westen & Gabbard, 2002). Confirmation depends on "the extent to which the [client's] projection meshes with aspects of the therapist's unresolved. . .conflicts. . ." (Meissner, 1996, 43). For example, some therapists have not resolved their own conflict over mothers being critical of their children in spite of the fact that they should accept them unconditionally. Their own mothers were routinely critical and, as a consequence, they hold templates of mothers as critical. It is likely that they will confirm their clients' projection of them as critical. They will engage in some form of fault-finding, noting, for example, that their client is a little late. On the other hand, therapists who have resolved their own conflict over mothers being critical will not likely confirm a projection of them as critical. They will not find fault with the client who sends them this particular projection. (1)

Interestingly, clients who project do not recognize what they project as their own. It feels foreign to them. Something that they dislike seems to be coming at them, but it is not theirs. They therefore sit back and criticize their therapist for what appears to be his or her negative trait or habit, oblivious to the fact that they are actually finding fault with themselves.

## Transference as Unconscious

Freud (1912) insisted that transference be regarded as fundamentally unconscious. Though clients may become aware of something calling forth their transference, they are not conscious of the relationship between that present stimulus and a past phenomenon. The transference of feelings about one's mother to a therapist, for example, seems simply a circumstance or an occurrence: something that just is.

Transference functions as a subtle, unconscious "meta-language" that carries meaning from client to therapist. Explained neuroscientifically, the right hemisphere of the client communicates emotional states in nonverbal ways to the right hemisphere of the therapist (Schore, 2003a). (2) Therapists receive the message on some instinctual, subliminal level that they have become their clients' mother figure and that their clients feel toward them the same way they felt toward their biological mother. When later asked, astute therapists might recall a gesture or posture of clients that probably served as a stimulus for their awareness, but at the time they were not conscious of anything. Their clients simply and mysteriously sent a message that they as therapists simply and mysteriously received.

Because transference is unconscious, it is no more accessible to clients than other unconscious processes. While they may become distressed by bodily sensations, fantasies, dreams, and other manifestations of transference, clients cannot ordinarily connect their distress with transferred material. As a consequence, they either move on to an issue of which they are conscious or attribute their distress merely to a non-displaced, purely here-and-now phenomenon. Clients who transfer to therapists their desire to be mothered by their biological mother, for example, might experience warm and tender sensations or unwittingly assume postures indicative of being held or make cradling gestures as they project a maternal role onto their therapist. But, if they try to find an explanation, they will simply attribute what is going on to their therapist's maternal ways. They will not be able to consciously access the material they have displaced.

## Transference as Fantasizing

Seen in a slightly different light, clients do not subject transference to reality testing, a process undertaken by the conscious mind to distinguish facts from fantasy. If the client's conscious mind does anything, it disregards the transference as an illusion unworthy of further attention.

Thus transference can be categorized as a form of unconscious fantasizing that requires conscious reality testing, a function of the left hemisphere (also called the left brain), to be held in abeyance (Herron & Rouslin, 1982). Right brain to right brain communication at the heart of transference by and large excludes activities of the left brain. The transference process involves erroneous perception and extremely simplified cognition that work together to distort reality. One or two similarities are recognized while many dissimilarities are dismissed. In particular, clients fantasize that their therapist is another person with whom they had a conflictual relationship, and they do not take time to evaluate whether that fantasy matches reality or is simply a figment of their imagination. (3)

Indeed, according to its classical definition, transference is merely a repetition of wishes, feelings, fantasies, attitudes, and bodily sensations initially experienced toward early-childhood figures and now inappropriately and unconsciously displaced to the therapeutic setting. The client's transferential experience is something like this: "I want an accepting mother and I do not perceive you as one, therapist. I perceive you as no different from my biological mother. As a consequence, I feel the same negative feelings toward you that I felt toward her."

According to the classical transference, the fantasy that begins and sustains transference can be accounted for by similarities between the therapist and an early-life significant other. The client's here-and-now experience of the therapist and the client's there-and-then experience of another become temporarily identical (Nunberg, 1951). The past is reconstructed in the present as the client regresses to an early-life stage, notices subtle similarities between the therapist and the early-life figure, and allows those similarities to guide perception. Thus the therapist becomes a person with whom the client is still conflicted (Freud, 1940).

Indeed, the past predetermines the present in that clients cannot help but perceive their revived ideas, feelings, and sensations as simply present realities (Chodorow, 1996). Transference just happens when something in clients' experience of their therapist, usually of a visual and/or auditory nature, serves as a clue to a similar past experience recorded in the clients' memory. "My critical mother had red hair and piercing eyes," the client recalls on an unconscious level, "and so does my therapist. My therapist seems to be my critical mother." Thus "transference is its own motivation"; [it is] "a built-in pattern that impels [clients] to engage in a particular type of similarity-judging, memory-priming pattern of behavior" (Levin, 1997, 1141). It is driven by a compulsion that Freud (1912) termed a repetition compulsion.

It takes little for clients to make fantasy-supportive connections. Slight resemblances such as hair color, facial features, gestures, tone of voice, or similarity in names become "kernels of truth" (DeLaCour, 1985) that allow clients to re-experience the entire pattern of their relationship with another person who is still significant on an unconscious level. They even sense the setting and atmosphere in which an encounter with the original person actually occurred (Rioch, 1943).

## Transference as Positive and Negative

Originally Freud (1912) regarded transference as either positive in that its inherent conflict is overshadowed by pleasant feelings, including and especially hope, or negative in that it is inundated by disturbing or painful feelings. In the case of positive transference, Freud (1912) wrote, clients displace the needs that a past figure did not meet to their therapist and hope that the therapist will meet those needs. A healthy part of the client hopes to create an outcome different from past experience. A healthy part of the client wants the present to be better than the past.

In the case of negative transference, while projecting their negative feelings toward a past figure onto their therapist, clients sustain their fear that their therapist will behave like the past figure. An unhealthy part of the client has a desire to repeat what is known, even if it is harmful, because it is familiar and safe Stark, 1994). It is invested in keeping things as they were. Freud (1912) advised therapists to simply ignore positive transference or regard it as an asset because it had the potential to help form the therapeutic alliance. In contrast, therapists were to interpret negative transference because it was a liability that, left alone, would weaken or destroy the therapeutic alliance.

In time, however, clinicians found that positive transference could easily become detrimental. It could encourage a "gentleman's agreement" (Wolstein, 1996, 507) to keep the therapeutic relationship non-confrontational and thus avoid difficult conflict resolution work. Hence, even Freudian theorists began to advocate interpreting positive transference if it seemed to interfere with the work that needed to be done. Similarly, they began to note that negative transference could become a positive experience if therapists were able to make their clients aware of their transference and embark upon the hard work of conflict resolution. (4)

## Transference as Conflictual

Though a paradigm shift within psychoanalysis has de-emphasized conflict in transferred material (Olds, 1994), the concept of conflict remains central to the classical definition. In simple terms, transferential conflict can be thought of as an incompatibility of conflicting desires "such that satisfaction of one such motive has a negative influence on another" (Westen, 1988, 172). Satisfaction of a sexual wish, for instance, can conflict with the moral values one has internalized.

Transferential conflict can also be thought of as a matter of a significant difference between what one needs or wishes and what one gets. A child who needs protection from a parent, for example, and instead is neglected will experience conflict. The child will find it difficult to reconcile his need to be protected with the neglect he experiences, thinking, "Should I not have needed protection? Or shouldn't I get the protection that I need?"

As will be explained in Chapter Three, conflict is to be expected even from a neuroscientific perspective because wishes, beliefs, values, and goals are likely to be processed by relatively independent neural circuits. In addition, each hemisphere of the brain forms independent self-representations or self-images, one stored in the left and one in the right, that are used again and again in new situations. Clients can wish for something that their right brain likes even as their left brain tells them it is illogical to have that wish. Similarly, clients can choose to endure what they experience as harmful. For example, to keep some kind of relationship with a parent, which would be in line with their right brain image of who they are in a family, clients can allow themselves to endure neglect at the hands of that parent, which would be a violation of their left brain image of themselves as rational and therefore unwilling to undergo harm.

Clients engaged in transference then attempt to resolve the ensuing conflict, not by dealing with the emotional pain inherent in it, but by repressing their memory of it or blocking it out of consciousness through dissociation. They hope to stop realizing that they have desired a relationship with a neglectful parent, for example, or have been neglected because they kept a relationship with parent. This repression or dissociation, of course, lays the groundwork for the phenomenon of transference to occur when new, similar circumstances remind clients of their old desires or experiences of not having their needs met. When their therapist has to cancel their appointment because of an avoidable emergency, for example, clients will recall the times they were neglected and feel neglected by the therapist.

## Transference: Totalistic Definition

The totalistic definition of transference, which is broader than its classical counterpart, was actually formulated early on as Freud's contemporaries disagreed about whether or not transference should be restricted to displacement of phenomena from the early past. Could it not also be based on clients' later experiences, they asked, even those occurring in the present outside the therapeutic setting? Could it not be interpersonal in addition to intrapsychic in that the therapist participated in, contributed to, or even instigated its formation? Indeed, if transference were to be a really useful construct during actual therapy, should it not include these experiences and interactions?

In addition, as early Freudians focused on parental figure links to patterns revealed in the transference, they found it more important to focus on clients' reactions to their therapists—as representing others in their present life—than to help clients discover the early-life origins of their problems. They also noticed that emphasizing the early-life sources of transferential patterns could strip clients of defenses they still needed for functioning (Bauer & Mills, 1989). They might not be able—at least at the present time—to face the fact that the parent who was more protective of them than the other parent actually failed to do so on a very significant occasion. They might need to defend themselves against that painful realization by engaging in a defense, called reaction formation, that allows them to keep, even embellish, positive aspects of their parent's image. However, they could deal with their disappointment in their current therapist. (5)

Hence, by the mid-1920's, Rank and Ferenczi (1925) theorized that focusing on displaced material that was impacting the therapist-client relationship—a here-and-now phenomenon—would eventually expose the conflicts the client still needed to resolve, whenever they originated. They seriously questioned whether positive therapeutic outcomes depended solely or even primarily on resolving the early childhood conflicts revealed in the transference. (6)

Thus for most theorists and therapists, including Freud, the concept of transference eventually acquired a more inclusive meaning that is now its totalistic definition. *Transference is the client's unconscious displacement of attitudes, feelings, sensations, and thoughts from another person in the client's life, past or present, to the therapist in an attempt to re-enact and resolve conflict; it presumes the therapist's unconscious participation in these efforts.*

The totalistic definition of transference becomes clearer when contrasted with the classical definition, point by point. (Shared elements of the two definitions will not be re-explored.)

## Transference as a Re-enactment

In the totalistic tradition, transference is a re-enactment rather than a repetition, as it is in the classical tradition. Motivated by a powerful desire for positive outcome, clients engaging in the reenactment unconsciously assign roles and functions, previously taken by others, to the therapist in the hope that these conflicts will finally be resolved. Transference is an "adventure from which [clients hope to] emerge changed and renewed," (Cooper (1987, 518).

Thus, in the totalistic tradition, transference is an unconscious activity in which both client and therapist engage. The client insists that the therapist be an active participant rather than a neutral screen. In fact, the client prods, provokes, and coerces; and as a result of this manipulation, the therapist unconsciously participates. The client, who unconsciously desires *"role-relationship"* with another, demands *"role-responsiveness"* of her therapist (Sandler (1976, 44). By engaging in transference, clients "actualize an internal scenario within the therapeutic relationship that results in the [therapist's] being drawn into playing a role scripted by the [client's internal world]" (Westen & Gabbard, 2002, 101).

The totalistic transference emphasizes the therapist's unconscious participation through a phenomenon called countertransference. The totalistic definition underscores an early observation of Freud himself: "It is a fundamental demand of all transference, underlying all the particular demands, that the [therapist]. . .should participate in a world endowed with particular meaning" (Freud, 1900, 747). As the client unconsciously attempts to re-animate problematic-interpersonal relationships, the therapist unconsciously cooperates. Client and therapist become enmeshed in a complex interaction, "a kind of psychic force field compounded out of intermingled transference and countertransference processes" (Meissner, 1996, 42). Countertransference is an integral part of a transference relationship in that every transference situation provokes a countertransference situation (Racker, 1968).

Freud (1912) alluded to clients' hope for conflict resolution through transferential reenactment when he wrote of the redemptive potential of transference. Transference is a self-taught attempt on the part of clients to heal themselves. It is motivated by clients' unconscious healing schemas that direct them to try to achieve psychological well-being by processing injurious, conflictual material. The privacy and intimacy of the clinical setting, the unconditional positive regard with which therapists hold clients, and clients' belief that their therapist will meet their needs all work together to provide a milieu in which clients' deepest longings to be loved, accepted, and treated well find expression. Through reenactment, clients unconsciously intend to bring flawed life dramas to wholesome finales. They fantasize that the present will redeem the past, for a benevolent person is replacing a malevolent one. The new version of an event will repair or heal the past (Wilson, 1993). (7)

However, as Freud (1912) clearly explained, clients cannot heal simply by engaging in transference. Transference in and of itself does not resolve mental conflicts, for healing depends on integration in contrast to unconscious re-enactment, let alone mere repetition. Healing is the fruit of clients' discovering non-integrated parts of themselves that had to be repressed, or dissociated from, at the time of original experiences, allowing those parts to develop, and then integrating them into what becomes a mature, functioning psyche (Rioch, 1943). (8) Healing is the result of transforming undeveloped and underdeveloped parts of the psyche into developed, functioning parts. In contrast, transference is simply a matter of clients' hoping that external, arranged, role-dependent interactions with their therapist will be positive enough to erase previous memories. Healing demands hard work. Transference is relatively effortless.

## Transference as Dynamic

According to the totalistic definition, transference is dynamic rather than static. It is produced by clients as they derive positive or negative meaning from their therapists' seemingly benevolent or even slightly malevolent verbal and non-verbal behaviors. Noticing such indicators of attitude as voice quality, degree of energy, level of professionalism, and person-to-person warmth, clients quickly project their feelings and attitudes toward pre- or extra-therapeutic persons onto their therapist. Moreover, they make their projections forceful and intense when they encounter a particular therapist who has relatively noticeable traits or capabilities that they associate with their relational conflicts.

Seen in a slightly different light, totalistic transference is dynamic in that it is an organizing activity in which clients unconsciously engage during therapy in response to a number of variables: early-life and later-life memories of others, current experiences with others, and the attitudes, words, and actual behaviors of therapists in the present (Stolorow, 1993). In engaging in transference, clients are imposing the organization of prior perception of experience upon the present and thereby trying to shape here-and-now psychic reality. (9) They are attempting to structure and organize experience in such a way that the past can come alive and be re-enacted in the present (Bachant & Adler, 1997). Said simply, the present experience will replace past memories, and thus clients can regulate their own feelings. Totalistic transference is not just clients' unconsciously reviving old pictures, thoughts, emotions, and sensations and perceiving them as present reality. It is not just, "You seem to be my parent." Rather, it is "You *are* my parent. I know so. I say so. Furthermore, you will love me as my parent did not and thus take away my pain. I will no longer be disappointed." Said simply, in the totalistic tradition, transference is an attempt on the part of clients to replace their memories of others' past behaviors and thereby regulate their own feelings. (10)

Furthermore, totalistic transference is dynamic in that it incorporates mental activities of therapists. First, they unconsciously behave in such a way that they offer clients an opportunity to re-enact past relationships. Therapists' own characteristics, interpersonal behavioral patterns, and traits make their transferential roles possible in the first place. Indeed, rather than simply and uncritically assuming the roles clients assign them, therapists unwittingly inspire the very roles their clients project. It is as if therapists assist clients in writing the scripts that define their roles.

Next, provided their countertransference is triggered—and it usually is—therapists unconsciously transform the roles their clients assign them in subtle, idiosyncratic ways. They shape a transference enactment by responding subjectively to the projections they receive. They give their clients "additional material" with which they can continue to enact their transference. Therapists who indicate that they even slightly disagree with something their clients say, for example, permit their clients to embellish their projection of a previous critical figure.

The original, classical definition already implied that therapists provided "kernels of truth" (DeLaCour, 1985) for clients. While consciously performing their roles, therapists also unconsciously contribute other, fragmentary, disguised variables that serve as reminders of persons in clients' conflictual past. Therapists momentarily use a harsh voice, for instance, and thus give clients the stimulus they needed to notice similarities between therapists and persons outside therapy who, by speaking harshly, verbally abused them.

The newer totalistic definition goes on to add that clients unconsciously send a message to therapists who have a certain potential that they have already activated that potential. Those who could be critical, for example, are being perceived as such. Therapists then unconsciously introject the message and, if their countertransference permits it, enact the role of a critical person. They might use a slightly disparaging tone of voice or use it to a greater degree than usual. (11) Thus the totalistic definition of transference emphasizes the powerful influence that therapists' personal, countertransference-based characteristics and behavior have on the content and shape of clients' transference (Cooper, 1987).

## Transference as Displacement of Any Interpersonal Experience in Life

Totalistic transference is displacement of any interpersonal experience in life, not just early-life experience. It adds the later past to the early past and the present to the past as sources of clients' conflicts (Strachey, 1934, 1969). The totalistic definition of transference adds what is going on interpersonally outside of sessions to what is transpiring in sessions and what has been going on intrapsychically in the client since infancy.

With Jungian theorists, the totalistic definition of transference has become so broad that it includes archetypal phenomena: universal and transpersonal material common to humanity throughout the ages and therefore able to serve as prototypic interpersonal templates. Universal archetypes, some of which will be more fully explored in Chapter Four, trigger transference, and transpersonal archetypal themes that form its content. Age-old, worldwide, collective, and transcultural material emerges as the client's own (Jung, 1966). The archetypes reveal their powerful relevance in generation after generation, culture after culture, and individual after individual (Dieckmann, 1976). Transference is both a new experience and an enactment of an old one. It is a here-and-now personal phenomenon based on a then-and-there universal memory. "I am an older sibling in competition with my therapist, my younger sibling," a client might fantasize, for instance, when being influenced by the Sibling Rivalry Archetype.

## Definition of Transference as Used in This Book

Because of the intended audience of this book, namely clinicians, students, professors, and supervisors, the definition of transference used in the rest of this book is an operationalized one based on key aspects of the totalistic definition. It is intended to give those not versed in psychoanalytic and psychodynamic theory a framework for understanding transference and its application to their work. It is meant to provide a concrete template to place on difficult-to-detect unconscious phenomena that occur during non-analytic as well as analytic therapy.

- During therapy, clients unconsciously and compulsively attempt to re-enact unresolved interpersonal conflicts originating in the past or outside of therapy.
- Clients unconsciously attend to similarities between their therapists and others with whom they have unresolved conflicts. They then let these similarities motivate them to displace past phenomena to the present therapeutic setting and to project qualities of past persons onto their therapists.
- Clients unconsciously organize their relationship with their therapist during sessions in such a way that, without consciously addressing past or present conflicts, they can reduce or eliminate their pain.
- Clients assign to their therapists roles originally played by significant others with whom clients are still conflicted in order to re-enact conflictual experiences and have them "turn out better."
- Concurrently, therapists introject or unconsciously take in their clients' projections: messages that they are like others and behave as they did or do.
- Clients also unconsciously permit their therapist to induce in them pre- and extra-therapeutic material that they can develop into transference phenomena.
- Clients unconsciously permit themselves to be influenced by universal

archetypes that suggest they play certain roles and assign corresponding roles to their therapist.

# Endnotes

(1) Some theorists, like Meissner (1996) hold that "projection…creates pressure in the interpersonal interaction to draw the other member of that interaction to fulfill the expectations and inherent demands of the projection." I prefer to make a distinction between projection and projective identification, wherein the latter—but not the former—creates the pressure. See Chapter Two for a more detailed explanation.

(2) See Chapter Three for a more thorough explanation derived from recent neuroscientific and cognitive research.

(3) For their part, therapists are to identify the conflictual wishes, urges, and fears originating in a very early time that energize clients to perceive something in the present. They are then to help clients subject these phenomena to reality testing (Freud, 1912).

(4) In addition, clinical experience led Freudian theorists to regard transference as a blend of positive and negative elements. Sooner or later, transference that appears to be positive reveals its conflictual base. Clients might perceive their therapist as a protective father, for example, but eventually notice he does not or cannot protect them from all pain. By contrast, transference that appears to be negative eventually shows its positive aspects. In particular, if clients can be helped to express their negative transferential emotions and can experience their therapist as non-retaliatory as he or she draws attention to the transference, they discover the positive affect under the negative transference. Hatred of the therapist who falls short in providing protection, for example, usually cloaks longing for and love of the parent who was projected onto the therapist.

(5) They also noticed that conflictual material was at least implied in issues that brought clients into therapy. Moreover, tensions and conflicts that occur during therapy were strikingly similar to those occurring outside of it, making therapy a virtual "slice of life." It was a slice of a particular client's life abetted by a particular therapist.

(6) Influenced by this thinking, many late-20$^{th}$ century theorists put major emphasis on here-and-now transference enactments during therapy (Kernberg, 1987; Binder, 1996). They advise therapists to interpret what is happening in the session at hand (Danvanloo, 1978; Malan, 1976b; Sifneos, 1979; Luborsky, 1984; Strupp & Binder, 1984). They hold that, although therapists can obtain information about clients' interpersonal history, they do not have to include that data in their interpretations (Malan, 1976a). Their first priority is to help clients understand that although their problems probably began in early child-parent experiences, they need to address the current situation rather than its past origins. Indeed, many contemporary clinicians who think of transference in a totalistic sense prefer not to make distinctions between past and present conflictual material. They see it virtually impossible to tease apart the past from present. Are clients angry simply because their therapist is criticizing them, or are they angrier than usual because they experience that criticism as similar to that of their teachers, adding injury to injury, so to speak? Asking clients may be helpful, for those who are particularly insightful may have vague suspicions, but clients' powerful emotions are likely to obstruct clear associations.

(7) Searles (1975) has given another explanation for clients' transferential re-enactment: clients are unconsciously attempting to contribute to their therapists' own emotional growth, integration, and maturation. Clients are giving their therapists an opportunity to resolve their own conflicts. Instinctively realizing that their own growth and

integration depend heavily on that of significant others, clients surmise that unless significant others become mature, their own maturity will be unstable. At the same time, clients unconsciously want others to change so that they do not have to make dreaded personal changes. They have identified with their long-lived immature emotional states and dysfunctional relational patterns to the extent that changing themselves feels like losing themselves. In addition, clients want to be mature without suffering the pain of personal change. The solution? Becoming mature by relating to a therapist who has become mature in the course of resolving the conflicts that they, as clients, have introduced into the therapeutic setting. Of course, this works no more than clients' attempts to heal themselves.

(8) Transference-based healing attempts miscarry in the end because they do not involve any real integrative processing (Ferenczi, 1909). Rather than requiring clients to subject distortions to rational scrutiny and, as a consequence, change the nature of similar present relationships, transference allows them to enact past relationships with all their distorted attributions and illusions (Freud, 1940). For example, clients may enact a parent-child relationship with their therapist, attributing to themselves neediness and inability to care for themselves and to their therapist resourcefulness and willingness to meet their needs. They do not subject these illusions to reality testing. They fail to take into consideration their own potential for self-nurturance or their therapists' perceiving them not as dependent children but as resourceful adults. As a consequence, the clients cannot integrate a capability for self-nurturance into their psyche. They retain an unrealistic need for others' nurturance and remain conflicted over others' refusal to meet that need, leaving their present relationships no healthier than their past.

Thus therapists must help clients "determine where…self-images and [interpersonal] patterns came from, how they may have been adaptive at the time they were initiated, and whether they are still adaptive or are self-defeating and maladaptive and therefore need to be changed" (Bollas, 1987, 3). Through effective therapy clients will see what they are doing to avoid pain—indeed they will run smack into the pain—and finally, by dealing with it, will discover from experience that they can face it, even embrace it, and survive. Thus identifying and dealing with transference becomes the primary means by which clients reduce, if not completely eliminate, their unique, historical and potential psychic pain (Lear, 1993).

(9) From a cognitive standpoint, transference can reveal itself anywhere along a continuum from simple or fragmentary thoughts to elaborate schemas or scripts that organize and give meaning to repressed experience. "This particular therapist resembles another person with whom I should have felt good," clients might unconsciously "think." Alternately, clients might use "Buxom, smiling women are mother figures who will make up for the nurturing I never got" as a schema whereby they classify each individual with those features as maternal.

(10) In general, totalistic transference makes use of a more powerful form of projection called *projective identification*, which is explored in Chapter Two.

(11) This activity will become clearer as projective identification and introjective identification are explored in Chapter Two.

## CHAPTER TWO

# THE PHENOMENON CALLED COUNTERTRANSFERENCE

## Countertransference: Classical Definition

Classical *transference* is clients' feelings and attitudes toward a significant, early-life figure being displaced to the therapist (Freud, 1912). *Classical countertransference, the mirror of transference, is therapists' own transference being elicited by clients' transference* (Freud, 1910a).

When defined as a *construct*, countertransference is therapists' unconscious response to clients' feelings and attitudes toward a significant past figure, usually a parent or sibling, being transferred to the therapists. It is a response triggered by the therapists' own unresolved conflicts. Countertransference is therapists' repressed, early-life, unresolved conflictual feelings and attitudes that surface in response to clients' repressed, displaced conflicts. Countertransference is a fusion of past and present. When old material is transferred to the therapeutic setting, the past becomes the present in the mind of the therapist.

When defined as a *process*, classical countertransference is clients' transferential communication "calling forth," from the unconscious mind of therapists feelings and attitudes related to their own early-life, conflictual experiences. Although there can be some exceptions, ordinarily this "calling forth" depends on two dynamics (1). One is that clients unconsciously send re-editions of early-life, conflictual experiences to their therapists' unconscious mind, and therapists unconsciously receive them. From a neuroscientific viewpoint, therapists' right-brain communication receptors are tuned in to their clients' right-brain communication expressions (Olnick, 1969). Using visual, auditory, and subliminal signals, clients project onto their unconsciously receptive therapist the traits or habits of persons that helped to create clients' early-life conflicts.

The other is that therapists already have unconscious memories of their own early-life conflictual experiences that can be "called forth" by clients' transference. They have conflict-based templates that permit them to transfer presuppositions or presumptions to the therapeutic setting (Herron & Rouslin, 1982). "You are my sibling. You have bullied me and are about to do so now," a therapist might unconsciously think about a client who has projected to his therapist subtle traits that characterize the sibling he once victimized. Thus countertransference "is determined by the fit between what [the client] projects into the therapist and what preexisting structures are present in the therapist's intrapsychic world" (Gabbard, 2001, 9).

In the classical tradition, countertransference is only those responses that are occasioned by displaced psychic conflicts: those that clients have transferred from an early-life relationship to the therapeutic relationship and therapists' own conflicts with persons from their early years. The conflicts are triggered by unconscious, right hemispheric, nonverbal communications of clients and therapists, but they are not based primarily on actual occurrences during therapy sessions. Consequently, they are not justifiable in terms of objective data. They are inappropriate or irrational. Therapists may be annoyed by clients who come late for a session, for example; but if countertransference is not at work, they are not outraged. If, on the other hand, therapists were frequently kept waiting because of the insensitivity of a parent and they are transferring that attribute to their clients, they easily become outraged.

Classical countertransference, like classical transference, is subject to a habit of the unconscious mind called repetition compulsion. Because of repeated projection and introjection, feelings and attitudes in the therapist's unconscious psyche are easily re-activated, not to be subjected to reality testing but simply to serve as grounds for therapists' re-using old perceptions and re-making old judgments. (2)

It is generally presumed that therapists introject clients' projections before clients introject therapists' projections, but it is more likely that introjection, like projection, is a simultaneous activity of therapists and clients. Or, clients may introject first as therapists provide "kernels of truth" on which clients can base their transference. (3) These "kernels" may be not only the therapist's piercing eyes—which are like the client's mother's eyes—but also the therapist's subtle habit of criticizing others that corresponds to her client's previously formed schema of mothers as persons who find something wrong with their child no matter how hard the child tries. Indeed, in the classical definition, countertransference is clients' transference activating therapists' unconscious templates of what life and people are like or should be like because of therapists' own early-life unmet needs and unfulfilled wishes.

An unconscious phenomenon, countertransference occurs spontaneously or automatically and is itself repressed or dismissed from awareness as soon as it is even suspected. Signs of its presence, called derivatives or manifestations, may be noted by the conscious mind—the therapist may become aware of shuddering in disgust, for example—but countertransference as such takes place within the inaccessible realm of the unconscious mind. That part of the psyche, which is simply called the unconscious, is a "receptive organ" (Freud, 1912, 115) or "delicate receiving apparatus" (Money-Kryle, 1956, 341) that has no choice but to introject what another projects as real or actually occurring. It is unable to use the conscious mind's reality testing function to distinguish between fantasies of its own making and objective reality. It fuses past and present and incorporates one person within another, distorting perception, impairing insight, and clouding judgment during the therapy session. "I am not this client's younger sibling," the conscious mind knows. "I feel like my client's younger sibling; I seem to be him," the unconscious mind concludes.

Classical countertransference is set in motion by therapists' conflictual wishes and needs. Therapists who have not resolved the conflict between their wish for their mother's unconditional love and her real-life limited expression of love, for example, tend to experience older, maternal clients as limited in their ability to cherish others, including their therapist. This, in turn, informs the therapists' attitude and behavior toward these clients. They feel distanced from them; they withdraw or at least minimize their verbal interactions with them. Thus, unless it is detected and processed by the therapist's conscious mind, countertransference undermines positive therapeutic outcome.

# Countertransference: Totalistic Definition

However complex countertransference already is in its classical sense, it becomes even more so in its totalistic sense, which it acquired gradually in psychoanalytic history. Because of wide disagreement on how totalistic countertransference should be defined, we will explore two of its more representative definitions before concluding the chapter with one that is operational.

At the start, it is important to note that the two definitions under consideration, like most totalistic definitions, presume the following elements of the classical definition. First, therapists' countertransference takes the form of emotions, sensations, and cognitions related to their clients. Second, countertransference involves unresolved conflict that has been repressed in the therapist's unconscious. Third, though countertransference involves more complex mental activities involving identification, it is still dependent upon projection and introjection.

## The Broadest Definition

According to Heimann (1950), totalistic countertransference is *all* attitudes and feelings that therapists experience toward clients, unconscious as well as conscious. It is the total reaction of therapists to clients in the therapeutic setting. It consists of therapists' unconscious, unresolved conflicts that are elicited by clients' transference as well as therapists' conscious, justifiable reactions to actual experiences during therapy: to what clients say and do in therapy and to what they report they are going through outside of therapy (Kernberg, 1987).

Thus the broad definition does not limit countertransference to unconscious, early-life material, to the past, to the subjective, or to fantasy. Rather, it is therapists' response both to real attributes of clients and to attributes that therapists merely impute to clients. A client might indeed be boorish, or a therapist might label him as boorish because he resembles a boorish person in the therapist's past. Likewise, countertransference is a response to present and recent material no less than early-life material. For example, if a therapist is being glorified by interns whom she supervises and unconsciously assigns similar adulatory roles to her clients, she is greatly disappointed when clients do not admire her.

Totalistic countertransference, which is subjective in that it arises within the mind of the therapist, may also have an objective component in so far as it is a response to clients' actual behavior in sessions. It is a product of the present therapeutic relationship as well as the past and present non-therapeutic relationships that both clients and therapists transfer to their therapeutic encounter.

In its broadest sense, totalistic countertransference consists of affect, cognition, and bodily sensations stemming from unmet needs of therapists as well as from affective, cognitive, and somatic communications coming from clients. It is occasioned by what clients do to therapists both knowingly and unknowingly. It is sparked by what therapists bring to sessions independently, what is "set to go" because of therapists' previously fashioned, conscious and unconscious schemas regarding people, especially people in therapy, and the professional roles that therapists believe they must play. They may transfer a maternal role to the therapeutic session, for example, when working with a distraught client who appears child-like. (4)

Totalistic countertransference is a matter of therapists' experiencing toward clients the feelings and attitudes that therapists originally associated with other persons with whom they had—and still have—significant and usually problematic interactions (Racker, 1968). It is also a matter of therapists' unconsciously assigning to clients roles peculiar to their own interpersonal experiences and the ways they define themselves in the present. Therapists send messages "asking" their clients to take certain roles that will meet their still unmet needs and fulfill their still unfulfilled wishes. Therapists who have suffered from dominating fathers, for example, tend to assign a dominating role to their clients, giving the clients an opportunity to refrain from dominating and thus meet their therapist's long-held need for self-determination. Similarly, therapists who see their role as quasi-medical tend to assign patient roles to their clients that will give the clients a chance to be healed and thus to fulfill their therapist's wish to heal others.

Therapists' countertransference also creates opportunities for clients' transference. In behaving in certain ways on their own, therapists create opportunities for clients to relate to them in ways reminiscent of clients' relationships: early, later, and even contemporary. As witnesses or recipients of therapists' behavioral tactics, clients experience their own unresolved conflicts and re-discover aspects of their conflicted selves. Therapists who are somewhat authoritarian, for example, enable clients to return to a student role if that role has remained conflictual for them. In the countertransference, clients find themselves, Sandler (1976) writes succinctly.

In addition, in its broadest sense, totalistic countertransference includes transpersonal and transcultural archetypes that emerge as therapists' own material and get transferred to the therapeutic setting. In fact, according to Jung (1966), archetypes are the major triggers of both transference and countertransference. Therapists might regard themselves as superior to their clients, for example, because of the God and Goddess Archetype. They might classify clients as inferior to them even as therapy begins or do so when time clients displace their sense of failure from a pre-therapy situation to the therapeutic setting.

Racker (1968) explained that totalistic countertransference depends not only on projection and introjection but on identification, a phenomenon wherein clients and therapists not only project and introject but actually see parts or aspects of the other person as belonging to themselves. Identification includes projective identification, a mental activity engaged in by one person; and introjective identification, a corresponding mental activity engaged in by another person. (Though both clients and therapists engage in identification, to keep explanations simple, projective identification will be attributed to the client and introjective identification, to the therapist.)

Melanie Klein (1946) first defined *projective identification* as children's fantasies of ridding themselves of unwanted feelings by assigning them to someone else. Today, however, most theorists define this construct as the omnipotent fantasy that we can split off an undesirable part of our personality, put it and the affects associated with it into another person, and then recover a modified version of what we put in the other person (Grinberg, 1962; Ogden, 1982). In that we pressure the person to identify with or own what he or she receives and they ordinarily succumb to that pressure, we experience a feeling of oneness with that person (Schafer, 1977). (5)

Schore (2003a) adds that those engaged in projective identification become dependent on the person into whom the part has been projected. They need the person in order to learn how to deal with the part. They might even need to collaborate with the recipient to manage the part. For instance, clients who have anger management problems first unconsciously put their rage into their therapist. They then unconsciously observe what their therapist does with the rage, noting how the therapist momentarily stops talking, for example, in order to think of how to speak calmly. They might also unconsciously talk in a very calm way in order to help their therapist regain composure.

In the course of projective identification, clients unconsciously put into their therapist a part of their identity they are unable or unwilling to admit or own. Concurrently, the therapist participates by unconsciously internalizing that very part of the clients' identity in a process called introjective identification.

Clients engaged in projective identification put into their therapist a part of themselves—a feeling, an idea, or a trait with its accompanying negative self-definition—that they find distressful for one of two reasons (Hinshelwood, 1999). In the first, the part is associated with the memory of an experience in which others treated the clients badly, which implied that they were bad persons. In the second, the part is the cause of the clients treating someone else badly, which also implies that they are bad persons and, on an unconscious level, makes them not want to own what they are doing. It is either, "You are abusing me and therefore distressing me; I must be a bad person" or "I am treating you badly and cannot stand that in myself. I cannot stand being a bad person."

When they become recipients of what their clients' project—sometimes called *projective fantasies*—therapists identify with their clients or with those who have been significantly impacted by their clients. Grayer and Sax (1986) note that in any given session, the therapist usually moves back and forth: identifying first with the client, then with a person who was affected by the client, then with the client, and so forth.

To begin the rapidly occurring, three-step process of projective identification, clients unconsciously put into their therapist an undesirable part of themselves in order to defend themselves against psychic pain (Ogden, 1982). They unconsciously scapegoat; they place in their therapist something in them that feels so unbearable that it must be expelled (Heath, 1991). Indeed, they do this so completely that they attribute what they expel no longer to themselves but to their therapist. Clients who are abusive, for example, and are unable to tolerate that trait in themselves perceive their therapist, not themselves, as abusive when they engage in projective identification. They really believe their therapist is abusive.

Next, clients exert pressure on their therapists to experience themselves and behave in a way congruent with the projective fantasy they have received (Ogden, 1994). Clients stimulate in their therapists intense, unexplained, and ego-dystonic emotions (Maroda, 1995), which causes therapists to undergo an affective experience commensurate with what they receive: feeling abusive or abusing another, for example, and in either case disliking it (Kernberg, 1987). As aversive, subjective emotional experience accompanies therapists' reception of projective identification (Schore, 2003a), therapists resonate with what they have received and internally amplify the emotions connected with it.

Projective identification is a form of nonverbal communication. By placing the pain of being abused in their therapist, for example, clients enable their therapist to know by experience how painful it was for them to be abused. This is particularly important to clients when they cannot find the words to express what they have experienced.

*The client denied being sexually abused. In fact, he laughed when he heard the suggestion that others with his symptoms have usually had inappropriate sexual experiences. Yet his therapist experienced a vague, partly-comfortable, partly-uncomfortable sexual attraction to her client. It was not as if she perceived the client as physically attractive; it was simply an attraction "out there" by itself.*

*In time, when the therapist disclosed her countertransferential reaction, the client revealed sexual play at the age of five. He enjoyed it, he said, even though he had no other fond memories of the babysitter who introduced him to it.*

*As she and her client talked about what had occurred when he was a child and he might be trying to relate to other females, it became clear to the therapist that what happened to her in therapy was an enactment of her client's original experience. She realized that though her client said he enjoyed it, in fact he was also conflicted over it. He enjoyed what he later learned he was not supposed to do. When he placed into his therapist his projective fantasy of having a sexual relationship with his therapist, however, he could enjoy the memory of the original experience without having to own it.*

Finally, clients engaged in projective identification unconsciously attempt to recover the part they have expelled in order to get the feel of what their therapist has gone through and what the expelled part is like now that the therapist has had to deal with it. They usually believe that their therapist has actually felt what they themselves could not tolerate and has not only tolerated it but also dealt with it. As a consequence, the part is less terrifying, and the negative feelings that accompany it are more manageable (Ogden, 1994). In the above vignette, for instance, the client would have fantasized that that his therapist managed the sexual fantasy he had projected even if she had not shared her countertransference.

Thus clients engaged in projective identification are able to fantasize that they can safely take back or re-own the traits and feelings related to their original experiences. They have benefited from their therapist's unconscious modeling. They can now imitate their therapist. They can manage their feeling of being controlled, for example, by rebelling against it, as did their therapist. Or, because they have observed their therapist, now a control freak, struggle to abdicate control or control in a benevolent way, they can manage their trait of controlling others. (6) The therapist has modulated the negative affect accompanying the projection, allowing the countertransference that it triggered to be acted out, not grossly or completely, but partially (Schore, 2003a).

This partial acting out, in turn, proves critical to the client's implicit learning of a corrective emotional experience. It represents an important opportunity for the client to perceive—in real time—that although the therapist is affected by the client's projection—indeed struggles to tolerate its negative affect—he or she ultimately manages to contain it (Pick, 1985). (7) It allows the client to enjoy a "safe" interpersonal environment wherein negative affect can be "metabolized" into something positive (Schore, 2003b).

According to Grinberg (1962), who was among the first to link projective identification with countertransference, projective identification accounts for transference-countertransference enactment or role-responsiveness. Projective identification is a form of pressure exerted by clients to get their therapist to help them process affective experience they have not been able to deal with (Schore, 2003a). In that the therapist becomes as much an active participant as the client (Plakun, 1999), projective identification is noticeably interpersonal, rather than being merely intrapsychic as Melanie Klein (1946) conceived it. (8)

In the case of *introjective identification*, therapists experience a feeling state that clients have put into their therapist in an attempt to disown it. For their part, the therapists have identified with their clients' projective fantasy. They have unconsciously appropriated it or owned it as their own.

Introjective identification can take one of two forms. In the first, called *concordant identification*, therapists recognize the feeling state belonging to their client as their own and therefore feel like their client. A therapist feels abused, for example, and feels sorry for the client who has put into his therapist his experience of being abused by his mother. The client's subjective reality seems to the therapist to be based in his or her own current reality. Thus concordant introjective identification functions in the course of countertransference to increase therapists' empathy with clients and their subjective experiences.

In the second, called *complementary identification*, the therapist who has identified with a client's feeling state feels the impact of what the client has done to another person. The therapist experiences what the recipient of the client's actions has experienced. As a consequence, the therapist empathizes *not* with her client but with the person with whom the client has interacted. To use the last example, the therapist experiences the frustration of the mother who resorts to abusing an obstinate child. Thus this second form of identification, in particular, yields valuable information to therapists who can detect it, decode it, and use it in their treatment plans to help clients realize what they contribute to their problems.

## A Narrower Definition

Some theorists, like Blum (1986a), find the broad definition of totalistic countertransference to say so much that it hardly says anything. Consequently, they offer one that is less comprehensive: countertransference is not all feelings and attitudes of therapists toward clients but only those that are *unconscious, irrational, and inappropriate because they are displaced; and only those that are conflictual or at least problematic*. If clients actually act badly in the session and therapists are angry, that reaction is called a counter-reaction, not countertransference. If, on the other hand, clients project onto therapists an early-life "picture" of themselves as acting badly—while not actually acting badly in the session—and therapists introject that old "picture," their angry reaction is termed countertransference. Thus countertransference is labeled irrational and inappropriate; it defies logic, strictly speaking. (9) The present is *not* the past. One person is *not* another, however much they resemble each other. In this narrower definition, countertransference is comprised of only those responses of therapists that are unconscious: only the imagined or fantasized perceptions of which therapists are unaware.

Furthermore, countertransference involves only conflict-based reactions of therapists. If a therapist has resolved her conflict over expecting her mother to meet her needs and finding that mother in fact neglectful, projection, but not countertransference, will occur. The client who resembles a mother might project her own unresolved conflict related to the neglect to the therapist, but the therapist will not feel neglected.

Thus the narrower definition of totalistic countertransference restricts transferred material to that which is problematic. Relatively mild and short-lived positive displaced feelings are not included. Negative feelings, on the other hand, or positive feelings that endure and become relatively intense are included. In brief, whatever displaced emotional reactions and attitudes weaken or destroy the therapeutic and working alliances, make termination a negative experience, or otherwise reduce the effectiveness of therapy are considered countertransferential.

# Descriptors of Countertransference

Whether defined classically or totalistically, countertransference can be described in the following ways.

## Countertransference Is Subtle

Though signs of broadly defined countertransference can be obvious—wanting to lash back at mouthy teenagers is easy to detect—manifestations of countertransference are usually subtle. They tend to be disguised or vague feelings, desires, images, gestures, fantasies, associations, bodily sensations, urges to respond differently from the way one usually does, silence, boredom, fatigue, fragmentary thoughts, and various combinations of these phenomena (Grayer & Sax, 1986). In response to a client who dislikes women, for example, a female therapist might feel chest pains, difficulty speaking, or performance anxiety. Or she may entertain the image of a person she dislikes, a fantasy of being humiliated, or a desire to end the session.

## Countertransference Is Unique and Varied

Like transference, countertransference takes both a unique form, indeed many forms, in every client-therapist relationship. As in the case of transference, it would be more accurate to say there are countertransferences rather than countertransference. Particular clients remind therapists of other persons, and therapists unconsciously impose idiosyncratic templates on the therapeutic relationship and assign specific roles to their clients. In addition, when clients and therapists represent different ages, ethnic groups, genders, religions, political affiliations, and socio-economic strata, their effect upon each other can be highly distinctive. Even with the same therapist-client dyad, in no two sessions do countertransference phenomena tend to be identical.

## Countertransference Is Both Simple and Complex

Countertransference, like transference, involves simplified perceptual and cognitive processes. In order to associate a client with a person whom a therapist dislikes, for example, the therapist must dismiss all aspects of both persons except the common element of the trait or behavior the therapist dislikes. Even before that or at least along with that, the therapist must accept the client's transferential message that the therapist reminds him of a disliked person with whom the therapist has relatively little in common. Perhaps it is their age. Perhaps it is their age and the slightly authoritarian tone of their voice. Perhaps it is their age, their authoritarian tone of their voice, and similarity in their clothes. But it is not the hundreds of similarities that it should take for one person to be actually identified with another.

At the same time that countertransference demands simplification, it also demands complex fantasizing. After focusing on select data, therapists go on to embellish their fantasies. To use the previous example, they might add to the common element of dislike such "evidence" as physical sensations of being punched in the chest, performance anxiety that reveals itself in confused thought processes, stammering speech, and even an urge to get rid of a client who reminds the therapist of another person he or she dislikes. Of course, the more therapists acknowledge and deal with material coming from their own unconscious, the less prone they are to fantasizing. None of them, however, can ever complete the work of self-understanding and resolving interpersonal conflict, for new clients uncannily call forth deeply repressed, only partially examined conflictual material. As a consequence, though therapists vary in their susceptibility to countertransferential fantasizing, none can completely avoid it (Herron & Rouslin, 1982).

Countertransference is complex in yet another way. It is a convoluted process that not only begins with anxiety-riddled, repressed material but is itself repressed because of the additional anxiety it induces. It then re-occurs when similar conditions arise, only to be pushed into the unconscious once more.

## Countertransference Is Both Positive and Negative

Freud (1910a) originally regarded countertransference as negative. It was therapists' undesirable reaction to their clients' transference. Because it interfered with therapeutic work, it was to be roundly dismissed from the therapeutic process. In time, however, theorists noticed that countertransference was either positive in that it seemed to be conflict-free or negative in that it contained discernible conflict.

Finally, in the course of developing their totalistic definition, theorists began to regard countertransference as having both negative and positive aspects. On one hand, countertransference ordinarily arouses discomfort—usually anxiety—in the therapist, who must use energy to repress it or dissociate from it. This, in turn, limits insight, clouds thinking, interferes with communication, and leads to misunderstandings that mar treatment, including therapists' taking judgmental positions or acting-out their feelings. On the other hand, if decoded, countertransference alerts therapists to what is going on in their relationship with clients (Racker, 1968). It increases therapists' knowledge of their clients' personal traits and interpersonal patterns. In fact, some of these traits and patterns may only be accessible through therapists' countertransference reactions (McDougall, 1978; Cohen, 1962).

## Countertransference Is Governed by Laws of the Unconscious Mind

Besides being governed by an unconscious law of the human psyche to repress what is too anxiety-ridden and painful to handle, countertransference is governed by what is called the law of talion: respond to every positive tranference by positive countertransference and to every negative transference by negative countertransference (Racker, 1972). This happens quickly and automatically, that is, within milliseconds and at levels beneath awareness (Sternberg et al., 1998). It is not a matter of conscious intention.

Consider, for instance, falling asleep, which usually makes therapists feel guilty. At least initially, however, therapists will attribute their dozing off to clients' being boring, their habit of dealing with nonessential material, or their repeating *ad nauseam*. Because they are unaware of transferring material themselves, therapists will not realize that they are retaliating in returning negative countertransference for negative transference. It is likely, however, that this is precisely what is happening, in addition to the client's actually being somewhat boring or engaging in some other form of counterproductive communication. When accurately decoded, the countertransference will more than likely yield its talionic motivation.

Another law of the unconscious mind and hence one to which countertransference is subject is the law of elaboration: "Build on, flush out, and give detail to fantasies." Hence, just as dreams are elaborate to the point of being confusing, even bewildering, countertransference includes therapists' inclinations to feel and behave fully in accordance with the identifications they are making. In subtle and varied ways, therapists play roles and perform functions once associated with figures in the clients' or their own past in the course of both therapist and client enacting their transferential fantasies (Bion, 1961).

## Countertransference Can Be Revelational

Countertransference inaugurates a revelational process once it is detected and accurately decoded. It reveals to therapists how they are influencing the therapeutic process, for better or worse. If they like the elderly because of their sweet grandparents, for example, and convey that message to elderly clients, the latter feel valued and accepted. The therapeutic alliance is quickly and soundly launched. If, on the other hand, therapists dislike the elderly because of their disgruntled grandparents, they are likely to focus on even subtle forms of negativity in their clients. As a consequence, the latter feel devalued and rejected, and the therapeutic alliance is fragile at best. Similarly, if therapists continue to associate their elderly clients with their sweet but failing grandparents, they might excuse them from hard work. (10)

If detected and accurately decoded, however, countertransference gives therapists data about what is going on between them and their clients as well as about how they and/or their clients are influencing the therapeutic process. Countertransference opens the door to a "slice of life": the client's life, the therapist's own life, and the life that client and therapist share in the therapeutic process. It gives therapists a first-hand experience of what feelings and thoughts their clients are unconsciously communicating.

Indeed, the true message of clients is understood primarily in what their communication does to therapists. Far more important than what clients consciously say to therapists are the attitude and affect with which they unwittingly say it, for in these elements lie both the fullness of meaning and the impact of clients' communication on others. "The way the therapist feels impelled to feel and behave because of the client's transference may be as important" as what the client says and perhaps more important (Pally, 2001, 91). A client's "What should I do?" for instance, can inspire a therapist to give advice, help the client think through alternatives, or turn the question back to the client, all depending on whether the therapist's countertransferential response is one of pity for one without experience being forced to act immediately, confidence in one who desires to become more analytical, or impatience with one who wants to stay dependent. In sum, therapists stand to gain their most significant insight into how they need to plan their work with clients by decoding their own countertransference.

For this reason, Brodbeck (1995) asserts that countertransference, even more than transference, is the central instrument of therapeutic work. Countertransference is "the map guiding the clinician through the hidden shoals of the transference," write Davies and Frawley (1994, 152). Countertransference is the most valuable instrument of research into the client's unconscious that the therapist has, concludes Heimann (1950).

## Definition of Countertransference as Used in This Book

Because of the intended audience of this book, namely non-analytic clinicians, students, professors, and supervisors, the definition of countertransference used in the rest of this book is an operationalized one based on the narrow totalistic definition. It is intended to give those not versed in psychoanalytic and psychodynamic theory a framework for understanding countertransference and its application to their work. It is intended to provide a relatively simple, concrete template to place on a difficult-to-detect phenomenon that occurs during non-analytic, no less than analytic, therapy.

- Countertransference is an unconscious process whereby therapists "allow" clients' transferential, nonverbal communications to elicit their own transference: their unresolved conflicts. Therapists respond to clients' transferential messages according to the significant, conflictual relationships that they, therapists, have previously or are presently experiencing, or experience as a result of archetypal phenomena at work in their lives and those of their clients.
- Countertransference is an unconscious process whereby therapists attend to similarities between their clients and others with whom they have unresolved conflicts, which then permits them to displace past or extra-therapeutic conflictual experiences.
- Countertransference occurs when therapists unconsciously take in their clients' projective fantasies and identify with the clients or with those affected by clients' verbal and non-verbal behavioral patterns. They experience the affect once felt by their clients or the recipients of their clients' behaviors. In the first case, therapists tend to empathize with clients in the course of experiencing their subjective world. In the second case, therapists tend to empathize with those with whom clients relate in the course of experiencing what clients do to them. Thus countertransference sheds light on how therapists can plan to help their clients.
- Countertransference is an unconscious process whereby therapists assimilate clients into the thematic structures of their own subjective, conflictual world. Therapists come to their work with unconscious schemas, templates, or images independent of clients and impose them on their clients. Therapists unconsciously assign to their clients roles originally played by significant others with whom therapists are still conflicted in an unconscious effort to meet their own needs and fulfill their own wishes. Thus countertransference sheds light on what therapists must do to meet their needs and fulfill their wishes outside of therapy and thereby be free to concentrate on their clients during therapy.

# Endnotes

(1) "Transference and countertransference *sometimes* (italics mine) occur without a transference/countertransference interaction" (Meissner, 1996, 307). However, the view of countertransference as inherently interactive has become increasingly operative (Gabbard, 1994).

(2) Therapists unconsciously introject what is given them: "messages" about roles, functions, self-definitions, and traits. Because these "messages" are given repeatedly,

therapists "hear" them, "read" them, take them to heart on an emotional, non-cognitive, nonverbal level without being conscious of what they are doing. In other words, introjecttion is ever present as a companion to projection.

(3) There is an element of reality in that those being given a projection have some of the objectionable attribute or at least the potential to act in the objectionable way (Searles, 1975).

(4) For instance, therapists might experience frustration as a result of their "good client" template when clients say little or nothing even though they came on time. However, therapists are also being influenced by their clients' unconscious need to punish them for exacting promptness of them, as did their parents, no matter the cost to them. Clients' actual present behavior is a manifestation of clients' transference as well as the countertransferential communication that they have received from therapists.

(5) These terms are defined differently in various theoretical schools, making it impossible to offer definitions acceptable to everyone. What is important, however, is for therapists to be aware of powerful forms of identification that inaugurate transference and countertransference. As a consequence, they unwittingly act and react toward their clients in negative ways they would not consciously choose.

(6) But the traits are not the same as they were originally because the recipients have contained and managed them in their own unique ways without even being aware of them. Under most circumstances, the recipients have lived with the undesirous traits without having "allowed" them to damage other aspects of the self (Little, 1957) or the self as a whole. Ironically, if the traits were not totally ego-dystonic to recipients, in some way the recipients may have even enjoyed them. Controlling people who need control, for example, can feel pleasant to those who control.

When the recipients are criticized for the traits, however, they find what has happened problematic. To the extent that there is a "kernel of truth" in recipients' having at least some aspects of the unwanted traits, they become defensive. They are caught between becoming aware of painful feelings related to the unwanted traits and denying them.

(7) If the therapist cannot tolerate the projective fantasy, however, she confirms the client's belief that his feelings are indeed unbearable and unmanageable. The client then feels even worse. Instead of meeting his need for hope, the client experiences hopelessness and despair (Bion, 1967). See Chapter Nine for a full exploration of steps therapist must take to ensure their proper use of what they have introjected.

(8) Therapists must remember that it is not just clients who engage in projective identification. They do so themselves, unconsciously, of course. For instance, they project their fantasy of omnipotence, which is easily transferred from an earlier narcissistic period of development; assign their clients the role of patients healed at the hands of their therapists; and then pressure their clients to be "cured." Thus therapists must own and process their projective identifications no less than help their clients do so.

(9) Winnicott (1965) regards the fact that therapists bring their own unresolved conflicts to bear upon the therapy situation as unrealistic, even abnormal. It is both abnormal and unrealistic, for example, to desire to be exacting with an older woman client simply because she is like women teachers who were exacting with the therapist in the past. What would be normal and realistic, by contrast, would be the same therapist's urge to hold the older woman client strictly accountable for being prompt for her sessions, as the therapist does all clients. The client's promptness ensures income each week, additional income from the next client, and the therapist's sense of accomplishment, all of which reflect the therapist's work ethic and personality.

(10) See Chapter Eleven for a more complete explanation of why keeping a positive alliance is not as benign as it may seem.

# CHAPTER THREE

# SCIENTIFIC DATA SUPPORTIVE OF TRANSFERENCE AND COUNTERTRANSFERENCE

## The Integration of Psychoanalytic Theory and Science

Researchers in contemporary cognitive science and neuroscience have discovered an enormously complex human brain whose structure and activity are supportive of what were previously thought to be only the psychoanalytic constructs of transference and countertransference (Westen, 1998). (From now, the two terms will be coalesced into transference). (1) In the light of this, it is reasonable to conclude that neuroscientists and cognitive scientists who describe certain activities of the body and brain of clients and therapists are referring to what psychoanalytic theorists call the process of transference. For their part, when theorists describe the past imposing itself upon the present in the therapeutic setting and therapy participants being assigned roles by each other, they are talking about what scientists refer to as brain activity related to self and others and information-processing. (2) Different vocabularies are representing roughly the same things (Grobstein, 2005; Pally, 2005).

Pally (2001), among others, has determined that "the nervous system does not so much collect information about the world as generate a model of it, act in relation to that model, and then check incoming information against the predictions of that model" (Grobstein, 2005, 6641). Early interpersonal experiences play themselves out later in therapy, causing both clients and therapists to unintentionally experience unfounded emotions and engage in inappropriate behavior prompted by unresolved, unconscious conflicts. (3)

Clients and therapists transfer to each other attributes and functions once belonging to significant others in accordance with the models—called schemas by cognitive theorists—that their mind has created.

Relatively recent neuroscientific data also reveal that conscious processes primarily involve the left hemisphere's neo-cortical circuits. In contrast, all unconscious processes, including transference, primarily involve the sub-cortical circuits of the right hemisphere's autonomic nervous system. (4)

> The right hemisphere holds representations of the emotional states associated with events experienced by the [client and therapist]. When [the client or therapist] encounters a familiar scenario, representations [or schemas] of past emotional experiences are retrieved by the right hemisphere (Shuren & Grafman, 2002, 918).

In the case of transference, they are displaced to the therapeutic situation. The right hemisphere is acting without the left hemisphere being able to put into words what is going on. (5)

Then, when therapists interpret transference, the right and left hemispherical circuits work together for the first time to resolve the conflict. As consciousness-connected parts of the left hemisphere focus on previously unconscious material presented by the right hemisphere, the unified brain is able to weaken the neural networks that support its faulty models. (6) "The therapist is not my mother," clients who process their transference finally conclude, "I cannot continue to demand that she nurture me in my mother's stead." Similarly, after therapists process their own countertransference, they finally decide, "I do not have to mother others. I can help my clients assume that responsibility themselves."

Said succinctly, transference, which involves models of interactions between the self and others, presents to clients and therapists an opportunity to correct their interactions. Neural-networks that "pull" therapy participants into unconscious, compulsive re-enactments of a conflict weaken as conscious, more objective and appropriate neural networks form and therapy participants gain insight. (7)

## Neuroscientific Data Supportive of Transference

Space permits only a summary of select neuroscientific research findings related to what accounts for transference: the implicit memory and nervous system communication, the limbic system, the right hemisphere, and biochemicals in the brain.

## The Implicit Memory and Nervous System Communication

Compelling neuroscientific data suggest that products of the implicit memory, termed implicit memories, account for the schemas that are the "building blocks" of transference. Put in a slightly different light, "the transference reaction, in and of itself, . . . represents an expression of the [client's] implicit perceptions and implicit memories" (Schore, 1999, 170).

Whereas explicit memories are consciously encoded in words, implicit memories are unconsciously encoded in feelings, sensations, and images. Whereas explicit memories consist of facts, concepts, and ideas that are mediated by the hippocampus, implicit memories are records of feelings, sensations, and images encoded directly in the cerebral cortex, (8) after having been mediated by the amygdala, through slow, incremental changes in the strength of connections between cortical neurons (Vaughan, 1998). (9) The implicit memory stores and recalls what it learns experientially (Gabbard, 2001).

Unlike explicit memory activity, which begins around age three, implicit memory activity is very prominent and robust in children under three, whose underdeveloped hippocampus permits little explicit memory activity. Hence, both childhood amnesia and the "rules" one has for how to relate to others—based on early life experience— explain the phenomenon of transference. In particular, interactions with caregivers form representations—in the unconscious mind—of procedures for relating to others and create prototypes of oneself in relation to others. When these interactions and the representations and prototypes they create meet a person's basic needs, relatively speaking, all is well. When they do not, the psyche attempts to use the repetition or reenactment that constitutes transference to resolve the psychological conflict it is experiencing. "I should be loved though I have made a big mistake," a client believes because of her basic affiliative needs. I will give my therapist a chance to love me in spite of the mistake I have made," the client "thinks" unconsciously.

Then, when the therapist uses a transference interpretation to make the client's implicit transference memory explicit, saying something like, "Are you asking me to overlook your coming late, the way you wanted your parents to treat you when you were a child?" "the origin of that memory is also made explicit, and the [client] can better understand the causal chain of events that led from past experience to present functioning. Simply put, the translation of implicit memories allows the [client] to gain insight regarding the relationship between past and present experience" (Bornstein, 1993, 341). Thus therapy that includes transference interpretations "acts as a growth-facilitating environment for inducing structural alterations in the [client's] preconscious regulatory systems" (Schore, 2003a, 241). (10)

## The Limbic System

Understanding the limbic system, especially its amygdala, is also fundamental to a neuroscientific explanation of transference. For it is on the middle or paleomammalian level of brain development, which includes the amygdala, that functions most likely to leave unresolved conflicts, such as mothering and protecting, emerge (MacLean, 1990). (11)

The limbic system's amygdala, which is almost mature at birth, plays a major part in transference (12) although the system's hippocampus, which begins to mature between ages two and three, also plays a role. The hippocampus processes data that make sense of experiences within the time line of personal history and record the sequence of the experiences. The hippocampus tags time and place to memories so that they can be stored as narrative memories (Schore, 2003b). In contrast, the amygdala processes and then facilitates the storage of emotions and reactions to emotionally charged events, such as early life experiences with caregivers. The amygdala also directs sensory information to the right hemispheric cortex for use in what will be explained later as pattern matching.

Subsequently, when therapists interpret transference and clients attain "explicit knowledge through the temporal lobe memory system and other cortical areas involved in conscious awareness" (LeDoux, 1998, 265), clients strengthen their cortical control over the amygdala. Rather than being left to operate on its own, the amygdala is made to coordinate its activities with those of the more conscious cortex (Grigsby & Stevens, 2000). As a consequence, emotionally charged events that result in psychic conflict get subjected to the workings of the conscious mind: to reasoning, evaluation, and judgment. Psychic conflict no longer has the power to motivate behavior on its own. "I might want to be comforted," the client who deals with transference begins to realize, "but I don't *have* to demand that others comfort me."

## The Right Hemisphere

The nature and activities of the right hemisphere also explain the unconscious phenomenon of transference, for "the emotion processing right hemisphere is the neurobiological substrate of the unconscious" (Schore, 2003a, 247). Compared to the left hemisphere, the right hemisphere is more involved in the background-holistic, subconscious processing of information (Prodan et al., 2001) and thus in bonding and in transference. "Lower-level right limbic activity and its associated psychobiological states are expressed in…transference" (Schore, 2003a, 241)

The right hemisphere not only develops more quickly than the left during infancy but also plays a major role in storing sensory input. (13) In particular, it recognizes faces and "reads" them in a search for signs of others' acceptance. (14) If signs of acceptance are present, bonding occurs. If not, conflict ensues, which sets the stage for transference. Clients with unresolved early attachment conflicts use their right brain to look for signs of acceptance in the therapy setting, which mirrors early infant-mother interaction in that it is highly right brain limbic: unconscious and preverbal or averbal (Wilkinson, 2003). They transfer early attachment experiences to their therapy in an effort to resolve their original unresolved conflicts.

Hence transference, no less than bonding, is said to be right-brain mediated. Transference is a matter of right brain to right brain communication through the use of slight, sometimes even subliminal, signals (Meares et al., 2005)

Clients may also bring to their therapy conflicts arising between the ages of three and four because of contradictory self-representations, one formed in the right brain and the other in the left brain. (15) The child's right brain may "see" that it needs to be loved, for example, and expect a caregiver to meet its need. The child's left brain, on the other hand, may hear the caregiver scold and then refuse to talk, at least in a loving way. This leaves the child with two self-representations: "I am a person who deserves love" and "I am a person who is not loved and perhaps does not deserve it." As Schore (2003a) explains,

> [The] dual-hemispheric system [of the human brain] allows for cooperation but also competition between the right hemisphere and the left hemisphere and [consequently] the presence of conflict, especially those involving sexual and aggressive forces that are active between three and four (245).

This conflict, in turn, is likely to be displaced to the therapy setting for psychic resolution.

Another function of the right hemisphere is to regulate the distress accompanying conflict, whenever and wherever it originates. The right hemisphere projects transference fantasies (16) in an attempt to manage the negative emotions it is experiencing (Schore, 2003b). The right brain of the client sends to the right brain of the therapist what is disturbing it. Then the right brain of the therapist sends to the right brain of the client a message that it has received the disturbing feeling. (17)

> Just as the left brain communicates its states to other left brains via conscious linguistic behaviors, so the right brain nonverbally communicates its unconscious states to other right brains that are tuned to receive these communications [as are clients and therapists who are forming a therapeutic alliance] (Schore, 2003, 76).

> Nonverbal transferential interactions that take place at pre- or unconscious levels represent right hemisphere to right hemisphere communications of fast-acting, automatic, regulated and dysregulated emotional states between [clients and therapists] (Schore, 2001b, 315).

Said succinctly, the right hemisphere of the client and therapist communicate their unconscious states non-verbally (Schore, 2001a). (18) In a state of receptivity and openness (Olnick, 1969), the therapist's right-brain countertransferential affective-receptive communications are tuned to the client's right-brain transferential affective communications, with more empathic therapists activating their right brain more than those who are less empathic (Alpert et al., 1980).

With its capacity to modulate negative transferential affect and to handle complex, internally contradictory and ambiguous information (Rotenburg, 1994), the right brain also enables therapists to experience clients' transferred feelings but contain them rather than act them out overtly and grossly (Schore, 2003a). Therapists' right brain activity allows them to let clients know through subtle signals that they have been affected by transference projections and are struggling to tolerate their negative affect. However, they will manage what they are experiencing (Pick, 1985). (19)

In a related light, beginning at about 18 months, the human mind acquires a unique capacity to travel through time mentally and reflect upon what it is doing. (20) Its right hemisphere stores cognitive schemas in visuospatial areas (Tucker, 1992) that use a nonverbal processing mode not accessible to language. These schemas enable the right brain to "mentally represent and become aware of subjective experiences in the past, present, and future" (Wheeler et al., 1997, 331). Thus the right brain is specialized to process new information by comparing it directly with context information (Federmeier & Kutas, 1999).

## Mirror Neurons

Exciting research findings in the last fifteen years that reveal what are called mirror neurons in both macaque monkeys and humans shed additional light on the phenomenon of transference. Located in the pre-motor cortex of the monkeys, mirror neurons fire not only when the monkeys do something but also when they see another human or animal perform the action. In humans, motor-evoked potentials—signals that a muscle is ready to move—occur even when humans watch someone else move muscles (Rizzolatti & Fadiga, 1995). This neural activation is involuntary and automatic. It simply happens.

Furthermore, this phenomenon occurs in non-motor areas, such as emotional centers. Wicker (2003), for instance, found that both smelling a noxious odor and simply watching a film of an actor smelling the odor activated the anterior insula, which registers olfactory data. As a consequence, those watching experienced the emotion of disgust no less than the actor.

Thus it seems reasonable to explain transference, at least tentatively, in the context of mirror neurons. Parts of the brains of therapy participants automatically and unconsciously communicate with each other simply when activity in one brain occurs. Activity in either the client's or therapist's brain causes mirroring activity in the other participant's brain. "You are my mother," the client "says," whereupon the therapist receives information regarding his maternal assignment and role. The therapist also sends information to the client as he even "thinks" of playing the part of the client's mother. "I have received your message to be a mother to you," the therapist communicates to the client. "I feel like your mother and am inclined to play—even beginning to play—a maternal role."

## Neuromodulators and Neurotransmitters

Biochemicals that mediate prototypic representations which account for transference include neuromodulators (21) and neurotransmitters. Neuromodulators called glucocorticoids prevent memory encoding (Bremner et al., 1993) whereas norepinephrine, also a neuromodulator, enables encoding (Lewis, 1995). Yet another neuromodulator, the adrenocortico-tropic hormone, facilitates activation of memories (Rothschild, 2000).

At the same time, dopamine, a neurotransmitter, activates reward centers, called u-opioid receptors, in the brain. The right number of receptors and amount of dopamine that remains in synapses between neurons "communicate to the brain that an event or experience is important and should be set in memory for the future" (Tancredi, 2005, 140). On the other hand, fewer than optimal receptors or dopamine that remains in the neural synapses for too short a time render a person less responsive to rewards. It would seem likely, then, that too much dopamine or dopamine remaining in the synapses for too long would make memories stronger and more lasting. If they were conflictual, they would easily surface as transference material when similar circumstances arose.

Furthermore, dopamine plays a key role in human attraction in that it is linked to the prediction of reward (Larsson & Ahlenius, 1999). Its presence in larger amounts and/or a longer time than usual in neural synapses is likely to increase the attraction a client has to a particular therapist. For example, a therapist with positive maternal qualities would quickly trigger the Mother Archetype to play itself out. This attraction would be even more pronounced when the therapist maintained appropriate eye contact, for fMRI scans show greater activation of dopaminergic regions of the brain when the gaze of one person rests on another (Kampe et al., 2001) as happens routinely in therapy.

To summarize, even though the conscious mind cannot encode a significant intrapersonal or interpersonal conflict because of young age or overwhelming distress, the body does. Neuromodulators and neurotransmitters bring about brain changes that, among other things, account for preverbal or averbal body memories (Ware, 1995). The fact that the body keeps score (van der Kolk, 1996) permits transference to occur when an individual is in circumstances similar to those involving painful conflict. In particular, brain imaging studies provide evidence that when clients are reminded of trauma in even subtle ways, they can have a full-blown neuroendocrine stress reaction (Yehuda, 1998). "Whether the trauma is physical, psychological or sexual, it sets off a ripple of hormonal changes that organize the brain to cope in a hostile world" (Wilkinson, 2003, 237). (22)

A substantial amount of research also supports the finding that once neural pathways have been activated by significant stress, even lesser subsequent stress, associations, or contextual cues can activate these pathways and memories of the stress. This, in turn, causes a person to relive trauma in flashbacks or nightmares (Wilkinson, 2003; Reviere, 1996) and to engage in transference in an effort to process them.

In summary, transference is easily activated from a neuroscience perspective. If it is not ubiquitous, it is at least close to that.

# Cognitive Theory and Research That Explicate Transference

Cognitive theory and research has also revealed that transference is easily activated—and done so so often that it is called ubiquitous—from an information-processing perspective. Moreover, more than under other conditions, transference is likely to be activated in therapy because "...the act of presenting for treatment evokes a set of highly specific wishes, fears, affects, and cognitive constructions, including expectations about helping relationships" (Westen & Gabbard, 2002, 123). Transference is "a crucial step in a cognitive/affective sequencing of information processing that builds and exploits emotional data bases of mind and brain" (Levin, 1997, 1136).

## Transference: Pattern Matching and Prototypic Schemas

Cognitive theorists now have enough research data to explain transference in terms of pattern matching: the brain is constructing and reconstructing thoughts, feelings, and ways of behaving in the context of new relationship experiences that can be understood only in the context of old ones. The person engaged in transference is not so much repeating an old—usually conflictual—experience as interpreting a present situation with a bias toward what occurred in the past (Pally, 1997). "Transferential processes always reflect an integration of current and past experience, as patterns of activation resulting from current life experiences...interact with enduring ways of responding...." (Westen & Gabbard, 2002, 130). Thus transference reactions are combinations of clients' and therapists' enduring dispositions to react in particular ways under particular conditions. They are highly dependent on the nature of the therapeutic situation: an occasion to confide and receive intimate, personal information (Westen & Gabbard, 2002). (23)

It may seem as if we just "take in" the world as it exists—as does a camera—but in fact our perceptions are actively constructed by our brain (Gazzaniga, 1995). Acting like a feature detector, the brain uses already existing sensory cues based on prior experience to see and hear and feel what it saw and heard and felt before (Pally, 1997).

Said simply, the brain does not perceive the external environment as it actually is. Rather, it "searches for a match between the current pattern of neuronal activation [related to what it is experiencing in the present] and patterns stored in memory [from prior experiences]" (Pally, 1997, 1021).

It finds patterns of neuronal activity within itself. It makes "a quick assessment of just enough details to find a 'good enough match.' When a 'good enough' match is found, perception occurs" (Pally, 1997, 1025). "This therapist looks and sounds like my mother," a client notes. (24)

"Since the brain only requires that the match be 'good enough,' current perceptions are strongly biased by previous experiences" (Pally, 1997, 1026). Because the brain only looks for a 'good enough' match, when a current situation activates a pattern that is similar to one stored in memory, "the brain may conclude that two different situations are the same. For this reason we tend to 'see' what we have seen before" (Pally, 1997, 1026). We transfer the past to the present. "This therapist, who looks and sounds like my abusive mother, is actually abusing me," the client notes on an unconscious level.

Cognitive scientists use the term *schema* to help define how people function. Schemas are generalizations that have become encoded in associative networks and re-enforced through later experience. They may be actual in the sense of personally experienced. But they may also be inherited or simply fantasized.

The concept of schema dates back to Piaget (1926), who suggested that people form prototypes for categorization of classes of people. These prototypes are then used when characteristics of a person in the present fit prototypic features. Thus one's understanding of another person through the use of schemas is an active process. Clients who enter the therapy room will bring with them a schema of what the therapist should be like and use that schema during their sessions. "The past serves as an analogy for the present" (Andersen et al., 1996, 1109).

The schemas clients use, like all analogies, are both somewhat accurate—therapists do tend to behave in very similar, well-known ways—and somewhat distorted because of the ways the clients have learned to think as well as the motives they have for entering therapy. Clients who want to be accepted for who they are and nurtured into mental health, for example, will primarily employ a mother schema, provided their own experience of their mother was one of acceptance and nurturance. Clients who have been sharply reprimanded by authority figures, on the other hand, are likely to employ a demanding authority figure schema. They might even unconsciously vilify their therapists in an effort to avoid hearing something painful from them (Westen, 1994).

Schemas brought to therapy, like all schemas, are multimodal. They are constellations that consist of "associated semantic, sensory, and emotional components, with links to a wide array of other such constellations" (Gabbard, 2002, 103). In addition, schemas are composed of generic knowledge or facts, episodic knowledge or memories of specific events, procedural knowledge or "how to" knowledge or skills, affects, and motives. Thus activating schemas triggers a range of cognitive and affective processes, the majority of which are unconscious. "Multiple process, active simultaneously, provide the shape of clients' patterns of relating to [their therapists] Gabbard, 2002, 108.

In sum, schemas are components of transference in that they divide cognitive activity into enduring organizations of self and others, goals and values, types of relationships, and mental states (Slap & Slap-Shelton, 1991). Schemas form because underlying emotional circuits of the brain "initiate, synchronize and energize sets of coherent physiological, behavioural and psychological changes that are primal instinctive solutions to various archetypal life-challenging situations" (Panksepp, 1998, 123). Schemas endure because their use solves a problem. They make sense out of life's experiences. They address the issue of newness. They lower the anxiety one feels when faced with the unfamiliar.

When therapists and clients meet in therapy, through a phenomenon called schema-triggered expectancies, they both expect the same pattern of liking or disliking, as well as being liked or disliked, as was characteristic of their relationship with prototypic significant others. They unconsciously use their pre-existing schemas to make sense of their therapeutic relationship.

Said in a slightly different way, both clients and therapists have representations or schema-triggered expectancies—that exist as potentials for activation—regarding the therapeutic setting. Consequently, they instinctively assimilate various aspects of the therapeutic setting to their pre-existing schemas (Cantor et al., 1982). (25) In particular, schemas related to the intimacy and intensity of parental care and concern and—to a lesser extent sibling rivalry in the home environment—are easily set in motion as well-trodden neural pathways that "house" the schemas are activated. The nature of the infant-caregiver relationship becomes internalized and is reactivated again and again in similar relationship contexts throughout life (Emde, 1988).

But this is not the whole story. Matters are even more complicated because one schema builds upon the next developmentally in the sense of early images of relationships becoming integrated into later schemas. "Old schemas never die: they . . . are incorporated in various ways into subsequent schemas, or are repressed and periodically activated without conscious awareness" (Westen, 1998, 331) as human needs call upon similar information processing channels.

In the intimacy of the therapeutic relationship "schema-nesting" is likely to proliferate. In early sessions, clients and therapists tend to use parent-child schemas with each other. Clients see therapists in terms of those with resources while therapists see clients in terms of those without resources.

Concurrently, clients and therapists are likely to use idealizing schemas with each other, playing out their unique versions of what will be more fully explained in Chapter Four as the God and Goddess Archetypes. Clients expect near-perfection of their therapist, for they bring with them schemas of those with special skills, extensive knowledge, and the power to help them end their distress. For their part, therapists tend to apply these same schemas to themselves as well as see their clients in terms of schemas of those without skills, knowledge, and power to effect change. Their clients are mere subjects of the gods and goddesses. They will be not only compliant but most grateful for whatever help they receive.

In time, however, when clients and therapists let down their guard—perhaps simply respond to the pressures of having to appear god- or goddess-like and subject-like—they begin to notice that they are now siblings vying for the same realms of power and control. As a consequence, they unintentionally employ a variety of schemas proper to the Sibling Rivalry Archetype, which will also be explored in the next chapter. It seems as if there is danger in not having control of the therapeutic relationship. It seems as if both client and therapist must compete for control of the therapeutic process.

As a consequence, in time clients and therapists find themselves employing schemas related to completion of the self. They desire to make up for loss of external control. They have not competed as successfully as they desired. They must find within themselves the strengths of both genders to offset their defeats. They must make use of schemas related to what will be explained in the next chapter as the Animus and Anima Archetypes.

What becomes problematic then in the course of therapy is clients'—and to a lesser extent therapists'—transferring their intrapersonal and interpersonal struggles to each other as schema-nesting occurs. What becomes extremely important, as a consequence, is for therapists to help clients look for various and complicated patterns in the conflictual relationships that lie at the heart of their presenting problems and get displaced in the course of therapy (Westen, 1998).

At the same time, therapists must also examine their therapeutic work for nesting patterns of their own. They must bring to consciousness and deal with the complicated relational patterns inherent in the schemas they and their clients transfer from other relationships to their therapeutic relationship..

But this still not the whole story. Neither therapy participant can fully rest, for, in spite of significant, overt progress toward goal attainment, the covert work of therapy can never be fully completed. As explained by cognitive theory and supported by cognitive research, transference is an ever-present potential because the neural pathways of schemas remain intact even though they may be weakened or even made temporarily unusable. "Although perhaps inhibited, [neural networks] are capable of reactivation in certain circumstances" (Grigsby & Stevens, 2000, 97).

This has extremely important implications for therapeutic work in that it suggests the need for vigilance during the termination phase of therapy as well as consideration of as "booster sessions" after clients have terminated.

## Transference: Similarity Judgments and Their Questionable Validity

Cognitive scientists have described transference not so much as an unconscious repetition or reenactment in an attempt resolve conflict as an interpretation of the therapeutic situation with a bias toward what has occurred in the past (Pally, 1997). An aspect of the present is priming the recollection of a whole past experience (Levin, 1997). Something in the present is serving as a cue to a similar past situation that the memory has recorded. The part is "printing out" the whole because the client or therapist has noted structural similarities between the present and the past.

Cognitive theorists explain that clients and therapists instinctively attempt to adapt to therapy, which is a new situation, by means of assimilation or accommodation. They note that the new experience closely matches an old, prototypic one. Hence, they can simply assimilate the therapeutic setting into an already-existing one. If clients and therapists find that the therapy situation does not match perfectly, however, they tend to alter the original representation—through what is called accommodation—in order to place the new experience in the old one. Though the old one becomes somewhat different, it remains basically the same.

If neither assimilation nor accommodation are workable, of course, clients and therapists create a new category. But this does not happen often. Rather, in adapting to therapy, clients and therapists use a method that is computationally cheap in that it calls for their brains finding and exploiting a small number of deep structural similarities and ignoring a larger number of relatively superficial dissimilarities. Clients and therapists are using relatively little time and allocating few resources of working memory (Levin, 1997).

Explained in this way, assimilation and accommodation account for transference. The past is transferred to the present as clients and therapists assimilate and accommodate.

Clients and therapists are especially prone to engage in transference when they are experiencing emotional disturbance. Needing to regulate the affect that disturbs them (Westen, 1998), they try to adapt to the disturbance by searching for an old experience into which it can be placed (Slap & Slap-Shelton, 1991) in a way that is as valid and emotionally tolerable as possible. "This is not totally new," the brain wants to think. "It is something I have handled before. I can do it again." The brain of the client then goes on with a specific unconscious thought, "My therapist looks angry because I do not have the money to pay today. So was my mother when I couldn't do what she wanted. The therapist is my mother." At the same time, the brain of the therapist is prone to think unconsciously, "My client is my child who notes my anger when she has not brought her money."

Said succinctly, transference is a matter of the brain taking a specific event and putting it into a general category. Thus the brain deals with newness, especially when it is characterized by ambiguity and colored by affect, in a temporarily satisfying way. (26)

Then, when therapists use transference interpretations and invite clients to explore transference collaboratively, clients get the opportunity to examine what they have unconsciously done. Their categorizations may be relatively valid because new experiences are almost identical to old ones. The therapist is angry as was the client's parent, for example. But their categorizations may be more invalid than valid because the new experience, while seemingly identical to the old, is really quite different. The therapist has a right to expect the client to honor his fee agreement, to use the same example, while the parent did not have a right to expect a child to be prematurely responsible. Or the therapist is expressing her anger in a polite, assertive manner while the parent resorted to punishment.

During the course of their interpretive work, clients may also gain the insight that psychological models or schemas that encode original experience may or may not be based on actual happenings in their life. They may be inherited or reflect the "random play" that results in pure fantasy (Globstein, 1994). Hence, their therapeutic work can result in new, or at least partially new, and considerably more accurate schemas for future use. "By learning how to exploit transference for its optimal learning potential, [therapy participants] convert potentially . . . dangerous perceptual 'mistakes' . . . into an opportunity" to adopt new, more effective patterns of relating to others (Levin, 1997, 1147).

# Endnotes

(1) It is actually more appropriate to refer to transferences than transference because of the complexity of the human mind. At any given time multiple representations are activated in different neural networks. Thus effective therapy is a matter of deactivating aspects of problematic mental links and creating new associative links as replacements (Gabbard, 2001). In this book, however, the more common transference will be used.

(2) Cognitive and neuroscience research also provides support for the constructivist notion that therapists exert a significant influence on clients' transference, just as clients do on therapists' countertransference. Clients elicit feelings, sensations, and images in therapists, and therapists reciprocate.

(3) A study by Shevrin et al. (1998) provides support for the existence of unconscious conflict. When participants were given words that captured their conscious experience of the symptoms that they had reported some time before, if the stimuli were presented subliminally, they put the unconscious conflict words in the same category. If the stimuli were presented supraliminally, however, they did not. The implication is that the material was transferred unconsciously rather than consciously.

(4) One of two things happens, both of which affect the sub-cortical circuits of the right hemisphere. The first is repression, wherein the pathway between the right and left hemispheres is blocked. Consequently, subcortical circuits of the right hemisphere are unable to communicate emotions, particularly anxiety, to the left hemisphere. The second is dissociation, wherein the pathway between the limbic system and the cortex is blocked. Consequently, subcortical circuits of the right hemisphere are unable to communicate emotions, particularly terror, to the cortex. In both cases, the feelings must be stored subcortically in the right hemisphere.

New neuroscience imaging research suggests that the adaptive operations of the unconscious mind are best described—not in terms of repression and dissociation—but in terms of nonconsciously mediated processes that are essential components of normal and abnormal cognition. Such dynamic operations are nonconscious because they occur too rapidly to be at levels of conscious awareness. However, "these early automatic appraisal processes which allocate attention and inattention to salient, valued aspects of the external environment shape the subsequent conscious processing of a stimulus" (Schore, 2003a, 247).

(5) This is but one example of unconscious procedural learning occurring in the brain whether or not it is accompanied by conscious knowledge (Willingham et al., 2002). The right brain learns to regulate affect without the left brain being able to put into words what is occurring.

Also of great interest is recent neuroscientific theory that early trauma may result in severe pruning or sculpting of neural networks in the orbitofrontal cortex, the "senior executive" of the emotional brain (Schore 2001a). The weaker orbitofrontal connections and the stronger amygdala connections that result from this make fear that marks trauma difficult to escape, let alone manage.

(6) One can only conclude that neither the conscious nor the unconscious should have primacy; they function best as an interdependent loop with each influencing the other: adding, subtracting, changing, and correcting (Grobstein, 2003).

(7) Freeman (2000) defines insight as access to the unconscious mind of another. Insight results from preconscious scanning of bodily states.

(8) The orbital prefrontal (OBF) system accesses memory functions and operates the implicit memory. OBF dysfunction is associated with "a failure to distinguish between currently relevant and previously encountered information," that is, between "now" and "the past" (Schnider & Ptak, 1999, 680). Affect-focused treatment during therapy, which would include processing transferential feelings and attitudes, literally alters the OBF system of the brain.

(9) However, the distinction between implicit and explicit memories does not negate the fact that as the brain develops, implicit memories are "reworked" by the explicit memory through the activation of memory networks. Because memory networks can include generic knowledge, episodic knowledge, procedural knowledge, affects, and motives, network activation often triggers a wide range of cognitive and affective processes. The two memories, though somewhat independent, usually function in concert, complementing one another. Thus verbal elements connected with beliefs and expectations proper to the explicit memory system combine with affect, imagery, and sensory data as transference continuously "takes shape" or gets activated. At the same time, though, transference does not involve conscious memories. The neural networks it activates involve processes that are inaccessible to consciousness.

(10) Processing transferential feelings and attitudes literally alters the orbitofrontal system of the brain.

(11) Lewis (1995) conceptualizes transference as a special form of remembering. It is unconscious remembering that is partly rooted in cognitive, procedural, or paleomammilian brain memory processes, which are pertinent to functions from which nursing, mothering, and early play patterns emerge.

(12) The amygdala ends its growth phase in the second year of life, but it continues to get cerebral blood flow more than the left hemisphere and its hippocampus until age four.

(13) In fact, the infant's prototypic representations are basically somatosensory. They take the form not of thoughts but of "visual images, sounds, smells, tastes, or bodily sensation such as pain" (Hackmann & Holmes, 2004). Hence when these representations are displaced in the course of transference, they manifest themselves physiologically. Transference reenactments generate intense somatic reactions in empathic and engaged therapists (Benatar, 2004).

(14) When efficiently functioning, "rapid-acting OBF appraisals of the social environment are accomplished at levels beneath awareness by a visual and auditory scanning of information emanating from an emotionally expressive face" (Schore, 2003a, 206).

(15) At this age, right to left orbitofrontal communication is still poor. Thus the right brain cannot communicate its distress to the left brain and expect reasoning to reduce the distress (Schore, 2003a). The right hemisphere is also dominant for mediating pain and pain endurance (Hsieh et al., 1995) and modulating distress states via a right-brain circuit of inhibition and emotion regulation (Porges et al., 1994).

(16) "Defensive projective identification (PI), an early-forming right-brain survival mechanism for coping with interactively generated overwhelming traumatic stress, is

activated in response to subjectively perceived social stimuli that potentially trigger imminent dysregulation" (Schore, 2003a, 75). "At the moment of the projection, the patient's disorganizing right brain (fragmenting self) switches from a rapidly accelerating, intensely dysregulated, hyperactive distress state into a hypoactive dissociated state" (Schore, 2003a, 75).

PI arises in a developmental context "of asymmetrical influence, with both internal-structural and behavioral communication aspects, in which one person pressures another to experience as part of herself something that the first person cannot accept within his own self-experience" (Seligman, 1999, 143).

(17) See Chapters One and Two for a fuller explanation of projection and projective identification.

(18) In contrast, the cortex of the left hemisphere, which begins an accelerated growth period toward the end of the first year of life, seems to have a more intimate relationship with the hippocampus in that it depends on language for processing information. Left cortex development continues as language develops. At the same time, the hippocampus matures, enhancing the baby's capacity to make sense of the environment. It too will eventually play a part in transference processing as therapists offer transference and countertransference interpretations and clients accept, reject, or modify them.

(19) As explained in Chapters One and Two, initially therapists cannot prevent themselves from experiencing what their clients unconsciously want them to experience and being who their clients want them to be. However, therapists must become aware of what is happening and desist. Their identification with what their clients are projecting should only be transient, for therapists to behave otherwise would be a denial of responsibility for countertransference (Finell, 1986).

(20) Happening at the time when the obitofronal cortex has become mature, this is called autonoetic consciousness or awareness.

(21) Neuromodulators are substances that affect the functioning of neurons. They do not act as neurotransmitters, however, (Grigsby & Stevens, 2000).

(22) Stress hormones are secreted when a client is abused or neglected. By contrast, when therapists convey care and concern, the secretion of these hormones is reduced and the neuroendocrine system shifts toward homeostasis (Adler, 2002).

(23) Linkages that exist in memory between self and significant-other representations are activated in transference. The nature of the infant-caregiver relationship, in particular, becomes internalized and is reactivated in similar relationships throughout life, including—perhaps especially—in the client-therapist relationship (Pally, 2001). The needy-infant transference draws forth a "nurturant response" even between adults (Pally, 1996). Similarly, a therapist's involuntary responses may be activated by the client simply as an expression of how human beings normally relate with one another (Pally, 2001).

(24) Indeed, recent cognitive research has demonstrated that transference is characteristic of everyday social perception. When people meet a new individual, they unconsciously activate an already exiting significant-other representation or image and apply it to the new person. Through a phenomenon called transference in social perception, they thereby retain their representation-consistent memory and habit of evaluating their world (Andersen et al., 1996). Through a phenomenon called schema-triggered affect, people feel the same way towards a similar new individual as they did toward an earlier, prototypic person. With a new person who resembles a significant other, people seem to be motivated to seek the same level of (or lack of) closeness as they have (or have had) with the prototypic significant other.

Furthermore, as Knox (2001) explains, we have a state-dependent retrieval of memory habit, meaning that we are more likely to remember something which occurred under certain specific conditions if those conditions are reproduced at the time we endeavor to recall the event or the conditions are simply there.

(25) The way in which a therapist feels compelled to act toward the client may be the result of innately encoded responses to the client's nonverbal transferential manifestations, which originate in early life needs for affection, attachment, understanding, and soothing. A therapist may engage in self-protective responses to an extremely needy and demanding client, for example. In turn, the client may shut down and become depressed just as babies do when their mother separates from them. Alternatively, clients may become anxious when the therapist endeavors to understand them, simply because never being understood in early life leaves them unprepared for it later (Pally, 2001).

Seen in a slightly different light, no thought or feeling is free of past influences, any more than it is free of current ones. All mental processes reflect the "on-line" integration of previously established potentials with new patterns of perception and thought (Pally, 2001).

(26) Our brain seems to be intolerant of ambiguity. It organizes available data into organized coherent explanations even though they are clearly confabulatory. This is essentially the same as what is called the defense mechanism of rationalization (Grigsby & Stevens, 2000).

# PART II

## TRIGGERS AND MANIFESTATIONS OF TRANSFERENCE AND COUNTERTRANSFERENCE

# CHAPTER FOUR

# TRIGGERS OF TRANFERENCE AND COUNTERTRANSFERENCE

## Introduction

Countless and varied stimuli—psychological and environmental, personal and interpersonal, conscious and unconscious—trigger transference and countertransference in everyday living. The realms of the unconscious mind wherein transference and countertransference "reside" are multi-structured, multi-layered, and multi-faceted. Unconscious psychological life is no less complex than biological life.

During the course of psychotherapy, however, transference and countertransference are triggered more often by what are called archetypes than other material for two reasons. First, therapy is a highly interpersonal process that draws from its participants primordial, transcultural interactional patterns, such as taking care of infants and children and appealing to more powerful others when in need. Specific cultures might have developed somewhat unique forms of caregiving and turning to one with power, but all cultures have learned to survive by enacting the Mother Archetype and God and Goddess Archetype.

Second, therapists and clients hold beliefs about universal archetypal situations that tend to occur during the course of therapy. Those in danger of decompensating, for example, must depend on those who know how to protect them, as embodied in the Father Archetype.

Hence, the focus of this chapter: archetypes, the manner in which they trigger transference and countertransference, and the expectations of therapists and clients that make archetypal material difficult to manage. The chapter focuses on the five archetypes that clearly cast therapists and clients in corresponding developmental roles and thereby occasion significant transference and countertransference conflicts that appear and reappear in various culture-influenced forms and intensities during the course of therapy (Dieckman, 1976; Kernberg, 1975). The chapter also focuses on these particular archetypes because they evoke the three major dynamics more likely than others to enter the treatment relationship: attachment and intimacy, authority, and sexuality (Westen & Gabbard, 2002).

## Archetypal Material as Embedded in Culture

According to Jung (1966), universal themes, collective beliefs, transcultural images, and primitive interpersonal scripts known as archetypes frequently attract the attention of the unconscious mind wherein they reside. They even become structural elements of the human psyche and demand to be used as patterns for life's interactions. Thus they prompt therapists and clients to resonate with them, even enact them, in the therapeutic setting. As Schafer (1959) explains, because of their empathy, "therapist[s] become in certain respects mother, father, sibling, child, and lover of the [client] as well as...the [client] himself" (354) as more than one archetype is activated during therapy, even during one session.

However, the exact nature of the transference and countertransference depends on the client's and therapist's culture(s), with culture being defined broadly to include ethnicity, age, socio-economic class, political affiliation, gender, sexual identity, religion, and other demographic characteristics. Being a mother in a Latino culture wherein the material role is central to family life, for example, would be different from being so in an upper-class northern European culture wherein some maternal functions are performed by nannies. Similarly, sibling rivalry in a Korean culture defined by a gender and age hierarchy as well as the influence and interference of in-laws would be different from its expression in a single-parent, Anglo-American family culture that is characterized by individual responsibility even among young children. Thus important lens through which therapists must observe archetype-based transference are the interwoven and ever-evolving cultures with which the client identifies.

At the same time, however, therapists must continually note long-lasting similarities among cultural identifications and be wary of a client's manipulation of culture as a defense mechanism. "All Latinos are late," for example, may not be so much a valid excuse on the part of a client as an attempt to limit interaction with the therapist because of shame or fear triggered by the God and Goddess Archetype.

In addition, therapists must be wary of their own unconscious bias against cultures other than their own. Should they see them as inferior, for example, they may not hold high expectations of certain clients. They may unconsciously pathologize certain clients or stereotype them, regarding them as exotic or too entrenched in their ways to change.

Unfortunately, space limitations do not permit detailed exploration of the impact cultural phenomena might have on transference and countertransference. Periodically, however, culture-relevant questions placed in parentheses will stimulate further thinking.

## The Mother Archetype

Jung's (1966) Mother Archetype is by and large the most relevant to therapy because, like the prototypic mother-child relationship, therapy involves repeated, intimate contact between two persons through conscious and unconscious channels of communication (Tower, 1956). Therapy easily becomes an opportunity for clients to find once more the vanished mother figure (Ferenczi, 1909) and enjoy again the mother-infant quasi-union of the first months of life (Greenacre, 1954). Similarly, therapy easily becomes an opportunity for therapists to play the maternal roles of creating and nourishing new psychic life.

When two people are all alone for an extended period of time as they are in the therapeutic setting, they cannot help but concentrate on each other's feelings and attitudes (Greenacre, 1954). Therapists closely attend to their clients, as did clients' mother figures. Clients experience understanding, non-judgmental professionals (Macalpine, 1959) who make no emotional counter-demands (Greenacre, 1954) and thus afford them another experience of original, early-life pleasure. Regardless of gender, most therapists come across in the typical therapeutic setting as having a maternal nursing attitude toward a suffering patient-child (Greenacre, 1954). Even when therapists fail to gratify their client, they replicate clients' early experience of mother: a combination of gratification and deprivation (Greenson & Wexler, 1965).

Thus therapy gives clients a perfect chance to recreate their infantile life in the transference (Bollas, 1983). Seeing their therapist in terms of a mother, clients can unconsciously displace their experiences with the original caregiver (Tower, 1956). They can expect that their therapist will satisfy all needs and repair all injuries (Horowitz et al., 1984). If they only please their therapist—usually in combination with making themselves appear needy and overusing negative self-descriptions—they can induce their therapist's care (Goldin, 1985). [What special impact might some Asian cultures have?]

For a client, the Mother Archetype is tantamount to secure attachment and uncomplicated intimacy: being loved unconditionally. It corresponds to the client's, indeed any person's, need to be valued, if only by one person. It permits the infant to discover his or her personal capacity "to light up the mother's face," an experience that becomes the "fundamental basis of self-image and self-esteem" (Casement, 1991, 93).

At a fundamental, unconscious level, clients, like infants, hold non-verbal expectations of symbolic bodily contact, of being held, fed, and kept warm and dry. They believe that their therapist will not only give them continual, empathic attention but also respond to both obvious and subtle indications of what they need. At an even deeper unconscious level, clients, like infants, entertain fantasies of returning to the mother-infant symbiotic state wherein they are no longer separate individuals (Benedek, 1953). They fantasize a psychological, pseudo-biological merger in which they enjoy undivided attention.

Concurrently, the Mother Archetype promotes in therapists complementary parental, care-giving attitudes and behaviors. These variables, in turn, prove key to establishing a nurturing, interdependent environment supportive of the therapeutic alliance.

Though clients' journey to independence rightfully includes an experience of dependence on their therapist, this dependence must foster healthy independence from the therapist. It must be transitional and temporary, not permanent.

Unfortunately, however, one "hazard" of the therapeutic profession is that therapists consciously attempting to maintain rapport during the working alliance can unconsciously habituate dependence. In working with clients, who are professedly dependent to one degree or another and want to be cared for (Chused & Raphling, 1992), therapists can unconsciously try to make clients regard them as *primary* change-agents. In subtle and sundry ways, therapists can cross over the line of objectivity and neutrality by assuring clients that they are not only profoundly interested in them and their needs but also intent on meeting those needs rather than helping clients assume that responsibility themselves (Plakun, 1998).

Another danger inherent in the Mother Archetype is clients' expectations of being mothered perfectly compared with therapists' actual performance. Therapists inevitably "mother" imperfectly; they do not, indeed cannot, fully compensate for clients' early experiences of deprivation. Thus therapy can become an occasion of powerful transferential conflicts within the client and between client and therapist as parental functions promoted by the Mother Archetype supercede key attitudinal and behavioral variables needed to sustain goal-attainment during the working alliance.

Gabbard (1996) exposes yet another danger. Clients with cogent needs to be mothered may also have a strong urge to defend against the therapist-client merger they covet. Clients may then withdraw and become resistive. They may even try to seduce their therapist, for a sexualized relationship may be preferable to the threat of a merger.

But even if seduction attempts do not occur, positive outcome depends on how successfully therapists balance clients' need to be "held close" and their need to be "held separate." Therapists must give clients "space" in which to find, on their own terms and in their own time, the "breast," the person who feeds. They must allow clients' self-sufficiency and autonomy. They must even allow clients to pursue a narcissistic desire to have "omnipotent" control of caregivers, or at least to oppose them as they strive for self-sufficiency, and still experience the caregivers' unconditional acceptance and positive regard.

Therapists who unconsciously hold the belief that they are and should be benevolent and self-giving and that clients should be able to use their therapists to obtain whatever they need are especially vulnerable to acting out the Mother Archetype. At first, their belief, which is itself based in the Mother Archetype, appears benign, even beneficial. For it assures therapists that they can be as unconditional as most biological mothers in their positive regard of their clients and their willingness to provide empathic support.

In time, however, this belief proves malevolent, for although therapists want to be instruments of their clients' healing, they grow weary. As their own need for self-care mounts, they cannot sustain the posture of being used by another. Furthermore, therapists, like all other human beings, have an instinctual sadistic trait against which they cannot endlessly defend (Pick, 1997). It is only a matter of time before they rebel against a system—in spite of having set it up—whereby clients can make endless use of their therapist.

In a similar way, it is only a matter of time before the seemingly positive enmeshment engendered by the Mother Archetype appears negative. Therapists who are eager to help clients make progress, for example, begin innocently by using an educational intervention. By overusing this intervention ever so slightly, however, they unwittingly give clients a two-fold message: because therapists know considerably more than their clients, *they* can bring about change; their clients cannot. In time, these therapists actually begin to do the work that clients should be doing while clients are relatively passive.

Clients who do not do the homework that they agree to do, for example, stimulate positive countertransference as they assume the role of needy students and therapists project their need to be a knowledgeable "teacher." Then, if their countertransference remains positive, therapists who have introjected the role of "teacher" unconsciously transform that role into "instrumental learner." In the end, as clients become proficient in non-participation, therapists experience disturbing countertransferential anxiety, which, in turn, gives rise to negative transference and the likelihood of treatment failure. Thus because of the Mother Archetype's profound influence on the unconscious of both client and therapist, therapists must maintain a delicate balance between allowing clients control and direction and refusing to assume their responsibilities.

Equally important, therapists must be neither insistent upon preserving closeness with their clients nor determined to maintain separateness from them. Therapists must be neither silently detached nor intrusive. They must remember that their client's need to feel secure in therapy by being "held" is figurative, for the client is a "child" within an adult, not a biological child (Casement, 1991). At the same time, however, therapists must keep in mind that a carefully selected intervention, such as an accurate, well-timed transference interpretation, can give the client a sense of being held physically that is more real than if "a real holding or nursing had taken place" (Winnicott, 1988, 61). Conveying understanding through language can seem to clients as if the therapist were "holding [them] in the past, that is, at the time [they] needed to be held, the time when love meant physical care and adaptation" (Winnicott, 1988, 62).

To summarize, in therapy no less than actual life, the Mother Archetype engenders developmental needs and empathic responses even as it generates personal and interpersonal conflict. In the hands of therapists who provide security by "holding" their clients even as they facilitate growth toward autonomy by allowing them to "move freely" the mother-archetype can facilitate significant therapeutic progress.

# The Father Archetype

The Father Archetype also influences the therapeutic process, for it speaks to another essential element of human development in early life: morality and its foundation in authority. The father represents the conscience, that psychological phenomenon that facilitates doing what is right and good for others, even if it is personally difficult (Nunberg, 1951), in order to preserve and protect life. Thus the Father Archetype speaks to that human instinct to sacrifice oneself for the good of the species. It encourages one to protect and defend life even at the cost of one's own life. *[Would Islamic cultures have a special impact in the case of the Father Archetype ?]*

Freud once said that the death of a man's father is the most important event in his life (Reik, 1937). It could hardly be otherwise for both men and women when that protector and defender of life departs—never to return.

Clients easily displace conflictual material from their biological father to their therapist because a major, if not *the* major, reason for coming to a therapist is to protect or restore their intrapsychic and interpersonal life. This is true regardless of the therapist's gender.

Equally natural is therapists' assumption of the paternal roles that clients assign them, for therapists want nothing more than to preserve or renew psychological life.

Transferential conflicts arise from the Father Archetype, however, because the preservation and protection of life is a matter of change, even of oneself, and clients tend to not want to make personal change. Rather, they want either to change others or to have their therapist change life for them. They do not want therapists to use their authority, which is bestowed on them by clients, to hold them responsible for personal change. Effective therapists, however, help clients realize that it is *they* who must change, even to the point of sacrificing what is dearest to them. Hence, conflicts within clients and between clients and their therapists inhere in the Father Archetype.

The Father Archetype appeals to therapists, for most choose their profession because of a deep-seated "savior" complex (Little, 1951; Cohen, 1952). They unconsciously believe that they are meant to save both themselves and others. In fact, by introjecting father archetypal transference, they can save themselves by saving their clients. As a consequence, they find it appealing to set a treatment framework, suggest a treatment plan, and impose certain expectations on their clients, for they thereby establish, intentionally or not, an authority relationship with their clients (Westen & Gabbard, 1996).

Therapists who unconsciously believe themselves to be omnipotent and innately powerful authority figures are especially vulnerable to the Father Archetype. They easily adopt a corollary belief: they are absolutely necessary for clients need to be rescued, healed, and protected, and they are rescuers, healers, and protectors *par excellence*.

Therapists who fail to recognize this related belief can even harbor unconscious prohibitions against their clients' getting well, for illness makes the therapist's presence a necessity.

Danger then arises for at least two reasons. First, though most clients want to get better on a conscious level, on an unconscious level they want to remain ill. Their symptoms enable them to feel connected with early, omnipotent caregivers.

> [Clients] want to hold onto [an] imagined perfect, or at least powerful, [person] from their past. [They...color the therapist with free-floating transference feelings. [They] fight to see the therapist as omnipotent rather than face the disappointment of seeing the real therapist (Alpert, 1992, 147).

Second, therapists are especially vulnerable to reparative functions, and clients become persons to whom therapists wish to make amends (Little, 1951; Pick, 1997). Indeed, repressed desires to rescue and perform reparative functions are the very basis of countertransference in the therapeutic setting (Volkan, 1995). When therapists hear about—indeed share—their clients' pain, they want to restore them to a pain-free emotional life. If clients let themselves be restored, all is well. If not, therapists become increasingly anxious, which, in turn, increases their desire to heal. And the vicious cycle begins again. (1)

Particularly vulnerable are therapists who have had a depressed mother. Unless they have done considerable personal work, their depressed mother, alive or deceased, continues to induce rescue and reparative fantasies. If she has also operated in a punitive motivational paradigm, she continues to provoke guilt. In turn, her therapists-children want to assuage their guilt or have grounds to deny it (Racker, 1972).

While on the surface this need would seem to be positive or at least harmless, it inevitably becomes harmful for three reasons. First, as already implied, reparative needs are susceptible to becoming reparative impulses, which, in turn, are susceptible to the repetition compulsion (Little, 1951). As therapists keep clients impaired because they want to make them well again and again, therapy becomes a travesty. Second, therapists' reparative needs cause them to unconsciously identify with clients' unconscious prohibitions against getting better that stem from their primitive aggressive instincts. Thus as clients express their early aggressive tendencies by thwarting therapists' efforts, therapists unwittingly exploit clients' sickness for what it does for them (Little, 1951). Third, therapists' reparative needs impede clients' growth from being victims to whom reparation is due to becoming survivors who choose to renounce victimhood and assume responsibility for their own welfare. Victimhood may be painful, but self-pity and the attention of others are powerful reinforcers of behavior.

# The God and Goddess Archetypes

Based on an eventual, developmentally appropriate need for autonomy, Jung's (1966) archetypes of god and goddess promote the twin fantasies of omnipotent control and self-sufficiency (Klein, 1957). *[What might be the impact of majority cultures? of high socio-economic class? of gender?]* They nurture the authority-based illusions of being smart enough to outwit "the gods" and powerful enough to rectify wrongs by punishing and rewarding others. (2)

Gabbard (1996) believes that the archetypes of god and goddess are especially influential in therapy because of clients' feelings of inferiority in the presence of their therapist. Especially for clients with an impoverished sense of self inherent in narcissistic traits or tendencies, therapists' ability to use therapeutic interventions effectively can serve as a painful reminder of others' superior creative powers and their own inferiority (Epstein, 1977). In fact, envy is aroused in some clients principally by their therapist's interpretative ability, Melanie Klein (1957) writes with penetrating insight. Ironically, while therapists want to increase clients' insight by interpreting, actually doing so may be a therapeutic mistake. (3)

*He was an attractive but needy client who had just been jilted in love. However, he was also seducing a vulnerable married woman who had little experience in being attractive to men.*

*When the woman finally decided to end their emotional affair, the man was furious and his fury extended to plotting revenge against the woman. He would reveal the affair to the woman's husband, he decided, and would hear of no reality testing that his therapist attempted to introduce.*

*His therapist wondered whether she should stand back and simply reflect her client's feelings even as he took steps to carry out his plan or share her countertransferential fear and anger.*

*She chose the latter, only to find her client resort to terminating his therapy. He could not—he would not—entertain thoughts of personal responsibility for harm he might do to others. He perceived himself as a god above reproach. He wanted to believe that he had the right to punish others without examining his role in failed relationships. He wanted to establish his personal omniscience and omnipotence.*

In hindsight, the therapist realized that it would have been better for her to continue to make intrapersonal diagnostic use of the transference, learning gradually why the client was resentful of suggestions that he focus on his personal responsibility. Once those reasons were addressed, the client might have been able to renounce his defensiveness and take personal responsibility for his actions. The client may never have assumed that responsibility, but premature termination eliminated even the possibility. Instead, the God and Goddess Archetypes set the stage for an unsuccessful outcome in spite of a well-intentioned attempt to address conflict.

Ironically, clients' unconscious insistence on failing in therapy is "inspired" by the God and Goddess Archetypes, for it is a control issue (Schafer, 1997). If clients are not successful, Grinberg (1997) points out, they continue to suffer, but they thereby outwit and punish their therapist. Their authority is covert but potent.

Clients who experience failure of the parental holding environment are especially inclined to embrace the God and Goddess Archetypes. Because they have had to be to sustain and nourish themselves, they instinctively adopt the position that they are omnipotently self-sufficient (Modell, 1980). They even believe that they must parent their therapist, much as they once did their parents. The more ill the clients, the more powerful are their transferential role reversals due to original parents treating them as if they actually were parents whenever they were thoughtful and considerate (Searles, 1975).

Paradoxically, clients' fears of being personally omnipotent are also embedded in the God and Goddess Archetypes. They fear the unending power and authority which that state conveys and, even more so, their not being able to find well-modulated support: an equal or at least a powerful companion-other (Stein, 1993). *[How might the Filipino culture, with the emphasis it puts on debts of gratitude to elders, exacerbate this problem?]* At the same time, clients fear domination and absolute control by their equal because they interpret great power with great enslavement. They regard having such a companion as risking exploitation, even annihilation (Modell, 1980). (4)

For their part, therapists who hold the belief, which is largely unconscious, that they are superior to others because of their education, experience, and professional success are especially vulnerable to enacting the God and Goddess Archetypes. They assume that they are gifted, remarkably skillful in their perception, analytic and synthesis abilities, instinct, and ability to deal effectively with affect. They are almost magical (Grand et al., 1985).

Then, because these therapists actually have a certain amount of *a priori* knowledge due to their experience and education, they succumb to fantasies of having innate power and authority (Bion, 1967). When, in addition, clients transfer to therapists their cultural-based reverence and awe for professionals called "doctor," the therapists are tempted to believe that they actually are superior human beings, superior to their clients and, perhaps, superior to people in general (Cohen, 1952). Unsuspected and unacknowledged in the unconscious, this countertransferential force becomes "larger than life." It becomes a "recipe" for ultimate therapeutic failure: therapists assume knowledgeable authority-figure roles and relegate their clients to relatively uninformed subject-figure roles.

These assignments become doubly dangerous in that the God and Goddess Archetypes also "inspire" fantasies of ideals with which therapists unconsciously identify (Grand et al., 1985; Racker, 1972). They begin to treat a challenge to their ideas and interpretations, even those based on minimal cues that clients unconsciously provide, as unwelcome interference. They let humiliation by clients, particularly blatant shame projected by clients with borderline or narcissistic personality disorders, plunge them into deep depression. They allow poor evaluations by clients to increase their fear that these same clients will disclose their "incompetence." They blame treatment failures on clients.

These therapists then adopt the belief that therapeutic failures cannot and will not be tolerated. Although they do not consciously deny that mistakes are part of being human, they unconsciously regard them as reasons to defend themselves against what would otherwise be wholesome feedback. Thus they fail to learn the lessons that therapeutic mistakes teach and sharply increase the probability of future failures.

Unfortunately, in response to countertransferential fears of failure and of owning mistakes, many clients persist in developing negative therapeutic reactions and treatment-destructive resistances. They even begin to hate their therapists (Blum, 1997), which, in turn, makes therapists with omnipotent self-beliefs progress from frustration and confusion to dislike, even hatred, both of themselves and their clients. They may even wish to attack or annihilate the clients they hate and, finding this unacceptable, project it onto their clients. When clients, especially adolescents, receive this projective identification, the worst proves true. They engage in self-destructive behaviors or activities dangerous to others (Ogden, 1994), both of which undermine focused therapeutic work.

*The therapist thought that he liked his adolescent client in spite of the terrific challenges she was providing. Besides not going to school, she was running away from home and, most likely, using drugs. The therapist reflected often on how he thought that he really listened to his client; in fact, he listened and listened and listened. He responded empathically; he seldom challenged her, and when he did so, he was most respectful and gentle. Yet his client continued her self-destructive behavior.*

*"Am I really able to like this client?" the therapist began to wonder. "I want to so badly that perhaps I am fooling myself. Maybe that is why my client periodically refers to parents who can hardly stand her."*

*Finally, the therapist had to admit that the time and energy that he was spending on helping someone change who apparently would not change might be leading to more negative countertransference than he would like to admit. He decided to let that possibility be voiced, hoping to see if it would help his client.*

*"I find your behavior so frustrating," he said to his client. "No matter what we plan, indeed what you say you will do, you hardly ever do it. Maybe my negativity is something you sense. Maybe you won't change because you sense that I don't like what you are doing and therefore don't like you."*

*The client listened attentively but said nothing. At the end of the session, however, she made reference to no one really wanting her, not even her parents. Listening intently and respectfully, the therapist simply held his client's pain. And he held it in subsequent sessions until it finally lost its grip on his client, and she no longer had to act it out.*

As this vignette reveals, therapists' unwitting denial of unpleasant truths about themselves and thus their enactment of the God and Goddess Archetypes can weaken, if not destroy, the therapeutic and working alliances. It is only when therapists recognize, and perhaps humbly acknowledge, their negative countertransference that the truth of the therapeutic relationship can serve as an invitation to clients to deal with similar truths.

Another way in which therapists unwittingly enact the God and Goddess Archetypes is by engaging in manic interpretive activity as a way of controlling depressive anxiety related to feelings of clinical impotence (Epstein, 1977). But manic activity only makes matters worse, for though therapists' assuming direction and control of the therapeutic process is usually seen as positive early in therapy, it soon becomes clearly negative for two reasons.

First, clients are actually ambivalent both about the therapeutic bond (Fox, 1998) and the power and authority that they presume their therapists possess. They both love and hate their therapists; they both idealize them and depreciate them (Olinick, 1996). They both want to receive their therapist's attention and destroy his or her position and authority (Freud, 1915). They desire to surrender to their therapist's authority—even turn over self-responsibility—but still stay in control. If clients actually surrender, sooner or later they rebel and demand that the all-benevolent, all-powerful therapist return their power but without their self-responsibility. In that way, they can do what they want without facing consequences. They can be assured that their therapist will set things right. Indeed, writes Schafer (1997), clients' refusal to take responsibility for their life ranks well above their use of self-abnegation to solicit reassurance. (5)

Second, therapists' assumption of direction and control becomes negative because it implies their personal right to respond negatively when therapeutic success is minimal or absent. They begin to justify their urge to express anger in ways that feel good at the time: punishing, getting revenge, and paying back. They even justify hating their clients. In time, however, this persistent countertransferential hatred is registered and experienced by clients. It then becomes a significant factor in therapeutic stalemates and failures (Blum, 1997). (6)

Yet another way in which therapists enact God and Goddess Archetypes is by rationalizing their character traits of rigidity and always having to be right. Therapists allow them to assume the legitimacy of valid approaches that justify corresponding therapeutic techniques. They become rigidly self-righteous about what they do and how they do it and reclassify clients who object to what is happening in their treatment as simply uncooperative.

Finally, some therapists enact God and Goddess Archetypes by unconsciously believing that they can use any available therapeutic measure, even sexual involvement with clients to ensure therapeutic success (Searles, 1975).

It is no wonder, then, that therapists' fantasies of omnipotence are a chief obstacle to effective therapy (Bion, 1967). Undiagnosed or misdiagnosed god and goddess archetypal phenomena are exceedingly dangerous.

## The Sibling Rivalry Archetype

Jung's (1966) archetype of sibling rivalry promotes expectations of getting one's way, winning over competitors, and placating others if victory is not within reach. Though therapists may first appear to be parents, as they reveal their shortcomings, they soon become "mere siblings" competing for some obscure prize or preferred place in the larger, interactional, relational world. This often happens when clients begin to find out that therapists have other clients, Ferenczi (1909) explains.

Just as the Mother Archetype inspires clients' need to escape merger, sibling rivalry occasions their need for space that protects them from being impinged upon by the environment, which is comprised of both non-persons and persons, including the therapist. (7)

The Sibling Rivalry Archetype challenges therapists to become aware of their need to assume that they are necessarily the focus of their client's internal world. It challenges therapists to provide both time and opportunities for clients to discover them gradually, that is, in ways dependent upon their role as clients in an emerging relationship.

Therapists who unconsciously believe that they deserve to be liked, even loved, for all the good they do are especially vulnerable to enacting the Sibling Rivalry Archetype. This belief lies along a continuum of therapists' expecting simple gratitude for services rendered to demanding that clients complete their therapy successfully to expecting that clients actually meet their therapists' affiliative, achievement, and power needs. Maintaining a line between use and abuse, this belief clearly excludes being abused.

However, that line is difficult to maintain, for therapists who feel used for more than a short time begin to feel abused. Even if they are not hostile, clients who are demanding can soon cause their therapists to dislike them. Even nondemanding clients who share their pervasive negative feelings with their therapists are asking that the latter absorb that negativity session after session. Consequently, therapists can have strong needs to retaliate, which causes them to resent their clients.

Relying heavily on getting gratitude from clients is particularly dangerous, for therapists who work hard and long to deserve that gratitude do not always take the time to develop outside relationships. In fact, to the extent that therapists feel loved and appreciated in their work, they can fall into the insidious trap of devaluing non-therapeutic relationships. When they meet their attachment and intimacy needs in their work, they unconsciously conclude that they do not have to meet them otherwise. Therapists may then rely on clients to comfort and renew them. They may even expect clients to meet their intimacy needs. Therapists may unconsciously act-out their arousal by encouraging erotic feelings in clients for their own gratification, ask for details of clients' sexual fantasies, or make phallic, "penetrating" interpretations too often and too soon (Gabbard, 1996).

Similarly, therapists may unconsciously encourage clients' erotic fantasies about them, only to become cold and aloof in response to clients' longings. They may insist that clients focus on problems brought in from outside and thus give clients the message that sexual feelings are unacceptable, even disgusting, which may sadly mirror clients' own feelings.

Clients who detect their therapist's aloofness will experience a form of negative attachment, even victimization. Caught in the transference-countertransference cycle, they may actually wish to prolong this victimization and avoid responsibility for behaviors that may correlate with past persecution or abuse. They may not want to face the fact that in some cases and to some extent their own immature thinking and irresponsible behavior contribute to ongoing victimization (Schafer, 1997). (8)

In other cases, clients who feel abused by their therapist will identify with them and become persecutors themselves, all the way from experiencing security in their therapist's presence to imitating them or surpassing them in abusing others. They may respond overtly by engaging in manic or aggressive activity or covertly by attempting suicide or otherwise maintaining a depressive state (Racker, 1972). (9) They may somatize or abuse their body.

If they are unable to detect the self-hatred of depressed or physically ill clients, therapists may make the mistake of sending "messages" to clients demanding that they become well. Some will rebel by resisting or even terminating therapy (Ogden, 1994). Others will comply, at least outwardly and for the time being. None, however, will satisfactorily address issues stemming from the Sibling Rivalry Archetype.

A similar sibling rivalry archetypal issue is clients' insistence on progress in therapy. They desire and expect success much too early in the therapeutic process. Shafer (1997) explains that if clients are consistently and quickly successful, they may be dealing with relatively superficial material rather than holding themselves responsible for making difficult personal changes. Conflicts then arise for therapists who want to support clients' efforts to be successful and yet need to challenge them to work on truly important issues.

In sum, the Sibling Rivalry Archetype challenges therapists to manage their clients' and their own competition for dominance. As equal partners, clients and therapists can rightfully vie for control of the therapeutic hour. Though clients ultimately decide content, therapists can and must sometimes introduce unwanted material. Though therapists hold ultimate responsibility for process, clients can and must influence timing and the order of activity.

## The Animus and Anima Archetypes

The Animus and Anima Archetypes hold expectations of completion, the strengths of one gender being added to the other. The Animus, an archetype within the female psyche, is "the deposit...of all men's ancestral experiences of woman" (Jung, 1966, 209). The Anima, a comparable archetype found in the male psyche, is a detailed outline of women's ancestral experiences of men. Men are compensated by a feminine element, as women are compensated by a masculine element in the course of both genders searching for wholeness, completeness, and unity (Jung, 1966). Both men and women achieve strength and power through attachment to what they are not.

The animus brings with him the paternal, the logical and the cognitive, especially the ability to discriminate. The anima brings with her the maternal, the relational, the emotional, especially the connectedness so needed in interpersonal relations (Jung, 1966).

The Anima and Animus Archetypes play out in therapy in clients and therapists expecting each other to compensate for what they do not have themselves, as they have with members of the opposite sex in the past and are likely to be doing outside of therapy. Rather than work to develop their own capacities, therapists and clients expect the other to do so for them.

If transference and countertransference become fully operative, the animus, partial as he is to argument, can best be seen at work in women in disputes wherein both client and therapist "know" that they are right. They have an unshakable feeling of rightness and righteousness. "Men can argue in a very womanish way, too, when they are anima-possessed and have thus been transformed into the animus of their own anima" (Jung, 1966, 153). With women—therapists or clients—the argument soon becomes a matter of personal vanity and touchiness rather than content. With men—therapists or clients—the argument becomes a matter of power, be it truth or justice or some other "ism" as their dialogue becomes marked by misapplied truisms, cliches, platitudes, opinionated views, insinuations, misconstructions, and misinterpretations. [*What might be the impact of American political affiliations?*] Nothing is important except proving one's point, with the result that the therapeutic alliance is seriously weakened, even destroyed.

Granted that most therapists manage the animus well enough to resist falling into an obvious argument, they can be righteous and judgmental in their interpretations and set on having the last word. They can be less than open to clients' rejection of their ideas, clients who themselves may need to reject whatever they hear for the sake of being right.

The anima can also disrupt therapy if transference and countertransference become fully operative. Bringing with her hypersensitivity, sentimentality, compulsive touchiness, and self-pity, the anima can make both therapist and client highly alert to each other's shortcomings and yet reluctant to explore their own contribution to difficult relations. Wanting to maintain an exaggerated positive self-image, [*What might be the impact of Japanese culture?*] client and therapist can consciously collaborate yet unconsciously resist honest interpersonal evaluation, becoming very offended at the implication of personal weakness and aborting fruitful evaluation by retaliating in passive-aggressive ways. If, on the other hand, client and therapist identify and work with the anima, she becomes for them a source of life-giving energy. With the help of their spiritual guide, they accept in themselves and each other a partly positive, partly negative self-image and thus enjoy elemental, feminine dynamism (Ulanov, 1984).

## A Final Thought

Therapists from cultures significantly different from clients would seem to have a special need to collaborate with their clients in order to increase their awareness of the ways in which archetypes impact transference and countertransference (Mishne, 2003). Therapists would then be in a position to help their clients "become aware of, review, and alter obsolete conclusions that determine their contemporary approaches to their lives" (Renik, 1990, 199). They would then be able to collaborate with clients to resolve the personal, interpersonal, and cultural conflicts that lie beneath various human needs and lead to unending aggression. They would not deny those needs, for they are universal and integral to psychological functioning, but would consider new, more appropriate ways of meeting them.

# Endnotes

(1) These therapists consciously conclude that failing with a client is much more than a personal problem (Sharpe, 1930). It means that clients will not get better, and therapists will be failures.

(2) Bringing gifts, asking for advice, and being careful not to disappoint one's therapist are likely to be other signs of the God and Goddess Archetypes.

(3) It is not unusual for clients to harbor a deep, passive wish to defeat the therapists that they love when they realize that therapists are much more resourceful and insightful than they. "You are so great, my fate lies in your hands; do your best and I shall yet defeat you" (Stein, 1981), clients unconsciously warn as envy surfaces. Like envious persons in everyday life, clients try to defeat envied others rather than acquire the skills they possess.

(4) The actual abuse that certain clients suffered presents special difficulties. For within the psychic structure of many victims lies a figure who is, paradoxically, both a protector and a persecutor image (Kalsched, 1996).

(5) Conflicts arise in therapy as therapists attempt to determine how and when to interpret clients' refusal to take responsibility for their lives and their therapy. Working most obviously within the God and Goddess Archetypes, therapists must balance their need to be ultimately responsible for the therapeutic process while their clients' need to decide whether or not they will take responsibility for their own lives, including their therapeutic "life."

(6) Blum (1997) believes that transference hate can become an even greater problem than transference love because it reaches even deeper into clients' and therapists' psyches than does their loving: it threatens their fundamental self-esteem. Nevertheless, transference hate and countertransference hate are easily repressed or denied because they seem contrary to the therapeutic alliance. "Clients should not hate their attentive, resourceful therapists, and therapists should not hate their needy, vulnerable clients," cultural and psychotherapeutic traditions hold. If hate is present, it must be denied, according to conventional wisdom. Then, like other denied and repressed emotions, hate intensifies on an unconscious level even as it is minimized or rationalized on a conscious level. As a result, hate can be unwittingly enacted by clients, and even by therapists. In turn, enactments of hate, such as holding a grudge, are powerfully reinforced by resultant experiences of self-enhancing power and enjoyable vindication (Galdston, 1987).

Hate tends to be strong when intimacy fears surface. However desperately clients want to be in a close, loving relationship, few have learned to tolerate the stress of that intimacy. When it surfaces and therapists do not draw attention to it–let alone help clients to deal fully with it–clients often resort to such hate-based maneuvers as significantly reducing the efficiency of their therapist. They induce guilt in their therapists, especially those who need to be needed, by acting-out and thereby destroying any concrete plan to improve (Herron & Rouslin, 1982).

(7) These therapists acknowledge that they may be used, as older sibling may be rightfully used by younger siblings, but they maintain that they must not be abused. They are not ultimately responsible for their "siblings;" unlike their parents, they can walk away if things get too bad.

(8) Therapists must resolve the thorny conflict of accepting their clients as they are while challenging them to grow in maturity and responsibility. Therapists must come to a satisfactory balance between respecting clients' perspectives and questioning the inevitable distortions they harbor, especially in the area of immature interpersonal relationships (Handley, 1995).

(9) Perhaps nothing causes greater transferential conflict than suicidal desires of clients and the anti-suicide stance of therapists, for the possibility of clients committing suicide reminds therapists many times over of losses they had to accept in their families of origin. Hence, therapists experience conflict over holding and containing their clients' suicidal desires and wanting to eradicate them at all costs and as soon as possible.

In turn, therapists' inability to resolve these conflicts satisfactorily can easily result in significant loss of rapport or even loss of the therapeutic alliance.

# CHAPTER FIVE

# MANIFESTATIONS OF TRANSFERENCE AND COUNTERTRANSFERENCE

## Challenges Inherent in Identifying Transference and Countertransference

Transference and countertransference challenge therapists in at least three major ways. First, because the conscious mind cannot have direct knowledge of phenomena "residing" in the unconscious mind, therapists can detect transferred material only in the vague, shadowy signs of its presence. They can discover it only as it manifests itself in words, feelings, dreams, fantasies, somatic responses, and behavior as each of "these voiceless and vociferous little parts of [the self] . . . do their best to add their 'two cents' into the final product" (Wittig, 2002, 143).

Second, because manifestations of transference and countertransference are a source of data but not a source of evidence (Smith, 1990), therapists cannot simply take them at face value. Rather, they must "unpack" them to the point of their yielding the truths they hold.

Third, therapists cannot forget that transferred material is characterized both by similarities across cultures and differences among cultures. Roles of women, for instance, are similar and yet distinctive in Asian cultures and American cultures, in Islam and Christianity, in the eyes of adolescence and those of senior citizens. Hence, therapists must attend to transcultural as well as within-cultural variables in order to expose the precise nature of transferred material accurately.

Categories of transference and countertransference manifestations, which overlap and merge, are artificial in one respect. Emotions, for example, find expression in words, facial expressions, gestures, and dreams even as dreams consist primarily of actions cloaked in affect. Examining these categories separately, however, permits one to simplify extremely complex phenomena and create manageable templates that can be placed over actual therapeutic occurrences.

## Words: Therapeutic Material

At least initially, therapists regard words that clients use as simply their means of communicating the problems and concerns of which they are aware. Therapists take these words at face value, that is, according to their dictionary definitions or denotations.

However, certain words with denotations that clients consciously use to convey meaning also carry connotations or affective associations of which clients may be relatively or totally unaware. Some words not only convey straightforward messages but also carry subtle, emotionally tinged nuances. A client who says that she wants to work on her relationship with her father, for example, may simply mean her biological father. But she may also be unconsciously revealing her need to improve her relationship with others she associates with her biological father: those in authority, those who provide for the weak, those who are simply older and male. Indeed, the client may even be implying her older female therapist. Similarly, a client who says, "I want to reduce my depression" may mean "my sadness, loneliness, and listlessness as they affect my daily life." However, a client who uses this statement may also be unconsciously referring to the depressing quality of a therapeutic relationship that closely resembles a previous affiliation. Thus therapists must be open to the possibility that the connotation-bearing words clients are unconsciously using to sharpen and refine their denotative communication are actually manifestations of transference.

But should therapists suspect the same of what they themselves say? Is it possible that the words therapists consciously choose reveal unconscious countertransferential phenomena?

Yes, according to psychoanalytic theory, for the unconscious mind is always trying to find ways to move its contents into consciousness. Therapists, like others, unintentionally say things that they consciously forbid themselves to say. "I am afraid I cannot schedule you next week," for example, may unwittingly reveal therapists' fear of their clients' imminent revelations. (1)

## Words: Extra-therapeutic Material

Therapists intent on discovering transference must also examine the extra-therapeutic, seemingly unrelated material that clients introduce during sessions. At times, in introducing extraneous material, clients are consciously intending to shed light on their goals, give background material, or provide information about who they are as persons. At other times, however, clients are unconsciously revealing the nature of their therapeutic relationship (Kahn, 1997), for it is either hindering or facilitating their progress. (2)

*In spite of the client's clearly stated goal to learn to be a better parent, she began her second session by speaking of not being called back to substitute teach by a local school. She wondered if she had not done a good enough job.*

*Her therapist, in turn, wondered whether his client was really asking about how well she had done during her first session. Had her performance been good enough for her therapist?*

*The therapist remembered that his client had called that morning to ask about the roads. Because heavy rains had made roads slick near her house, she wondered whether he thought the roads near his office were dangerous. Perhaps she really wondered whether her therapist would call her again, so to speak, or be like the school personnel? Was it dangerous to travel the "road" to therapeutic work?*

*The therapist decided to test his hypothesis that the call the client made to him was due less to the weather and more to concern about his evaluation of their first session. "Did I seem disappointed in our session?" he asked. "Did you call to find out how emotionally dangerous it might be to drive to my office?"*

*She breathed a sign of relief and answered thoughtfully. Yes, there were similarities between him and the school personnel. Yes, he too was an evaluator who might find her wanting. Yes, it felt dangerous to her to think of returning for a second session.*

*Subsequently she returned weekly, revealing in detail how her early years were marked by poor grades for performance in the "book" of her father. She explored the basis of her feeling inferior as a parent and teacher.*

As this vignette reveals, when talking about a third party, clients may be displacing *toward* their therapist: unintentionally revealing their feelings about the person with whom they are working and who *they* are in relationship with their therapist. (3)

Clients' urge to do so—to reveal self-in-relationship—is unusually strong in the closeness of the therapeutic setting, for it is there that their unconscious desire to share what is really important but too threatening most easily breaks through the barrier between the conscious and unconscious minds. It is "intended" on an unconscious level.

*He complained bitterly of his religion teacher, saying how stupid and out-of-it the teacher was. He couldn't stand her or her class.*

*His cognitive-behavioral therapist listened attentively, waiting for moments of insertion, hoping to help her client recognize the value of doing his assignments for religion class in spite of his feelings toward his teacher. For not doing homework and skipping class were the client's presenting problems. Though he was bright and capable, he was failing.*

*One morning , through a frantic call from the client's mother, the therapist learned of her client's drug problem. He had been expelled from school for smoking pot, and it wasn't the first time. Realizing she should have decoded the client's hatred-for-teacher remarks much sooner, the therapist said, "You never even mentioned you were having trouble with drugs."*

*Her client looked painfully embarrassed but quickly shot back with, "I can't talk to you about certain things. You're too old. You don't understand what it's like to be me."*

Too late, far too late, was the client's real message becoming clear. Had the therapist only decoded the transferential meaning of her client's complaints about his teacher, she could have afforded him an opportunity to explore his belief that closeness in age was a key prerequisite for therapeutic collaboration. Without that, he could only presume that his therapist was as much "out-of-it" as was his teacher. He could not focus on his goals because he could not count on his therapist to assuage the pain of making the changes they required.

Extra-therapeutic material clients bring in at the beginning or end of sessions is especially noteworthy. Enigmatic, mysterious, and seemingly totally unconnected to hardcore therapeutic work, it often holds important transferential messages.

*He walked in feeling very, very tired, saying he couldn't get enough sleep. "Was he also saying that he was very tired of their therapeutic work?" his therapist wondered. Was his therapist's insistence on his becoming self-sufficient tiresome for him?*

*"Maybe," the client answered when asked about his in-session fatigue. "I am tired of people trying to change me," he admitted. "It started back in grade school. The teachers always had something hard for me to learn. It made me wonder when it would ever end."*

*After a brief period of silence, the client breathed a sigh of relief, saying "Nobody ever cared about how hard it was for me before today." Then he moved with uncharacteristic interest and feeling into what he himself needed to change.*

# Feelings

## Transferential Affect

Transferential feelings are those displaced to the therapist because of subtle similarities between the therapist and persons outside of therapy. Clients whose parents were intolerant of them, for example, may experience their therapist as intolerant because of displaced feelings triggered by a "kernel of truth:" the therapist's slightly intolerant behavior. (4)

Though single, obvious feelings would not appear to require decoding, what appears to be a simple feeling may indeed be complex emotion with a second or even third feeling at the periphery of the obvious feeling. Anger due to a therapist being slightly intolerant, for example, may actually include fear of the therapist's rejection and sadness because of it.

*"She cancels for so many reasons," her therapist thought. Some seem legitimate, but others seem flimsy. The therapist recognized that the material on which the client was working was intimate and embarrassing but wondered, "Could it be that our therapeutic relationship is even more of an obstacle to her coming?"*

*When her client finally came for a session, the therapist listened and watched for displaced material that might help her decode what on the surface appeared to be positive feelings. She also opened herself to decoding her own countertransference: her annoyance that sessions were being cancelled and her fears of a premature termination.*

*Finally, when her client described her mother-in-law as controlling and said she was going to set firm limits with her, the therapist decided to use a transference interpretation to ask if her client felt able to set limits during therapy sessions. Her client said that she wasn't sure. Noting that ambivalence, however, the therapist began helping the client explore possible negative transference. The client, in turn, stopped canceling her sessions.*

Theorists vary as to which transferential feelings are most probable in therapy. Racker (1972) tells therapists to expect first what is nearest to consciousness. Clients want to partner, if not bond, with their therapist and therefore hope to be found worthy of their therapist's efforts. Beneath this hope, however, can lie fear of being judged. (5)

Other theorists tell therapists to expect transferential feelings most likely to contribute to the therapeutic alliance, regardless of their closeness to consciousness. On the positive side are feelings of love, calm, and relief resultant from experiences of unconditional acceptance by others being transferred to the therapist who, in turn, provides "kernels of truth" in the form of unconditional positive regard. But even these feelings might be coupled with fear of the unconditional acceptance becoming conditional.

On the negative side are feelings of distrust of someone appearing too good to be true, fear of being engulfed, sadness because of previous broken promises, embarrassment because of shame assigned by others, or any combination of these feelings transferred from experiences with others. Since bonding experiences are at least partly negative, primitive negative feelings can easily combine with each other and with positive feelings. In fact, earliest bonding experiences commonly consist of a positive experience of having one's basic needs met on demand, followed by a negative one of learning one has asked too much or too often.

To decode feelings, then, is to derive the true meaning of complex, labile emotions that originally appear to be simple and stable. It is to study body language, especially the prosody of the speaker's speech, for voice quality is the truest indication of emotions (Bostanov & Kotchoubey, 2004). It is to listen carefully to reports of dreams and fantasies, consider the connotation of words clients choose with particular attention to those suggesting affect, and note whether there are contradictions between these seemingly reliable manifestations of transference.

*She came late, saying that she had rushed to get to her appointment. She was unsettled, overwrought, and uneasy. When her therapist asked about her rushing, she simply explained that she had not left the house in time. The therapist then had to decide whether to take at face value a poor judgment of time and distance or whether to decode her client's words.*

*Noticing her client's uptight body language and clipped sentences, the therapist decided to ask directly about whether leaving the house late might be connected to reluctance to come to her appointment. She then received what was a far truer answer. Her client said that she was not sure that the particular therapist she had chosen could really help her.*

*A fruitful exploration of the exact nature of their work and the relationship it implied followed, during which it became clear to the therapist that the client was transferring her disappointment with former teachers to her therapist.*

## Countertransferential Affect

Even as therapists decode transferential affect, they must be alert for countertransferential affect, for it can reveal both the interpersonal weaknesses of clients and the work therapists themselves must do to facilitate therapeutic progress. Having had negative experiences with teenagers, for example, therapists can perceive youth as crass and self-centered even as they enter the therapy room. Adolescents sense this unspoken attitude, become self-conscious, and come across as crass in their anxious response to a person who somehow dislikes them. Others have disliked them and inflicted harm, which has taught them a simple lesson: "Harm others before they harm you." Especially challenging for therapists are countertransferential feelings resultant from the projection of displaced feelings that clients cannot tolerate, own, or even put into language because they precede the ability to speak (Modell, 1980). Like infants who deliver subliminal affect-laden messages before they are able to use language, clients unconsciously hand over their feelings of being unloved, blamed, or confused to therapists who have the ability and readiness to receive them. Thus by unconscious design, the truth about clients is discoverable first in what therapists experience on a non-verbal level and then in what their clients experience as their therapists put that initial truth into words.

As a general rule, therapists first discover the truth about themselves in feelings that seem excessive or inappropriate to what clients seem to be saying (Tower, 1956). Because these emotions are usually much nearer to the heart of the matter than reasoning, therapists' unconscious, affect-based perception of a client's unconscious mind is more acute and in advance of their conscious, cognition-based conception of the situation (Heimann, 1950).

Moreover, therapists' behavior or somatic response can signal already existing affect. Sleepiness, for example, might indicate that therapists have felt abandoned by clients who frequently intellectualize, speak monotonously, or talk in circles (Racker, 1972).

*She moved from topic to topic as skillfully as a skater circles a rink, returning periodically to certain issues but never completely dealing with them. Her therapist grew increasingly sleepy but tried to convince herself that a hot day and getting too little sleep was causing her head to feel heavy. She wondered, however, why nothing she did, including getting up to adjust the shades, alleviated her distress. "Should I be decoding" the therapist wondered, "because the client is 'saying' more by her language patterns than meets the eye?"*

*Finally, the therapist decided to test her hypothesis that the client's circling speech might be unconsciously intended to disconnect from her therapist. "When you circle from topic to topic, I simply can't follow you for long," she said. "I get so frustrated that I disconnect from you. Could it be that you want to disconnect from me?" she asked.*

*"I don't know," the client responded. "But I do know that this happens to me a lot. I've been so hurt by people not listening to me. Even as a child, when I said I wanted to play with other children, they never heard me. I need help with how to talk. I've needed it forever!"*

*Thus decoding a countertransferential response proved invaluable in terms of "unlocking" affect and exposing childhood experiences from which the client continued to suffer.*

Similarly, therapists' feelings can indicate enactments in which they have already become embroiled (Hinshelwood, 1999). Therapists' irritability, for example, may be in the service of staving off guilt feelings for having already acted out their dislike of a client (Schafer, 1997).

A closer look at therapists' countertransferential affect begins with grouping commonly experienced feelings into the four categories of sadness, anger, fear, and gladness, followed by a feeling rarely discussed: envy.

## Countertransferential Sadness

Countertransferential sadness usually combines discrete states of feeling demeaned, inferior, sorry for oneself, hopeless, helpless, and depressed. Therapists' depression, which encompasses the other feelings, merits special attention because remaining depressed can result in therapists' losing the self-esteem and self-efficacy they need to function. (6)

Arlow (1985) asserts that therapists' depression is basically a countertransferential reaction: a defense against the depression of clients. Clients come to therapy because of an unconscious sense of a bad self even as they consciously proclaim a good self in relation to bad others. Occasionally clients project a good self onto their therapist, but more often, they project a bad self (Epstein, 1977), which they subject to punitive measures in unconscious imitation of prior caregivers (Racker, 1968).

However, countertransferential depression also depends on therapists' own sense of self. Therapists with a positive sense of self and an internal "caregiver" are in a favorable position to realize that their depressed clients are engaged in projective fantasies with which they must first resonate and then reject. In contrast, therapists whose own self-definition is basically negative may unconsciously add self-punishment to negative transference. Even worse, when therapists experience the combined force of their inadequate internal self and their clients' projections, they can lose their capacity for rational, objective observation. Though they may never admit it to their clients, therapists can "agree" intrapsychically that they are inadequate (Epstein, 1977), as the following vignette illustrates.

*First the minister came to therapy; then his son. Their therapist ,who had experienced painful humiliation at the hands of adolescent males, thought that in this instance she was secure. As the surly adolescent attacked first his father and then other members of his family, however, she had to admit that she was becoming increasingly uptight. For his part, the father appealed to the therapist to set limits but still allow his son to express himself.*

*Feeling demeaned when the son shifted his focus from people to the "stupid" therapy sessions he was being forced to attend, the therapist articulated what she thought would be an acceptable agenda. People could express their feelings, but one would have to combine feelings with discussion so that both father and son could arrive at a solution they could both endorse. In formulating the plan, of course, the therapist was unconsciously attempting to lessen the negative impact that the adolescent was making on her, even as she was consciously steering the therapy from problem to solution. She was determined not succumb to the adolescent's negativity. She would side with the father in his need to get rid of it. She resolved to transform the adolescent's resentment into problem-solving energy and thus reduce the resentment that she felt toward him.*

*The therapist's failure to address transference and countertransference however, proved fatal. Imbibing his son's attitude, the father began to align with his son. He agreed that the family situation was so bad that it could not be fixed and that therapy was proving to be a waste of time and money. He implied that the therapist lacked the skills to help them.*

*However, rather than address her painful countertransferential feelings of inferiority and impotence, the therapist again set out to convince the father, if not the son, of the value of patience and hard work, both within and outside therapy, and to convey her hope that things could change. As her professional and psychological survival became uppermost in her mind, the therapist continued to de-emphasize her powerful countertransferential feelings.*

*Eventually, the therapist admitted to herself that therapy was going nowhere and that she could no longer count on her clinical expertise. When the father finally said that he would not make another appointment, the therapist merely mentioned her availability if he changed his mind.*

Thus the therapist's insidious sense of self-impotence and low self-esteem clouded her vision, leading her to self-destructive despair. Her acting-in contributed to therapeutic failure no less than her adolescent client's acting-out.

## Countertransferential Anger

Countertransferential anger includes hatred of abusive clients as well as disdain for victims of abuse combined with revulsion and disgust for what happened to them. Thus displaced anger manifests itself in various forms of acting-out: withdrawing from clients (Plakun, 1998); becoming irritable because of precious time being taken up with what seem relatively small problems, leading to restlessness; and feeling bored because of mundane therapeutic issues, leading to sleepiness. Countertransferential anger may also reveal itself as therapists' resentment of the emotional barrenness of clients' communications or helplessness and frustration (Cohen, 1952), all of which may induce sleepiness.

Therapists' extended frustration over lack of progress in therapy, which is often due to narcissistic transference in the sense of client's sense of entitlement to progress without effort, can also produce countertransferential anger. This, in turn, can result in inattention, annoyance, and forgetfulness (Schwaber, 1990).

Countertransferential anger can also stem from transferential guilt resultant from clients' inducing their therapists to act in an angry fashion in order to appease their own guilt (Chused, 1992). On the other hand, in response to aggressive transference, therapists may experience subjugation. In time, however, even submissive therapists feel vengeful and angry and subsequently fear these feelings (Racker, 1972). Then, if they actually attempt to resolve their discomfort through subtle recrimination, they experience their own guilt and anxiety.

At times, countertransferential anger can also be provoked by clients' rejection of a state of dependence that is being "asked for" by therapists who assume the role of "savior" (Racker, 1972). At other times, countertransferential anger can stem from therapists' inability to tolerate shame resulting from not living up to their clients,' their colleagues,' and their own expectations (Winnicott, 1958). Therapists' anger can serve as a defense against the experience of shame resultant from therapeutic failure (Lewis, 1987). (7)

Ironically, countertransferential anger can also be the result of therapists' efforts to prevent injury and protect themselves (Rothschild, 2000). It can be a response to having been threatened, hurt, or scared. Similarly, the fruits of elevated anger or aggression can actually be akin to a life force composed of activity and movement that can lead to loving, hating, or both as therapists interact with the object of their aggression (Winnicott, 1965).

## Countertransferential Anxiety and Fear

Countertransferential anxiety, a response to some internal stimulus (LeDoux, 1995), usually takes the form of therapists' feeling scattered and confused. They are unsure of relating to clients similar to others they have found difficult and uncertain of therapeutic progress (Schafer, 1997). (8)

Countertransferential fear, in contrast, is a response to the environment. It makes therapists feel disconnected, disorganized, and even unable to think in response to autistic clients (Gomberoff et al., 1990), attention deficit clients, or hyperactive clients. It causes therapists to experience disequilibrium in response to hyperactive clients. It causes therapists to experience disequilibrium in response to schizophrenic or manic clients (Kantrowitz, 1997) or terror in the presence of clients with an antisocial personality disorder.

All of these experiences can result in therapists' desire to get relief by imposing their own ideas and solutions on clients rather than patiently and painstakingly helping their clients to discover at their own pace what they must do to change. (9)

Therapists' fear and anxiety sometimes develop because they experience clients' hold on them as an unconscious fear of intimacy, seduction, engulfment, aggression, or dread of therapeutic regression (Langs, 1979). Therapists may become apprehensive, for example, when clients ask them for more time and attention than they can afford to give.

Paradoxically, countertransferential anxiety and fear may combine with guilt feelings and result in actions and words indicative of submissiveness. This submissiveness, in turn, may cause therapists to avoid frustrating clients, pamper those they already have, or search for quick resolution of complex situations in an effort to get relief (Racker, 1972).

## Countertransferential Gladness

Gladness runs the gamut from contentment to joy or elation. Gladness may also manifest itself in therapists' feeling superior and wanting to boast (Handley, 1995) or monopolize the therapeutic conversation.

At times countertransferential gladness lures therapists into engaging in the unwholesome practice of competing with their clients or other professionals, like teachers, working with their clients. Therapists can become insistent, for instance, that clients follow their advice rather think for themselves or consult competent others (Blum, 1986a).

However, the two-edged sword of countertransferential gladness usually reenkindles hope in clients and thus proves extremely helpful. It contributes to the formation or repair of the therapeutic alliance. But danger lurks even here, for gladness on the part of therapists may induce in them a desire for sustained positive feelings about therapeutic progress, feelings that are unjustified because they rest on denial of still-needed and difficult therapeutic work.

## Countertransferential Envy

Because envy of clients is considered so shameful and unprofessional even when it is not acted out, therapists rarely admit it. Unfortunately, however, therapists' desire to be helpful at the same time that they are determined not to be outshone by clients they envy is more common than therapists would like to believe (West & Schain-West, 1997). Envy of clients' real accomplishments or even their potential to achieve may lead to therapists not supporting or encouraging their clients (West & Schain-West, 1997). Envy of clients may even result in premature termination if clients feel their therapist's subtle rejection.

Decoding countertransferential envy begins with becoming aware of the anxiety that accompanies it (Racker, 1968) and, in time, the lack of joy and satisfaction as therapists focus on what their clients, not they, possess. Envy might also be suspected if therapists become competitive during sessions, need to prove their competence by knowing as much—if not more—than their clients, or feel confused, ambivalent, and uncertain.

## Dreams

Dreams that clients bring into therapy are rich sources of transference, especially when therapists are dream figures (Ferenczi, 1909). Therapists' dreams are also valuable sources of countertransferential material, particularly if dream figures are clients (Tower, 1956). Because they are highly symbolic, containing both primitive urges to act without regard to reality as well as rational motives for acting or not acting, dreams are often complicated, extended, and exceedingly confusing. They call for extensive decoding.

Only an in-depth presentation would do justice to the decoding of dreams, but consideration of the following account may at least reveal the value of doing so.

*The therapist noticed her client's uptight facial expression and her forced congeniality. She claimed she was eager to work on assertiveness; but even when her therapist began helping her with specific assertive skills, she remained tense. It was only when she introduced her dream that her therapist could decode its contents and understand what was really going on.*

*In her dream, the client was being chased down narrow halls from one room to another. Wherever she turned, doors opened into other rooms and never to the fresh, freeing outside. The "enemy" chasing her was so close that she even felt its hot breath down her back. The client thought that the narrow halls and rooms were those of her own home, and her critical, demanding husband was the "enemy" always breathing down her back with his instructions. She couldn't escape him. She couldn't get free.*

*While this interpretation may have been accurate, the therapist wondered about transferential implications. Could the rooms be the contents of the therapy sessions, which were packed with information but never let the learner breath freely and easily? Could the "enemy" chasing her be her therapist, whose words felt like suffocating hot air? Could the client be feeling as if she were being chased by a well-meaning therapist intent on doing good but nevertheless robbing her of her freedom?*

*Sharing the hypotheses that she derived from decoding, the therapist learned that her interpretation of the transference was also accurate. Had she not done her own decoding, she would have never realized that she was harming, not helping, her client.*

# Fantasies and Daydreams

*Fantasy* includes all mental images or sets of mental images created by needs, wishes, or desires, particularly daydreams occurring during non-sleep states. *Daydreams* are extended fantasies, even as fantasies can be thought of as "kernels" of daydreams. Though both may seem simple, fantasies and daydreams are actually intricate, detailed, and elaborate.

Fantasies and daydreams involve both primitive urges and believable presentations (Herron & Rouslin, 1982). They are means of accommodating to the environment, understanding what is occurring, internalizing environmental events, and discharging the energy from conflict (Piaget, 1962). Hence, they can reveal transference and countertransference.

Furthermore, as fantasies and daydreams bring ideals into reality, they become the basis for hopes and expectations in interpersonal relationships. As ideals, however, fantasies and daydreams aid and abet disappointment, confusion, and dislike, even hatred, of real persons who inevitably fall short of the ideals inherent in fantasies and daydreams. As representations of emotional "activity" needing to be understood and worked with, fantasies and daydreams provide clues about clients' emotional responses, including their reactions to therapists (Herron & Rouslin, 1982). They call for serious efforts to decode their messages.

However, clients seldom share fantasies and daydreams with their therapists because they see them as distractions not worth their attention. Consequently, therapists must be ever alert to their presence, suspecting them in their own daydreams and fantasies as well as in clients' subtle body movement and body language, particularly in lapses of focused attention or mini-dissociative episodes. Clients whose eyes become "glassy," for instance, may well be daydreaming. Subsequently, they may make verbal reference to the material. (10)

One fruitful way of decoding fantasies and daydreams in non-analytic therapy is to look for the needs that they encode, particularly those that can be met by others.

*After a chance encounter outside of the therapy office, the therapist found it difficult to stop fantasizing about her client for several hours. "Strange," she thought, "I have so many other things to think about. Why am I distracted by thoughts of the young man I see on Fridays? Why do I keep thinking of him way into the weekend?"*

*During supervision, however, the therapist became increasingly aware of her positive attraction to the client. His good looks, optimistic attitude, and refreshing viewpoints made him "the perfect client." "Still," she asked, "why do I need to fantasize about him?"*

*The therapist then began to notice subtle associations related to junior high when boy-girl crushes were rampant. The therapist hypothesized that this positive countertransference related to her own need to enjoy what are called crushes on someone of the opposite sex might well be reflecting exactly what her client also needed t o look at: the part he played in opposite-sex "rituals" that struck others as adolescent infatuation. Indeed, her client had said that, though he didn't agree, others described him as flirtatious.*

*The therapist worded her countertransference interpretation carefully during their next session: "I wonder if the thoughts I keep having about junior high days are originating solely within me or whether you are contributing to them? They're positive but out of place."*

*The client at first appeared bewildered; but when asked to take his time to respond, he realized his attraction to his therapist although he didn't think that his feelings were something that he could put into words. He never verbalized these kinds of feelings, he reported. He always tried to tell people that he liked them by "just being himself." "Could that be why people say I'm 'flirting'?" he pondered. Later, for the first time in his life, the client began to deal with behavior he had previously deemed inconsequential.*

## Behavior: Body Language, Complex Movement, and Somatization

Manifestations of transference and countertransference behavior—body language, simple movement, complex movement, and physical sensations—are messages from unconscious to unconscious through bodily means. Indeed, "the basic units of experience are [not words but] bodily interactions between self and others" (Fast, 1992, 449). The behavior of the body contains key information that determines exactly what clients and therapists are trying to convey to each other (Scaer, 2005). Both therapists and clients are being unconsciously influenced by a series of slight, even subliminal, signals. Details of posture, gaze, tone of voice, even respiration, are noticed and recorded by both therapy participants (Meares, 2005).

Moreover, because the body *cannot* lie, it is a source of truth about the present as it embodies memories of the past. (11) The body has "the ability to tune in to the psyche: to listen to its subtle voice, hear its silent music and search into its darkness of meaning" (Mathew, 1998, 185). Hence, in order to discover transferred material, therapists must decode their own and their clients' bodily behavior. (12)

### Body Language or Simple Movement

In the context of displaced material, body language or simple movement refers to inadvertent responses of the body to subtle, unconscious "messages" from the right hemisphere. "You are in some kind of danger," for example, is a common message that makes clients fold their arms in front of them. However, when asked whether their body language indicates feeling threatened, clients usually say "No" for the transaction that sent the message from the right hemisphere to the arms was unconscious. Thus it becomes extremely important for therapists to study their clients' and their own muscular movements, postures, gestures, and other somatic reactions during therapy.

Of particular importance are right hemisphere-controlled facial indicators, especially subtle movements around the eyes and mouth (Schore, 1994). For the left-hemisphere-controlled right side of the face registers socially appropriate affective responses whereas the right-hemisphere-controlled left side divulges hidden personalized feelings (Mandal & Ambady, 2004). (13)

While what happens on a one-time basis may not be worthy of much attention, body language that persists or repeats itself is especially noteworthy. For as in dreams, the unconscious mind produces again and again important material whose overlooked messages need to break through to the conscious mind (Jung, 1946).

*No matter what she talked about, the client sat back in her chair, keeping a safe distance, as it were, between herself and her therapist. "She has made progress, to be sure, but could more have been made?" her therapist wondered. "What needs to be done to increase her comfort, if that is indeed a prerequisite for further work? Rather than just space her sessions farther apart, I should address the sensitive topic of our therapeutic progress."*

*In the course of the exploration that followed, the client reaffirmed her difficulty with getting beyond the roles in which she had been cast as a child, roles so deeply cultural that someone from outside her culture would hardly believe them. It seemed as though the client needed to uncover the deterrents to changing her ways. She had to trust someone who could really understand how much she would be an exception to her group if she changed.*

*"She sits back for that reason," her therapist decided, "she is telling me in body language how alienated she feels." So the therapist said, "It's hard to trust someone from a different culture, isn't it. We seem so different though we may really have a lot in common."*

*To her therapist's relief, during the next session the client reported a shift in her attitude toward making a change. She hadn't actually made the change, she explained, but she was planning it in detail. And she leaned forward slightly when sharing her news.* (14)

## Complex Movement

In contrast to body language that encodes relatively simple messages, complex movement communicates several displaced feelings and story-like thoughts. Complex movement that puts transferred feelings and thoughts into action is often simply called enactment. (15)

Enactment is the last step of "information processing that builds and exploits emotional databases of mind and brain" related to displaced material (Levin, 1997, 1136). Thoughts and words become coercive action loaded with emotion that usually relates to figures in the client's or therapist's early years. It is action dictated by a "script" never actually seen (Field, 1989), one most likely written between conception and eighteen months, when tone of voice, facial ex-

expressions, and gestures served as primary means of communication (Meares, 2005).

In carrying out transferential enactments, clients assign to themselves and their therapist roles specific to past experiences that have remained conflictual. They "intend" to play a part and have their therapist play a related one for various, sometimes overlapping reasons. (17) They may be revisiting the past in order to have it turn out better. They may be unconsciously testing with their therapist a pathogenic belief acquired in childhood (Sampson, 1992), asking "Is that belief really true or will this person give me reason to negate it?" Then, by closely monitoring their therapist, clients hope for the evidence they need to substitute a new, wholesome belief for a disconfirmed pathogenic one (Silberschatz, Fretter, & Curtis, 1986).

Enactment of negative feelings and thoughts is simply called *acting-out*. Because it strains boundaries, acting-out is considered a regressive interaction "experienced by either [client or therapist] as a consequence of the behavior of the other" (McLaughlin, 1990, 595). It must be quickly decoded and, if necessary, examined lest it limit the capacity for therapeutic work and exacerbate extra-therapeutic interpersonal problems. For ordinarily, others soon find the "mind reading" required by acting-out overwhelming, if not maddening. Clients must learn that others greatly prefer words that describe feelings and attitudes.

Meissner (1996) notes that

> the potential for countertransference difficulties to influence the therapist's thoughts, feelings, attitudes, and words is great enough; the potential for these unconscious processes to find expression in the therapist's...behavior and action is even greater (51). (16)

The same is true, of course, for transferential difficulties influencing client's behavior. In turn, words used in therapy can become, on a subliminal level, incitement to action on the part of both clients and therapists (McLaughlin, 1990). Both unconsciously desire responses in themselves and others in line with their transference and countertransference schemas. Both want to "shape a happening, bring about an enactment, in accord with [their] fears and hopes," (McLaughlin, 1990, 599) fears that the present might otherwise be simply a repetition of the past and hopes that it could be better.

Countertransference enactment is often a matter of therapists' participating in the acting-out of clients' transference. (18) Therapists unconsciously collude with clients in mutual projective identification organized primarily around clients' unresolved conflicts (Plakun, 1998). Thus countertransference enactment conveys meaning regarding clients' transference conflicts (Sandler, 1976). Clients still conflicted over wanting to be nurtured *gratis* and finding parental figures unwilling to do so, for example, might fail to bring their copayment. Should therapists refuse to play a parental role, asking instead for payment, they will be actually addressing that conflict.

Countertransference enactment can also be a matter of therapists acting-out or communicating indirectly their own unresolved conflicts. Therapists with unresolved narcissistic conflicts, for instance, might repeatedly insist that they are right (Wilson & Weinstein, 1996). Those with unresolved aggressive conflicts might act belligerently; those with unresolved security conflicts, dogmatically (Casement, 1991).

At other times, countertransference enactment will be a matter of therapists' engaging in reaction formation as they attempt to counteract their own weaknesses. Those who are indecisive, for instance, may exaggerate their open-mindedness (Wilson & Weinstein, 1996).

*An in-patient adolescent ended his session by telling his therapist that another staff member regarded her as incompetent. Unable to process her embarrassment and anger sufficiently, the therapist set out to prove her competence. During a staffing hours later, she vigorously defended her client, blaming others for his bad behavior, and insisting on the soundness of her judgement. Unfortunately, exoneration was the opposite of what her crafty client actually needed, which was to take responsibility for his behavior.*

*Impressed with the therapist's reasoning, however, the staff pardoned the client, who in time not only repeated his behavior but took an even more adamant stand that he should not be held responsible. He was the worse for his therapist's erroneous defense. He had been significantly harmed by his therapist's acting out, a result of her blindness to both his manipulating her and her own unresolved conflicts over being regarded as competent.*

Ogden (1994) thinks of countertransference enactment as a powerful nonverbal "interpretation" being unconsciously conveyed to clients. The "interpretation" may take a simple form, such as ending a session early when stress levels are high. Similarly, therapists may use facial expressions that indicate confusion without asking for clarification. (19)

Countertransference enactment has been identified as an unconscious means of either indulging or punishing clients, both of which are harmful. By indulging their clients, therapists infantalize them: ask less of them than they are capable of giving, provide for them what they can already do or have the potential to do, and absolve them of their obligation to change. By assuming rescuer roles, therapists do clients the disfavor of not having to face their dysfunctional patterns.

Therapists unwittingly indulge clients by caressing them with words in order to quiet their persistent negative feelings. They speak in soft tones or assure clients that all things are passing. They praise clients for occasional, minor achievements that are more likely to be the result of chance than hard work. Similarly, therapists try to divert clients from painful countertransference-causing conflictual material by directing attention to non-countertransferential material. They avoid all mention of pervasive distress on their part, sparing their clients from painful self-discovery related to the way they treat others.

*The therapist was uneasy, not once but almost every time she met with her highly educated and wealthy client who had a subtle habit of demeaning her. She did not want to admit the uneasiness, however, either to herself or to her client. Instead, the therapist reasoned that she would be noticeably prepared when her client came and thus prove herself his equal. "Competition for outstanding performance is good for a person," she said to herself. "It makes people reach for the heights others have attained," she thought as she recalled seminars in which she felt inferior to male students.*

*Sessions appeared to go well, relatively speaking, as the therapist conveyed information the client professed to want. In his termination form, however, the client referred to a stifling atmosphere within his sessions. There was an absence of free exchange, he wrote, for his therapist seemed defensive. He couldn't say that he felt disrespected, he added, but he knew deep down that mutual respect was simply not there. Rather, there was some kind of a power struggle going on. In a primitive attempt to outdo one another, both parties were indulging each other on the surface but battling for superiority in the "deep."*

Sadly, by not addressing her countertransference, the therapist indulged both herself and her client. She failed to deal with the self-destructive interpersonal behaviors both she and her client were enacting. Thus she indirectly punished her client.

In contrast, punishing clients directly includes discounting them by unconsciously performing the exact opposite of the roles that clients assign. Plakun (1998) tells of a client who had been victimized assigning her therapist an abuser role. Instead of discussing the client's desire to be abused, however, the therapist assured the client that he was totally kind and caring. He refused not only to abuse her but also to accept countertransferential feelings of guilt. In doing so, he denied his client the opportunity to work through her experience of being victimized. (20)

Alternative ways of punishing clients are responding in a hostile, distant, frozen manner or taking a moralistic stance and condemning in clients what therapists cannot tolerate in themselves. Therapists may become excessively sympathetic to third parties, for instance, and "take clients to court in a superior or angry way" (Pick, 1985, 164). They may "forget" to bring up something important, become highly distracted, or dissociate. For extended periods of time, they are available for their clients in body only.

Therapists also punish their clients by simply becoming silent, whereby they strike a compromise between their hostility and its rejection. They identify with a persecutor at the same time that they withdraw from that identification (Racker, 1972). (21)

In brief, whatever its unconscious motivation, enactment is an extremely significant psychic operation that is directly or indirectly tied to the very reason clients enter a therapeutic relationship in the first place. Recognizing and dealing appropriately with enactment can finally resolve clients' conflicts. Conversely, not recognizing them or dealing with them inappropriately is one of the major reasons for treatment failure (Plakun, 1998).

# Somatization

Somatization, a source of truth known in the present but pertaining to the past, is the body's revelation of what happened earlier in mind and "heart." (22) Hence, it can reveal transference and countertransference. A client's smiling uneasily as she protests her love for her child, for instance, may reveal transference related to prior negative experiences with the child. Similarly, transference may manifest itself in psychosomatic illness aimed at drawing "the psyche from the mind to the original intimate association with the soma" (Winnicott, 1949, 254).

Transference often manifests itself in somatosensory form because so many unresolved conflicts occurred in a preverbal period. While somatization may originally be adaptive, it is usually a maladaptive learned response to a situation once uncontrollable but now controllable. Clients can experience "butterflies" before being able to use language to explain anxiety, for example. They then retain the ill physiological effects even after they can reason away or otherwise process the anxiety.

Somatization in therapists, a twin of depression and a form of acting-in, is usually a matter of either thoughts stimulating emotions that then find bodily expression or of emotions themselves finding bodily expression. Like transferential somatization, countertransferential somatization manifests itself in symptoms and bodily conditions that have no clear physiological cause. Relatively common are sudden stabs of pain, tears, trembling, or a growling stomach, strange sensations in the solar plexus, fits of coughing, poor sleep, sensitivity to noises; sleepiness, tightness in the chest, nausea, rising heat, abdominal cramps, barely perceptible odors or tastes, and sexual arousal (Boyer, 1997).

*She was more than tired after a certain session with a couple that she was counseling, the therapist noted. The clients were pleasant, even cooperative, and they were making some progress. Why was she so tired instead of relieved or energized?*

*It was only when her clients slipped back substantially that the therapist realized she was investing more energy than they in therapy. She was working harder than she did with comparable clients.*

*Like many clients, the couple was ambivalent about improving their relationship. Though they both agreed they had to make personal changes, they resented having to make the effort. Furthermore, they unconsciously resented the therapist that supported their doing so.*

*Being relatively sure of the countertransferential meaning of her fatigue, the therapist interpreted her countertransference. "I'm not sure why I'm so tired after your sessions," she said, "but could I be putting more into this work than you?"*

*"Now that you mention it," the husband replied, "we are always being asked to account for what we did or did not do during the week. There's more to life than doing therapy assignments!" After the conversation that followed, the*

*couple finally began to take more responsibility for their progress. Slow but steady, their progress matched their own timetable rather than their therapist's.*

As revealed in this vignette and explained in detail in Chapter Nine, it is important for therapists to stand in the spaces of different pieces of their self-experience and not use language too quickly, for words can never adequately substitute for bodily experience (Bromberg, 1991). Rather than telling clients what they think they know, therapists must be more interested in listening to their clients and to themselves from an embodied place. To understand their client's displaced relational patterns, therapists must become aware of what it actually feels like in their own body (Looker, 1998).

Damasio (1994) reminds therapists that somatization is common because emotions are actually conglomerates of sensations, which are integral experiences of the body. Each emotion has a different bodily expression, starting with a unique pattern of skeletal muscle contraction that is visible on the face and notable in body posture. Each emotion also feels different on the inside of the body, for different visceral muscle contractions are discernible as body sensations that are automatically and involuntarily transmitted to the brain. Shame, for example, feels like heat rising in the face and sadness, like wet eyes (Rothschild, 2000).

Thus therapists who are willing to experience their body subjectively will discover clues to phenomena occurring in clients' interpersonal past, especially at a time when no words were available, when psychic trauma could not be distinguished from physical injury (Balamuth, 1998). A feeling of deadness in therapists, for example, will reveal how clients were neglected or loved and then rebuffed and hence never really experienced the vitality otherwise natural to infants (Field, 1989). Being able to engage in only shallow breathing will reveal to therapists clients' unwillingness to experience their emotions fully.

# A Final Thought

Manifestations of transference and countertransference, whether verbal or non-verbal, affective or physiological, yield their tremendous power for contributing to positive outcome if only therapists, alone or assisted by clients, extract their probable meaning. Thus therapists must become experts at "reading" their own and their clients' actions and reactions and deciding whether they can be taken at face value or must be decoded.

# Endnotes

(1) Clients somehow know when their therapists are open to connotations carrying displaced material. They sense that it is safe to imitate their therapists: to look within themselves for exactly what furthers or hinders their wholeness. When therapists are not open to the possibility of countertransferential communication, by contrast, clients do not feel safe enough to proceed with their work (Kantrowitz, 1997).

(2) It can be argued that when clients bring in extra-therapeutic material for the sake

of dealing with out-of-session problems, it is more appropriate for therapists to accept it at face value and teach clients the rudiments or refinements of skill building. With this approach, however, the question remains of whether or not those skills are actually used outside of therapy. Clients describing their behavior may be merely relating how they hoped they acted. On the other hand, when therapists admit the possibility of the transferential meaning of extra-therapeutic material, they pave the way for making the therapeutic setting itself a venue for interpersonal skill building. As they get first-hand experience of clients' transferential behavior, therapists can instruct, coach, and all but guarantee skill acquisition.

(3) By comparison, when clients treat their therapists as if they were third parties, they may be displacing *away* from their therapists. They may be expressing their feelings, attitudes, and impulses toward third parties. It is likely that they are doing so because they have recognized themselves behind or in these extra-therapeutic persons and wish to reveal who they are by referring to the third parties (Giovaccini, 1967). When this is the case, if therapists are to really know the interpersonal styles of their clients, they must also decode this non-transferential material.

(4) The concept of transferential feelings implies that, ordinarily, the experience of similarity initiates the affect rather than the affect initiating the experience of similarity. However, it is more likely that either both are initially operative or the distinction is artificial. The feeling imbues the experience just as the experience imbues the feeling.

(5) Of the feelings striving for expression, fear appears to be the most pervasive. Consequently, it is the most common transference affect. At times, clients transfer to their therapist hostile behaviors and qualities that inspire fear. At other times, they let basic fear create the appearance of threatening behaviors and qualities in the therapist, for at the same time that early parental figures were nurturing and life-sustaining, they were also capable of withdrawing that care and sustenance at any time. Indeed, they held what felt like absolute authority and appeared to require clients to please them in order to win their love. If parents were displeased, their negative attention could inspire only fear. Thus clients knew no middle ground, softened emotions, or counteractive force. All was primitive: all-good or all-bad.

(6) Depression is regarded as a major form of acting-in because the anger and anxiety at its core are being turned inward and directed toward the self. Because these two emotions are less responsive to inhibitory efforts that reduce the likelihood of acting-out, therapists unconsciously conceal them in depression.

(7) Therapists are wise to decode their feelings of being punished in order to uncover their possible anger-base though they can explain neither the exact nature of the punishment nor the reason for it. It may be that in punishing their therapists, clients are asking them to respond positively to a negative experience. They are hoping to revise their beliefs about themselves and their interpersonal worlds through witnessing their therapists return good for evil. On the other hand, therapists' feelings of being punished may stem from their being taken for granted, used, or even abused. They may resent having to give precious time to clients whose issues seem mundane in comparison with the horrific problems of other clients. After therapists have worked with sexual abuse victims or have been victimized themselves, for example, they may find it difficult to appreciate clients' distress resultant from a relatively minor setback like receiving a poor grade on a paper.

(8) To a certain extent, of course, anxiety is characteristic of all countertransferential reactions, for in the process of being impacted by clients' transference, therapists lose cognitive control (Kantrowitz, 1997). Rarely, however, are they conscious of losing it.

(9) Therapists may rationalize their tendencies by saying that their clients need their

insight; but more likely than not, therapists are discounting their clients' insight more than adding to it (West & Schain-West, 1997).

(10) Because clients often conceal their fantasies and daydreams, methods like Eye Movement Desensitization and Reprocessing (EMDR) (Shapiro, 1995) are valuable interventions. When the bilateral movement sets that are central to EMDR stop and clients are asked to answer a question such as, "What is there now?" therapists often become privy to transferential fantasies that clients would not otherwise share.

(11) Space and time do not permit a full exploration of why the body reveals transferential truth, indeed why it cannot lie. But research suggests that memory is spread throughout the body in wavelike frequency patterns along a network of fibers on all nerve cells rather than stored in specific cells or even cellular tissues. Memory capacities, therefore, exist not just in cerebral neurons but in all parts of the body's nervous system and not just in the nervous system but in all cellular tissues of the body (Oschman & Oschman, 1995b).

Furthermore, because the body as a whole is a continuous, unbroken fabric and a living matrix, throughout its entire system it retains a "record or memory of the influences that have been exerted upon it, both as an individual and as a member of the race" (Oschmann & Oschmann, 1995a, 65). The body remembers both ancestral information through genetic transmission and personally experienced events, especially those charged with emotion (Schacter, 1996). Because of this highly developed capacity to retain memories, the body is constantly responding to present stimuli against a background of past experiences. Cells are being reminded, so to speak, of previous similar experiences, all the way from simple sensations to highly structured cognitions that give events meaning.

(12) Some theorists assert that all therapeutic behavior, including verbal behavior, is motivated by and reflective of transference and countertransference (McLaughlin, 1990). Most, however, find some therapeutic behavior, but not all, is rightfully connected to transference and countertransference. Clients may come late, for example, not because of early familial patterns but because of traffic problems or resistance to being in therapy in the first place, no matter how little their therapist reminds them of a parental figure. Thus therapists must discontinue decoding, when appropriate, no less than engage in decoding.

(13) Research reveals that body language or simple movement may prove beneficial to clients and contribute to positive outcome if it is truly a response to clients' attachment affect, namely sadness, fear and anger (Dreher et al., 2001). On the other hand, simple movement may be harmful to clients and contribute to negative outcome if therapists simply match the behavior of their clients. Therapists' smiling back, for instance, appears to be especially harmful when clients are feeling shame in addition to anger. Therapists may consciously intend to strengthen the therapeutic alliance by smiling even while feeling angered by what they hear from clients. Unconsciously, however, therapists may be denying the degree of their anger. In addition, their smiling may be countertransferential in that therapists learned earlier in their lives to smile when anxious about expressing their anger. Hence, it is therapists' responsibility to decode their urge to smile.

(14) Clients who lean forward may be indicating that they have come to trust their therapist enough to share intimate information. In contrast, clients who remain chair-bound may be "saying" that they do not feel comfortable enough to reveal what is painfully humiliating.

(15) Although it is appropriate on select occasions to show feelings in action, if doing so is the only way in clients' repertoire, they may need to discover that acting-out usually creates a mine-field of negative interpersonal relationships.

(16) Factors increasing the likelihood of countertransferential enactments originating in therapists are permeable boundaries, poor impulse control, inadequate education, excessive therapeutic zeal (Searles, 1979) and blind spots (Plakun, 1998).

(17) Transference enactments fall into two categories depending on how therapists respond to the roles they are assigned (Levin, 1997). In the first, which is the more common, therapists actually assume the role they are being assigned and thus fulfill their client's transference expectations. In the second, therapists refuse that role and thus fail to meet their clients' expectations. In fact, in order to help their clients realize that they are living not in the past but in the present, where they must assume responsibility for their own self-care, therapists may have no other choice but to decline their role assignment.

(18) Factors increasing the likelihood of countertransference enactments triggered by clients are certain personality disorders and the use of primitive defense mechanisms. For example, clients may worry their therapist excessively by splitting and considering an "all-bad" situation a justification for attempting suicide. Or they may replay the trauma that they are presently suffering outside of therapy, assigning roles of victims to themselves and abusers to their therapists. In contrast, they may reverse roles, becoming abusers themselves and making their therapists victims.

(19) Whatever their specific form or immediate cause, countertransferential enactments must be decoded lest they cause the therapeutic focus to shift unnecessarily from what clients need to achieve to how they are relating to their therapists. If clients' conflicts with their therapists closely resemble those with non-therapists, all is well. If not, however, clients must use precious time and energy dealing with the disconnectedness that has ruptured their relationship with their therapist instead of exploring their own issues. Therapists who are overly sensitive to slights, for instance, can revert to defending their treatment-related actions and blaming clients for not cooperating with them when clients complain that therapy is not benefiting them. Having to focus on their therapists' powerful defensive feelings, clients are not able to explore the negative feelings that explain why treatment is not working.

(20) The same kind of failure can result from therapists' insistence that clients are not and never were responsible for such a thing as participation in sexual abuse as children. Therapists may do so in the name of reality testing, Plakun (1998) explains, but they thereby prevent clients from processing the painful feelings of guilt that some sexual victims carry.

(21) This response contrasts with silence that is appropriate when content loses its importance or when interpreting strikes clients as nagging or doing something they could do (Bird, 1922).

(22) It also appears as if the human brain can exploit what are called holographic principles. Each part of the brain can contain both a fragment of a memory and the entire memory in miniature. Consequently, association upon association is possible, with every cellular tissue capable of "revealing" the truth the whole person "knows" (Pribram, 1971). Thus somatic memory may indeed hold the "truth" about what clients have displaced from significant, pre-therapy and extra-therapy persons to their therapists.

# PART III

## CLINICAL APPROACHES TO TRANSFERENCE AND COUNTERTRANSFERENCE

## CHAPTER SIX

# DIAGNOSING TRANSFERENCE AND COUNTERTRANSFERENCE

## Introduction

Therapists working within non-analytic paradigms must deal with difficult therapeutic challenges. They must form a therapeutic alliance, set goals, explore various approaches to accomplishing those goals, select interventions to facilitate these tasks, form a sustainable working alliance, and terminate therapy effectively. The purpose of this chapter is to explore the question of when therapists might diagnose transference and countertransference and thus position themselves for using their findings to perform these all-important tasks.

Clinical experience and empirical data reveal that successful processing of transference depends heavily on its interaction with other variables. Sufficient insight, in particular, reduces transference in successful therapy because with insight clients see their transferential reaction as distortions that can be and must be dealt with (Graff & Luborsky, 1977; Gelso et al., 1991). But must therapists actively foster this insight? If so, how and when?

Similarly, clinical experience and empirical data support the theory that therapists should resolve their own issues and thereby reduce the occurrence and strength of the countertransference that motivates them to act-out or act-in.
But questions remain. How can therapists effectively identify, understand, and monitor their countertransference in non-analytic therapy? Should they do so primarily by themselves, during the therapeutic hour or after it? Should they seek the help of colleagues or clients?

Chapter Six is intended to help therapists decide when and with whom to diagnose transference and countertransference, with the understanding that, although they may diagnose at more than one time and in more than one way, one time and way will usually work best for them. After considering the three approaches from a theoretical standpoint, readers will have an opportunity to examine data and evaluate general and specific observations.

## Diagnosing Transference and Countertransference Intrapsychically during the Therapy Session

One approach is for therapists to diagnose transference and countertransference on their own and primarily during sessions. But is it realistic to do this demanding work while focusing on clients' presenting problems and issues relating to them?

Theoretical support for diagnosing transference during sessions begins with the nature and power of transference. Transference is the most pervasive unconscious phenomenon operative in therapy, long-term or short-term. Regressing together (Tower, 1956), clients and therapists reconstruct unresolved, primitive conflicts even in non-analytic therapy (Gelso et al., 1997; Patton et al., 1997). Therapists need not "go in search of the past; the [unconscious] brings the past to [them]—through the past becoming dynamically present in the session" (Casement, 1991, 150).

Thus to refrain from diagnosing transference as it is happening is to ignore the heart of therapy. To diagnose transference, by contrast, is to begin the central task of therapy.

Transference can and must be identified even as it is happening because it is most often negative. Frequently, it is a continuation of the mother-child symbiosis and past-present fusion. Not identified, transference cannot be incorporated into the treatment plan. And if it is not incorporated, no matter whatever else is accomplished, clients will not be released from primitive relational patterns. They will not become individuals or achieve psychological adulthood (Searles, 1975). They will leave therapy highly dependent on others, and transference will have become a major contributor to a poor therapeutic outcome.

Even positive transference, which is as much a distortion as negative transference, can contribute to a negative outcome, for it consists in clients' distorting the image of the therapist (Gelso et al., 1997) and, consequently, their own image. Undetected, transference results in clients' relating to their therapist as all-good or mostly good mentors whose affect should be duly honored and whose ideas should be politely accepted. They, as clients, should remain pre-adult admirers, students, and disciples. They should not take a full participative role. Their therapists should accept responsibility for therapeutic outcome.

Moreover, therapists should diagnose transference even as it is happening because it is then that transference phenomena are significantly more concrete and therefore more readily verifiable than clients' reports of past or extra-therapeutic problematic relationships (Cooper, 1987). Less vulnerable to progress-impeding defense mechanisms, transference phenomena provide indispensable evidence of extra-therapeutic conflicts and unwholesome interpersonal patterns that clients are reluctant to address (Lipton, 1977). Clients can distort accounts of what actually goes on in their interpersonal relationships outside of therapy and even deny what they do during therapy, but they cannot hide from therapists what they do *to* them during sessions. Therapists have first-hand evidence of how clients affect other persons.

Theoretical support for diagnosing countertransference during therapy is based on the generally accepted belief that countertransference—no less than transference—is a "fact of analysis." Even in non-analytic therapy, countertransference is central, pervasive, ubiquitous, and potent. Depending on what is done with it, that is, how it is used or processed, countertransference becomes either harmful or healing even during the session (Little, 1951).

Countertransference that is ignored, overlooked, or underestimated can negatively affect therapy process and outcome (Singer & Luborsky, 1977; Hayes, 1997). It can easily lead to therapists attempting to meet their own needs rather than addressing their clients' presenting problems (Gelso & Hayes, 1998; Strupp & Binder, 1984; McDougall, 1978), for therapists cannot control what they do not comprehend. Since therapists are bound by professional ethics to do no harm, they cannot evade their responsibility to diagnose countertransference even as it occurs.

Moreover, it is inaccurate to say that the education and experience therapists have and the therapy they have undergone necessarily results in their being consistently mature. In fact, Racker (1953) warns, in the therapeutic setting therapists are prone to act like children and neurotics. They can act as dysfunctionally as their clients. What is equally bad, because therapists' acting-out influences clients (Little, 1951), unacknowledged countertransference facilitates clients' acting-out rather than dealing with their own dysfunctional behavior.

Even if therapists avoid acting-out, they are prone to acting-in. Therapists who do not deal with their own countertransference routinely tend to become depressed or experience negative physical states resultant from unresolved psychic conflict. As a consequence, their effectiveness is considerably reduced. On the other hand, therapists who have identified their countertransferential feelings can process them even as the session unfolds. They can model for clients how to deal with disturbing material.

Of even more importance, therapists who diagnose their own countertransference can, by their understanding of and empathy toward clients lay the foundation for a *sine qua non* of successful therapy, the therapeutic alliance (Ferenczi, 1909). Therapists cannot truly understand their clients by listening only to their clients' messages, whether spoken directly or concealed in the transference. For those messages are always filtered through personal experiences that therapists bring to therapy, material that reveals itself in countertransference (Spence, 1987). In contrast, even vague countertransference begins a revelational process that provides therapists data about their clients. Originating in clients' transference, countertransference is a direct source of information about clients (Heimann, 1960). It reveals what is really going on between them and their therapists and, by extension, what goes in clients' lives outside the therapeutic setting. It gives clues about the nature of obstacles standing in the way of clients' favorable development (Cohen, 1962).

In fact, some kinds of transference can be perceived only through countertransference (McDougall, 1978). Trauma that occurred before verbal communication, in particular, as is often the case of persons suffering from a psychosis, is usually accessible only through countertransferential distress. Therapists must use countertransferential information to accurately decode the distress that underlies these clients' confused communications (McDougall, 1978). Tower (1956) goes right to the heart of the matter: for clients to resolve transference, therapists must resolve countertransference.

Bollas (1983) also spares no words. If therapists truly want to find their clients, they must look for them within themselves. They must look particularly within their own countertransferential reactions, which are largely determined by clients' transferential material. Countertransference opens the door to the "slice of life" that reveals both the functional and dysfunctional attitudes, thoughts, and behaviors of clients. The resolution of transference depends on therapists' understanding their own countertransference (Zetzel, 1970), which they can do only when they diagnose it as it arises.

Successful therapy, Boesky (1990) adds, requires a complementary response in therapist-to- client conflicts, a response almost always characterized by discomfort and departure from neutrality. This is what is meant by countertransference. To diagnose it while it is happening is to prepare for the required complementary response.

Countertransference is also an instrument of research into what therapists are truly like. Though clients can transfer their own unresolved conflicts with significant others to therapists, the precise nature of a countertransferential response to transference depends on the therapist. As the creation of a particular person, countertransference gives data about that person (Heimann, 1950). Consequently, by diagnosing countertransference as it is occurring, therapists can distinguish what clients are contributing to countertransference from what they themselves are contributing. They can separate the defensive and acting-out elements from the constructive ones (Tower, 1956). They can then overcome their regressive tendencies toward splitting, in the sense of seeing their clients as all-good or all-bad, and projecting onto clients what they themselves are contributing to therapeutic difficulties (Racker, 1953).

Furthermore, if therapists postpone the diagnosis of transference and countertransference until after sessions, with the passage of time, memories of exactly what was being perceived—or even suspected—can fade or become distorted. Transference and countertransference that are not diagnosed as they are occurring grow vague and their implications, shadowy as discrete memories combine into complex memory clusters. As feelings combine into complex affective states whose connection to individual clients is vague at best and distorted at worst, therapists cannot recall the exact details of transferential and countertransferential material specific to each client. What therapists are then likely to do is to draw relatively faulty conclusions from incomplete or inaccurate memory fragments.

Equally important, waiting until after sessions to diagnose transference and countertransference can result in losing "teachable" moments. It is at the time that they are occurring that they are most in need of being addressed, either by means of interpretations or in adjusted treatment plans. If therapists discern that clients are transferring anger toward parents to them, for example, they can either refer to it directly or hold their own attention on that dynamic until they really understand it. They can also gently encourage clients to consider what they are experiencing, staying with it long enough for it to reveal its full dimensions. By contrast, not diagnosing and processing such transferential anger leads to its continued presence, which, in turn, reduces the level of cognitive work clients can do (Jung, 1921). Clients experiencing strong transferential emotions can think no more clearly than therapists experiencing strong countertransferential emotions.

## Diagnosing Transference and Countertransference Intrapsychically Primarily after Sessions

A second approach is for therapists to note the presence of transferred material during sessions but to wait until personal reflection time after sessions to diagnose it.

Theoretical support for the second position begins with a proactive premise: therapists must focus on what clients consciously bring to the therapeutic setting in order to build solid rapport. Non-analytic therapy, which is generally much shorter than analytic therapy, does not allow a therapist to do anything but focus on the problems clients have identified and on ways to facilitate clients' insight and skill building. If clients' problems are primarily personal, they usually need to gain new insight by focusing, in the short period of time that they have on how they think, what they do, and how they can act differently, rather than on client-therapist interactions. Similarly, if presenting problems are primarily interpersonal, clients need to gain insight on how they relate to others, insight into what is not working and what might work. Transference correlates with positive outcome not in itself but in its interaction with clients' insight (Gelso et al., 1997). Moreover, in addition to gaining insight, clients need to develop new interpersonal skills. Given enough insight and new skills, clients then are able to make their present and future more wholesome by giving up past conflicts lying at the heart of transference. Therapists do not have to spend energy and time understanding transference when clients are solving transference problems themselves.

Jacobs (1986) adds that focusing on transference during sessions restricts therapists' listening, which results in such a narrow focus that they "find" transference even when it is not there. Furthermore, focusing narrowly on transference can actually lead to a defensive collusion between therapist and client to avoid other anxiety-laden material.

Furthermore, therapists can use the quiet time between sessions to properly adjust plans for the next session, should that be called for, in order to deal with the transference. While not devaluing therapists' adjustments to observed or suspected transference and countertransference during therapy, theorists supportive of the second approach point out that this delayed diagnostic work is more realistic, and thus more effective, than diagnosing during therapy sessions, especially if transference is evoking heightened countertransferential reactions in therapists.

With regard to countertransference, theorists point out that countertransference is unconscious and therefore virtually unidentifiable. Therapists should not attempt to accomplish what is very difficult, if not impossible.

In addition, waiting until after sessions enables therapists to be less emotional about their own countertransference. Away from the "heat of the battle," sometimes as much as several hours, therapists can make fuller use of necessary cognitive functions and thus be considerably more objective. Countertransference is decoded well only after considerable effort and time, Meissner (1996) reminds therapists. During sessions, therapists should simply detect and manage countertransferential feelings. After sessions, when therapists are not expected to perform other critical therapeutic functions, they can step back emotionally and devote full attention to subjecting countertransferential material to thought (Pick, 1997).

Additionally, non-analytic clinical work should stay on the *ego* level (Reich, 1951), the level of perception, reality testing, and problem-solving. Unless extended, there is too little therapy time to engage in work on the more primitive level of the *id* on which countertransference usually operates. Allowing the continued regression necessary for diagnosing countertransference, in particular, is *id*-based work that is mutually exclusive of the *ego*-based cognitive work (Jung, 1921) characteristic of non-analytic therapy. To expose conflict through the working of the *id* is one thing; to resolve it through the working of the *ego* is another. Though it is often the functioning of the *id* of the client that reveals most clearly needed therapeutic work, it is always the functioning of the *ego*, first of the therapist and then of the client, that determines outcome.

Furthermore, countertransference might have little or nothing to do with particular clients (Freud, 1910b). Though instigated by clients, countertransference might simply reflect therapists' permanent neurotic problems (Reich, 1951), which they should address only on their own time.

Restated, countertransference pulls attention away from what is truly important, not only to clients but also to a successful process. Because countertransference is not a valid therapeutic tool, it should remain in the background (Reich, 1951).

## Diagnosing Transference and Countertransference with Consultants

A third way of dealing with transference and countertransference is to subject them to scrutiny during consultation between sessions. Diagnosing them in collaboration with a third, uninvolved party, of course, presumes that they have been noticed during sessions.

Diagnosing transference and countertransference with consultants permits greater objectivity and thus leads to greater accuracy. With the help of relatively uninvolved third parties, therapists can more surely identify what is really going on in the transference. Thus they can fashion more realistic treatment plans and prepare to use truly efficacious interventions.

Countertransference—and to some degree even transference—lies largely, if not completely, outside the awareness of therapists. More often than not, both detecting transferred material and truly understanding it depend heavily on collaborative work.

Furthermore, during the quiet of the consultation hour, consultants are in a position to actively decode material therapists are sharing. Besides listening to their words, consultants can focus on body language as it reveals affect. They can also ask about therapists' somatic responses and fantasies, knowing that they are offering valuable information.

The third approach does not exclude therapists' identifying transference and countertransference and hypothesizing about their meaning by themselves. In many cases, they can even begin to test their own hypotheses without risk. In many cases, however, therapists can place their clients and themselves at risk for misinterpreting what is going on between them and their clients by selecting from various hypotheses and drawing unsound conclusions on their own. The authenticity of transference—and more importantly countertransference—can often be judged only after further testing with the help of professionals outside the dynamics of the therapy session.

Furthermore, postponing processing of displaced phenomena is no different from moving from client to client each hour of the working day. Therapists have been educated to wait until consultation time to process difficult feelings, thoughts, and bodily sensations, all of which constitute transference and countertransference.

Although consulting can be challenging, especially for those in private practice whose offices are not by any means adjacent to those of their colleagues, phoning and e-mailing can be done with relative ease, provided arrangements have been made ahead of time.

A caveat with regard to the third position, however, deserves attention. Consulting can be difficult for consultants because they are usually not privy to first-hand observation. Having it reported is never as objective as either party would like it to be in that therapists bring their own countertransferential issue to reporting. Consultants never hear clients' unadulterated verbal messages or see the subtle non-verbal message that clients unconsciously communicate (Spence, 1987). Similarly, therapists never report what is actually the content or processes of the therapeutic hour, especially the part they unconsciously contribute. Unless sessions are videotaped, reporting includes just a fraction of the problematic dynamics.

Furthermore, consulting can also be extremely challenging for those who do it because of the countertransference aroused in them as they listen. For they, too, are filtering what they hear and see through the lens of their own unfinished business: the prejudices and biases that limit their personal objectivity.

On the other hand, in many cases consultants will not find their own countertransference aroused as they listen. And when they do, they can candidly admit it. They and the consulting therapist can then use the elements of combined countertransference to their advantage.

## Literature Review

Although Bernstein (1992) has observed that it is no longer necessary to "prove" the usefulness of transference and countertransference because of so much observation about their effects, it is interesting to note that empirical data actually do support the theory that transference and countertransference can foster or impede positive therapeutic outcome.

The earliest study is that of Wallach and Strupp (1960), who, using a 27-item questionnaire, found that 82 practicing medical psychotherapists developed both positive and negative countertransference rapidly in the course of reading case histories of neurotic clients. This experimental setting was sufficiently similar to real first sessions, the researchers claimed.

Results revealed that although therapists' attitudes do not statistically correlate with the kind of treatment plans they make, statistically non-significant trends exist. Countertransference appears to have an indirect relationship with therapeutic outcome in that it tends to influence some clinicians in their treatment planning. Therapists have positive countertransference when they perceive clients as capable of insight. They tend to make treatments plans implying closer therapeutic contact and work toward a more extensive change in the clients.

More recent research supports the relationship between transference, countertransference, and insight. The interaction of these phenomena correlates with successful therapeutic outcome (Atwood et al., 1989; Elkind, 1992; Mordecai, 1991; Nathanson, 1992; Pulver, 1992; Weiner, 1974).

More specifically, Gelso and others (1997) found in studying 33 time-limited cases that transference increased as therapy drew to a close in less successful cases. In contrast, in more successful cases transference increased during three-fourths of therapy but decreased during the last quarter. It was not transference alone that determined outcome, however; it was an interaction of transference and emotional insight. While these researchers did not address the issue of what therapists should do to deal effectively with transference and to foster clients' insight, their findings do support the theory that even in non-analytic therapy transference and clients' attainment of emotional insight can make a significant difference in outcome. They imply that therapists need to diagnose transference as soon as possible.

With regard to countertransference, Singer and Luborsky (1977) discovered that even highly experienced therapists act out their negative countertransference more frequently than is commonly supposed. In early sessions conducted by 40 therapists with a median of 9 years of experience, a significant number responded negatively and counter-therapeutically to clients' hostility, mistrust, inflexibility, and pervasive resistance. When clients communicated a fear that people would dominate them, for example, therapists became dominating. The result was poor outcome. Reviewing similar studies, Singer and Luborsky (1977) concluded that "the influence of clients' transference relations on [therapists] can be considerable, arousing strong feelings and stimulating distinct behaviors that can adversely affect [the] therapeutic style" (187).

Similarly, Henry and Strupp (1989) found that even experienced therapists engage in countertherapeutic interpersonal processes with difficult clients. Expression of hostility by these therapists then negatively affects the therapeutic alliance and outcome. Predictably, outcome can be expected after high frequencies of hostile exchange and complex negative messages given by therapists.

In addition, Kiesler and Watkins (1989) discovered that the strong hostile behavior of 36 non-psychotic clients, as measured by self report after the third session, evoked in them negative perceptions of the working alliance. Client hostility also evoked in their therapists countertransference of a distancing nature. By contrast, in order to feel comfortable about themselves and to stay in therapy, the clients needed their therapists to consciously transform their aloof countertransference behaviors into complementary reactions, that is, into connected, relational behaviors. Clients needed their therapists to confirm their self-presentations, not distance themselves from them. Countertransference appears to correlate with a key requisite for therapeutic success: continuance in therapy. Diagnosed, countertransference becomes an available correlational variable. Not diagnosed, countertransference can do harm.

Similarly, Mohr (1995) found in his meta-analysis that when therapists experience negative countertransference in the form of disappointment, anger, and hostility, clients can deteriorate, resulting in negative therapeutic outcome. Earlier, Strupp (1980) discovered that therapists were less warm, communicated less approval, and made fewer interventions with clients whose therapy eventually failed. Therapists were relatively cold and rejecting; they distanced themselves especially from clients whose transference was extremely hostile.

In addition, recent research supports the relationship between transference, countertransference, and insight. The interaction of these phenomena correlates with successful therapeutic outcome (Atwood et al., 1989; Elkind, 1992; Mordecai, 1991; Nathanson, 1992; Pulver, 1992; Weiner, 1974).

It must be acknowledged, however, that other data discourage therapists from spending time and energy diagnosing transference and countertransference. In analyzing the first 100 hours of one psychoanalytic case, for example, Gassner and others (1982) found that a client dealt with previously warded-off contents by himself. It was only a matter of time before the client became aware of repressed contents and worked with them, resulting in positive outcome. This implies, then, that therapists do not have to worry about their diagnosing transference during session. It is all right for them to simply follow what their clients are doing.

Along another line, the work of Joyce and Piper (1993) implies that though transference—and by implication countertransference—may be diagnosed during the course of therapy, therapists need time between session, alone or with consultants, to do the kind of work necessary for those challenging tasks. For it is not enough merely to identify transference and diagnose it in general. Rather, therapists must link transference with clients' problems and their relational patterns outside of therapy. Earlier Luborsky and others (1988) had also found that transference had to be linked with clients' main wishes regarding their therapists. By analyzing data from two early sessions of 73 non-psychotic clients, the researchers found that transference phenomena had to be connected with relationship themes at the core of clients' conflicts. By implication, time between sessions and, in some cases, consultation are needed for all but the most skillful therapists. Indeed, Hill and others (1996) found that therapists need supervisors or consultants during their entire careers.

## Observations

Although there are insufficient empirical data to support diagnosing transference and countertransference during therapy over doing so between sessions, either intrapsychically or with consultants, there seems to be enough to support beginning the diagnostic work during sessions and finishing it after sessions. If transference and countertransference are having a major impact on the course of therapy, it is imperative to diagnose them, at least up to a point, during the session. Then, they can be further diagnosed by therapists between sessions. Therapy notes taken during a session, for example, might include a notation about the therapists' strong urges to verbally abuse their clients, at which time therapists can monitor closely their actually doing so. Then, between that session and the next, therapists—alone or with consultants—can refine the nature of their urges, use the information to understand their clients more fully, and make suitable treatment plans for the next session.

Besides these general observations are the following specific observations, which are submitted to readers for their evaluation.

- Countertransference, and by implication transference, affects even experienced therapists.
- Negative outcome can result from failure to diagnose and somehow deal with transference and countertransference.
- Though it cannot be concluded that transference and countertransference affect outcome directly, they do affect determinates of outcome,

such as the therapeutic alliance, the working alliance, insight, and continuance in therapy.

- Because reasonably detailed and comprehensive diagnostic usage is likely to correlate with positive outcome, provided it does not interfere with rapport building and other essentials of therapy, clinicians are wise to diagnose both positive and negative transference and countertransference in order to give them serious consideration in treatment plan ning. They are wise to examine sessions periodically to decode transference and countertransference phenomena, study them carefully, and monitor their impact on the therapeutic process.

In conclusion, the three approaches to diagnosing transference and countertransference outlined in this chapter clearly bring with them both advantages and disadvantages. An individual therapist's valuing one over the others might be just that: a value judgment made on the basis of the therapist's comfort level and skill acquisition. Therapists will also vary their judgment on the bases of individual clients and the therapeutic phase in which they are working. They might also vary their judgment on the basis of yet another approach, namely, interreting transference and countertransference to clients, the focus of Chapter Seven.

## CHAPTER SEVEN

# INTERPRETING TRANSFERENCE AND COUNTERTRANSFERENCE TO CLIENTS

## Introduction

A fourth way of dealing with transference and countertransference—one distinctive of non-analytic therapy—is to interpret these phenomena to clients and invite them to enter into the diagnostic process. In this somewhat controversial approach, therapists articulate a hypothesis that they have arrived at through their intrapsychic or interpersonal diagnostic work and give clients an opportunity to confirm or disconfirm the hypothesis.

This approach should not be taken, some say, because it is intrusive, even invasive. Directly addressing the relationship between client and therapist brings out weaknesses, even abuses, in participants' treatment of each other and, by implication, of others. This is uncomfortable, even distressful, for clients if the interpretation refers to what they do. It is irrelevant to clients if it refers to what therapists do.

Others say, however, that this approach is extremely helpful to clients in that it exposes in a safe, nonjudgmental environment the contributions that they make to the very problems that brought them into therapy. Even if the interpretation refers to therapists, clients have somehow drawn out or occasioned their inappropriate interpersonal patterns. The insight that clients can acquire in the long run through this direct and concrete approach far outweighs the discomfort or distress that they may experience at the time.

We now move to an exploration of various positions regarding interpreting transference and countertransference to clients.

# Three Theoretical Positions and Corresponding Empirical Data

Research studies pertaining to interpreting transference and countertransference to clients can be classified according to three distinct theoretical positions. In the first, although diagnosing transference and countertransference intrapsychically and with consultants is important, diagnosing them in collaboration with clients is proscribed. In the second, transference interpretations (TRIs) are permitted under stringent rules while countertransference interpretations (CTRIs) are not. In the third, both TRIs and CTRIs are considered cardinal to positive outcome.

All three positions espouse therapists' diagnosing transference and countertransference intrapsychically. Therapists are to examine transference phenomena in order to identify therapeutic problems as early as possible. Therapists are also expected to identify countertransference in order to avoid harming clients and hindering therapeutic process. Equally important, therapists are to use both transference and countertransference material to discover clients' extra-therapeutic conflicts and skill deficits.

Furthermore, all three positions imply that diagnosing transference and countertransference during supervision or consultation sessions is appropriate and at times even necessary. Objective third parties are invaluable in discovering the exact nature of transference and, even more so, countertransference. Interpreting transference and countertransference in collaboration with clients, however, is clearly a separate issue. Beyond ruling out TRIs and CTRIs when clients' psychopathology severely restricts executive ego functioning and encourages dangerous acting-out, theorists hold widely differing positions, and researchers draw widely differing conclusions.

In the present investigation, empirical data supportive of three theoretical positions follows a concise definition of and representative example of each position.

## First Position: Prohibition of TRIs and CTRIs

In the first position, interpreting transference and countertransference to clients in an effort to elicit their collaboration is proscribed.

*Desirous of not having his client experience her therapist's upcoming vacation as abandonment, the interpersonal-oriented therapist told the client about it several times in advance. The week before his vacation, however, the client hinted repeatedly that her therapist was selfish.*

*Knowing how often the client's mother made unnecessary and lengthy excursions, the therapist attempted to link his vacation with the client's mother's absences and alluded to feelings of abandonment the client might have, whereupon she stomped out of the office, threatening not to return. When she didn't, her therapist realized that he had unwittingly "stomped" into a sensitive area that she wasn't ready or willing to enter, let alone have him enter.*

Research supportive of proscribing CTRIs and TRIs, as used in this example, begins with the work of Strupp and Hadley (1979), who found that psychodynamic therapists using TRIs had no more success than untrained college professors not using them. Outcome, which was measured by therapists, independent clinicians, and subjects, was not significantly different for the two treatment groups: male college students suffering from neurotic depression or reacting to anxiety. However, small numbers, inadequate sampling, and confounding variables make these results questionable.

A decade later, when Gassner and others (1982) analyzed the first 100 hours of one psychoanalytic case, they found that the client dealt with previously warded-off contents by herself. Repressed contents became conscious without interpretations, yet without anxiety. It was only a matter of time before the client became aware of repressed contents and worked with them, which resulted in positive outcome.

Nearly a decade later, Elliott (1991) also found that a client's development of an important insight did not follow specific interpretations. However, he did not clearly include TRIs in his definition of *interpretations*.

Using an impeccable research design that included extensive examination of hundreds of hours of interviews, Weiss and Sampson (1986) concluded that the unconscious mind can and does act autonomously to bring into consciousness previously warded-off phenomena. It does not need therapists' interpretations. It thinks, plans, and decides, without the benefit of TRIs, how to master conflictual material. The unconscious works without interpretations to change pathological beliefs by testing them in relation to the therapist.

> [Because clients] are sharply, unconsciously observant of the interpersonal reality of the therapeutic situation, [they] make considerable...progress on their own, that is, without interpretive help. [Clients] carry out a trial action in the hope that the therapist will not react as their beliefs predict (Sampson, 1992, 523).

Also supportive of the first position's tenet of using only those interventions that address presenting problems is the work of Silberschatz and others (1986). Using observational data and independent raters in a three-case study, the researchers found that TRIs are no more effective than other interventions. At least with clients suffering from dysthymia, the only criterion for an intervention to affect outcome was that it address conscious and unconscious motives and beliefs preventing goal attainment.

Other research data suggests that TRIs can even be harmful. In one study, Piper and others (1993) provided 20 once-weekly, dynamically oriented sessions for 105 persons, most of whom had affective, adjustment, anxiety, and impulse control disorders. Sixty-four participants from a balanced sample of those who completed the treatment were then categorized as either interpersonally mature or interpersonally immature. Immature persons were defined as those with a life-long predisposition for inordinate dependence, extreme reactions to real or imagined loss, and destructiveness; mature persons had a life-long predisposition to engage in mature give-and-take relationships. Results revealed that immature persons did not improve when offered TRIs that correctly linked negative transference with past conflicts. Even accurate TRIs affected outcome negatively.

Furthermore, Piper and others (1993) found that though mature men and women could benefit from accurate TRIs, an inverse relationship existed between their number and favorable outcome in the case of women. Mature women did not benefit from an emphasis on the conflictual dynamics of the client-therapist relationship. Interpersonal maturity served as a moderating variable in the effective use of TRIs in that mature women regarded the therapeutic alliance as weakened as TRIs became frequent. TRIs had to be used infrequently for them to benefit mature women.

Indeed, Postner (1994) had found already in 1971 that using too many TRIs correlated with a poor therapeutic alliance and, in some cases, negative outcome. Then, almost 30 years later, in studying the early sessions of 29 depressed clients, Connolly and others (1999) discovered that high levels of TRIs correlated with poor treatment outcome for clients with poor interpersonal functioning.

Piper and others (1993) also found that female clients had poorer therapist-rated alliance and post-therapy outcome when their therapists used more TRIs. The authors speculated that their negative reaction may have been a defensive response. Less successful clients may have elicited a high frequency of TRIs. Male participants in the study also had a poorer therapist-rated alliance and post-therapy outcome, though less pronounced than those of women, when therapists used more TRIs.

Hoglend (1993) corroborated this finding in his quasi-experimental, longitudinal study of 43 mature outpatients whose symptomatology ranged from major depression to personality disorders to various problems not due to a mental disorder. The use of few TRIs led to successful dynamic change in two out of three clients after two years and in three out of four clients after four years. In contrast, the use of many TRIs led to successful change in only one out of three clients after two years and in only one out of four clients after four years. When clients receiving additional treatment during the two- and four-year periods were removed from the statistical analysis, findings were even stronger

Furthermore, Buckley and others (1994) found that supportive interventions such as reflective summaries predicted better outcome than interpretive interventions. TRIs were high risk with clients with severe personality disorders, Bond and others (1998) concluded after their literature review. Similarly, Banon and others (2001) found that in the early sessions of seven personality-disordered males, increased defensiveness followed early TRIs unless interpretations of defense followed, even when there was a solid therapeutic alliance.

Finally, Grunebaum (1986) found that using TRIs to the exclusion of non-TRIs could leave clients feeling unsatisfied, even harmed. Interviews with 47 former clients, all mental health professionals, revealed that 18 rated their therapy harmful because of a distant and rigid therapeutic relationship. Of those, one-third complained that their therapists confined their interventions exclusively to TRIs. This study includes no control group, however, and relies on past, even distant, memories of knowledgeable observers of psychotherapy.

## Second Position: The Value of TRIs

In the second position, TRIs are considered efficacious and, hence, permitted under stringent rules. CTRIs, however, are not.

*The client set as her goal moving out of her parents' home but failed to take any steps toward that goal. Aware of his growing impatience over several sessions, her therapist finally asked if her stalling might be intended to render him as helpless as she, if her stalling might be "paying him back" for holding her accountable for goal attainment.*

*"Why should you succeed," she retorted, "if I can't? You piss me off by insisting I can change! Changing me has been the only thing my parents have cared about."*

*Soon thereafter, however, the client changed her residence as well as explored how resentful she was of parental insistence on fashioning and refashioning her into their likeness.*

Empirical support for the second position begins with Malan's (1976a & b) discovery of a positive correlation between favorable outcome and TRIs that link clients' present reactions to therapists with their past reactions to parents, namely therapist/parent transference interpretations, interventions acronymed T/P TRIs. Though the study included only 22 subjects and no control group, supporting evidence for favorable outcome was based on both clinical judgment and content analysis. Successful outcome was found to correlate with early, though infrequent, T/P TRIs and additional interpretation of transference.

Marziali and Sullivan's (1980) replication of Malan's study with a small but independent sample and stronger research methodology supported his findings. In brief dynamic psychotherapy, T/P TRIs were found to correlate positively with dynamic change for 25 subjects with a variety of diagnoses. Favorable outcome, as measured by independent sets of raters, was found to correlate with the frequency with which therapists' interpretations referred to emotions experienced in the transference relationship that were similar to those experienced in relationships with parents.

Marziali and Sullivan (1980) also found that TRIs referring to therapists, parents, and other important persons in the present—acronymed TPOs—were predictive of positive outcome. TPOs were found to correlate with clients' increased ability to relate more maturely with others, especially to make use of available sources of support that were experienced previously as conflictual. A TRI like this would facilitate positive outcome: "You seem sad because I can't meet with you next week. Are you reminded of your father's frequent trips and those your wife takes now?"

Later, however, Marziali (1984) clearly acknowledged that his and Sullivan's 1980 study lacked specificity. It needed to be followed by studies examining the exact behaviors of clients after hearing TRIs to determine which variables contribute to variations in outcome. He also acknowledged that studies were needed to examine TRIs in relation to a positive therapeutic outcome in the context of such variables as trust and mutual respect.

Marziali (1984) meant precisely the kind of study Gedo and Schaffer (1989) conducted five years later. In a single case study, the investigators found that the client's insights were noticeably responsive to TRIs immediately after they were given. The interpretations contributed to improved self-understanding. Subsequently, McCullough and others (1991) conducted a similar study of 16 clients with outcome data being collected both one month and 1½ years after treatment. They found that an interpersonal focus and active use of TRIs produced significant positive change in personality-disordered clients who underwent 40-session brief dynamic therapy, provided they responded to TRIs with affect. If instead the clients' behavior became defensive, TRIs did not correlate with positive outcome. McCullough and others (1991) also found that TRIs were more powerful than other interpretations in eliciting affect.

In a similar vein, in studying the transcripts of early sessions for seven males with personality-disorders, Banon and others (2001) found that TRIs followed closely by interpretations of defense enhanced therapeutic work. Defensiveness, which was dissipated, did not contribute to negative outcome. Furthermore, Banon and others (2001) found that not interpreting early negative transference caused problems in therapy.

The Banon and Bond study underscores a finding critical to evaluation of TRIs discovered by Pessier and Stuart (2000) in their analysis of three cases of women clients between the ages of 24 and 34. Because transference work is often very difficult, there may be a lag between the time the TRI is given and a positive response on the part of the client. The TRI may have an inhibitory effect to begin with, but in time, facilitate progress.

Piper and others (1986), who used both independent samples and a stronger research methodology than Malan (Frances & Perry, 1983), found that T/P TRIs correlated with favorable outcome as measured by general symptomatology and dysfunction. Again, however, the sample was relatively small, and positive correlations between favorable outcome and other TRIs were not found. Perhaps unsuccessful clients elicit a high frequency of simple TRIs while successful clients give therapists more opportunities to make T/P TRIs.

Similarly, O'Crowley (1999) found in a single case study that the client's anxiety and speech dysfluency both decreased in the course of discussing conflictual transference-related topics. The researcher concluded that interpretations addressing transference conflicts are crucial to resolving the conflicts. They are indeed mutative.

Gabbard's studies (1994, 1996) reveal that TRIs are the strongest predictors of positive outcome provided a strong therapeutic alliance has formed. Several other studies suggest a related point: interpretive work in general and transference work in particular correlate with successful outcome for clients capable of forming a strong therapeutic alliance (Bond & others, 1998). Those who are not capable do not do well with interpretive interventions in the beginning of their work because they need supportive interventions to form a strong therapeutic alliance (Wallerstein, 1990).

However, in another small study of six cases with a poor initial therapeutic alliance, Foreman and Marmar (1985) found that TRIs linking clients' problematic feelings toward their therapists with clients' defenses correlated with successful outcome. Not using these TRIs correlated with poor outcome.

But Winston and others (1993) failed to find that TRIs addressing defenses alone correlate with successful outcome. In four analyzed cases involving clients with personality disorders, TRIs needed to address wishes and fears as well as defenses in order to elicit the affect required for successful outcome. Therapists had to link clients' defenses with their wishes and fears in order for positive outcome to follow. They had to use a TRI like, "You want so badly to see your son, and yet you seem to be totally opposed to our working on the anger you have toward me during our sessions. If it also comes when you are with your son and you deny it, will you get what you want?"

Piper and others (1993) discovered that TRIs strengthen the therapeutic alliance with males, an important finding in light of a correlational relationship between a strong therapeutic alliance and favorable outcome (Horvath & Symond, 1991). However, the total number of both male and female subjects in the study was only 32.

Studying 60 short-term therapy cases constituting 1081 episodes, 28 % involving TRIs, Joyce and Piper (1993) found that accurate TRIs positively affected clients' responses and, ultimately, resulted in successful therapy. TRIs capitalized on emotional immediacy in the therapeutic relationship and promoted conscious revision of interpersonal scripts. However, TRIs had to correlate with formulations of clients' problems, give clear references to the here-and-now, and include support from known parallel relationship patterns. They also had to be used infrequently, that is in fewer than one out of five interventions, a finding supported by Hoglend's 1996 analysis of his 1993 study.

A few years earlier, when Luborsky and others (1988) analyzed data from two early sessions of 73 non-psychotic clients, they found a positive correlation between desired outcome and interpretations that accurately describe clients' main wishes regarding their therapists, their therapists' responses, and clients' responses toward the therapists. According to self-reports, therapists' evaluations, and clinical observations, clients improved when therapists accurately diagnosed and verbally expressed central transference patterns as they emerged in relationship themes at the core of clients' conflicts.

In a three-case study, Fretter and others (1994) found that TRIs affected outcome positively provided they accurately addressed clients' pathological beliefs resultant from childhood trauma. TRIs contributed to progress by disconfirming the beliefs. However, non-TRIs that met the same criteria also resulted in positive outcomes.

In another three-case study, Silberschatz and others (1986) found TRIs to correlate with productivity in clients, which contributed to positive outcome, provided the TRIs addressed clients' conscious and unconscious goals as well as the pathogenic beliefs that had prevented them from attaining their goals. However, other interventions addressing goals and beliefs also correlated with productivity.

In studying the records of 24 early dropouts, Vaslamatzis and Verveniotis (1985) discovered that TRIs used early in therapy correlated with clients' staying in therapy beyond 10 sessions. However, it was not just TRIs that correlated with positive outcome. A circumscribed problem, high motivation, and a crisis situation were also needed.

Finally, accurate TRIs made early in treatment have been found to correlate with positive outcome at termination. Even during only one session, accurate TRIs correlate with a positive outcome at the end of the session (Bond et al., 1998).

## Third Position: The Necessity of Using TRIs and CTRIs

In the third position, both TRIs and CTRIs are considered cardinal to positive outcomes, as explained by Stolorow (1993), among others. A process of synthesis within clients, from which a coherent understanding gradually emerges, can take place only when therapists discover insight alongside clients. Synthesis cannot take place when therapists dogmatically impose understanding. Rather, it calls for therapists to share their insights and invite clients to confirm, deny, or modify what they hear.

*Whenever the client came for therapy, his therapist fought to stay awake. The client's "story" was always the same: his plight, his victimization, his unchanging lifestyle.*

*Finally, the therapist admitted to his client his boredom and asked if these negative feelings toward his client might possibly explain his client's failure to change and his repetitious accounts of the status quo.*

*The client looked at the therapist intently, then recounted a childhood "must": he had to keep very quiet in order to stay physically near his sleeping parents. They were professionals who rarely nurtured him because of their extensive travel. Any physical movement on his part increased the risk that they would find him in their bedroom and banish him to his own. And, yes, he feared that his therapist could banish him at any time from therapy, from the one stingy hour his therapist gave him out of the 40 work hours available. "With one hour of your precious time, how could we get anywhere!" he challenged.*

*The two then explored this bittersweet childhood memory and the client's negative feelings toward his therapist. The client gradually came to see the link between boring his therapist "into sleep" by keeping therapeutic movement minimal and his unexamined need to preserve whatever connection he could with a parental figure who gave him just one hour each week. Shortly thereafter, the client's therapeutic progress met his therapist's expectations.*

The third position ranges from using TRIs and CTRIs exclusively (Langs, 1979) to using TRIs and/or CTRIs only in conjunction with confronting, clarifying, and/or using non-transference interpretations (Bond et al., 1998; Meissner, 1996).

Crits-Christoph and others (1988) found a correlation between correctly addressing clients' patterns of needs and wishes, followed by examining the responses of others, and positive outcome in the cases of 43 subjects with various diagnoses. Measuring outcome by adjustment ratings of clients and clinical observers and by benefits ratings of clients and therapists, the research team discovered that therapeutic success correlated with early-session interpretations that accurately linked subjects' needs and wishes with how others responded. These results suggest that similar interpretations, such as TRIs and CTRIs, also lead to successful outcome as clients become more aware of how their behavior contributes to others' well-being.

Furthermore, based on their discovery that clients dialogue internally about their therapists and therapy both during and after therapy, Geller and others (1981-1982) hypothesized that therapists' appropriate therapeutic behavior gives clients models for change. The researchers studied 206 therapists who themselves were clients and their use of mental representations of their therapists to continue the therapeutic dialogue after therapy sessions. A significant correlation existed between self-perceived improvement and use of the representations.

The findings of Gellers and his colleagues support earlier discoveries of clients with more expressive therapists tending to have more favorable treatment outcomes than those with less expressive therapists (Butler & Rice, 1963). However, the work of Geller and colleagues (1981-1982) neither disproves improvement of clients with unexpressive therapists nor directly suggests using CTRIs.

## Evaluation of the Research Studies

Though some findings are compelling, the number and quality of existent research studies of TRIs and CTRIs overall do not permit valid scientific conclusions. The first position of not interpreting and the second position of interpreting only transference are supported more impressively than the third position of interpreting both transference and countertransference, but one can draw only tentative conclusions for the following reasons.

First, most of the studies do not allow conclusions regarding causality because they have not been experimental or even quasi-experimental. In addition, research data remains conflictual because of uncontrolled correlational and predictive variables such as clients' gender and maturity, characteristics of therapists, and relational dynamics between clients and therapists.

Second, extant studies have not used standardized terms and measures of commonly recognized dimensions of outcome; they have not been based on an agreed upon definition of positive outcome. Neither has there been agreement about the relative weight to be assigned to outcome measurement at various times in the course of therapy in contrast to post-termination and longitudinal measurements. Furthermore, because very of the few studies, either case or non-case, have been longitudinal, they cannot speak to the stability and longevity of either positive or negative outcome.

Third, most of the non-case studies have not been sufficiently complex. They have oversimplified perspectives in assessment as well as in levels and sources of measurement.

They have used neither sufficient numbers of participants nor included the number of variables needed to accurately reflect the clinical situation.

Fourth, many of the studies have used neither sufficient numbers of objective theorist-clinicians and non-believing clinicians nor included inter-rater coefficients. Thus, they cannot rule out observer bias.

Fifth, few of the studies have used clearly articulated protocols. Even if they have, few of the therapy sessions have been systematically reviewed by objective peers as to their faithfulness to the protocols.

Sixth, even methodologically sound studies have not been replicated with other populations. Though key variables have been isolated and studied in some single case studies, the issue of generalization remains. Studies have provided insights into how given individuals change, but these insights cannot be generalized even to a series of case studies (Edelson, 1984).

Seventh, the validity of clients' retrospective reports, one of which has been cited, of what seemed beneficial in the course of therapy has not been established, let alone systematically studied Waldron (1997).

In summary, it is not possible to draw firm conclusions from studies conducted thus far of the interpretation of transference and countertransference in actual sessions. For conclusions to be drawn and valid generalizations to be made, future studies need to be methodologically sound and replicated with larger populations.

Within the context of the above research limitations, however, valuable observations from which treatment recommendations may flow can be made. Those that follow are intended to aid therapists in their evaluative work, with the understanding that students and therapists need to continue to assess the validity of the three positions.

## Observations Regarding TRIs

TRIs, long attractive to many long-term clinicians, may be cost-effective, but it is not possible to conclude that therapeutic outcome depends on their use. The role and function of interpretation, including TRIs, as distinct from the role of the therapeutic alliance, has not yet been systematically assessed (Waldron, 1997). Rather, empirical evidence leads only to the conclusion that successful outcome can be achieved through the use of many other inventions, with each case dependent on those which effectively launch therapeutic work and keep particular clients in therapy until it can be completed. If all interventions combined account for only 40% of successful outcome (Lambert, 2001), a given intervention, such as a TRI, can affect outcome but not determine it in and of itself.

However, accurate, sensitively timed, and occasionally used TRIs can make an indirect contribution to successful outcome by positively affecting correlates of that outcome, namely, rapport building, the therapeutic alliance, continuance in therapy, and the working alliance. Indeed, careful use of TRIs contributes to successful outcome with a variety of Axis I and II diagnostic categories and non-diagnostic populations provided clients' resistance is neither high nor repeated, and formulation, focus, and timing are varied according to degrees of pathology.

TRIs that clearly refer to clients' here-and-now core conflicts, including wishes and needs that underlie them, and/or connect therapists to parents and siblings contribute to treatment efficacy. Clients can also benefit from there-and-then parallels, particularly TRIs that link clients' needs and wishes with the responses of others, beginning with their therapist's.

TRIs are especially efficacious if combined with non-transferential interventions, such as confrontations, explorations, and clarifications.

## Observations Regarding CTRIs

As useful as CTRIs can be, research has yet to show that successful outcome depends on them. It can be argued that intrapsychic processing of countertransference, combined with consultation, is usually sufficient to counteract acting-out unless it is extremely subtle or unusually potent. On the other hand, because research reveals that even experienced therapists tend to act out countertransference, CTRIs are among the valid means of counteracting potential harm.

Especially when therapists use CTRIs to reveal their process-oriented experiential countertransferential bodily responses—their visceral reactions to what clients are saying—they give clients direct information about how they affect others. When therapists use CTRIs to recognize their countertransferential discomforting bodily states, followed by a "report" on how they are autoregulating the painful disruption in state triggered by their empathic resonance with clients, they are determining that countertransference is constructive (Friedman & Lavender, 1997).

CTRIs also encourage clients by drawing attention to universal human vulnerability as well as the capacity for self-regulation (Beard, 1992), for reflective thought rather than action (Feldman, 1997).

Furthermore, CTRIs that address positive countertransference expose for clients seemingly innocuous but actually detrimental motivational forces at work even in highly educated, experienced, and well-intentioned professionals.

> The key to [managing] countertransference may be a self-reflective function by which the [therapist] determines whether he/she is internally sensing his/her counterregulator reactions to the [client's] dysregulation, or is psychobiologically resonating with the [client's] chaotic state (Schore, 2003a).

In addition, CTRIs perform a useful modeling function. "The willingness to self-disclose on the [therapist's] part facilitates self-disclosure by the [client], and therefore productive dialectical interchange between [therapist and client] is maximized" (Renik, 1993, 529).

On the other hand, it is usually risky for therapists to interpret countertransference to clients with moderate-to-severe psychopathology. Less vulnerable clients can even be at risk. Similarly, in some circumstances, interpreting countertransference may be meaningless or even damaging in that it may be inaccurate or at least incomplete.

# RECOMMENDATIONS FOR PRACTICE

The following recommendations, which are based on careful study of theory and research data related to interpreting transference and countertransference presented in this chapter and the previous one as well as clinical experience, are submitted to readers for their serious consideration.

- Remember that unaddressed transference and countertransference can correlate with negative outcome even in the course of a single session.
- But also keep in mind that use of TRIs and CTRIs can interfere with rapport building and the formation of the therapeutic and working alliances by distracting from other essential functions, such as attending to material central to clients' presenting problems and observing non-verbal phenomena that confirms or contradicts speech.
- Distinguish relatively overt and blatant transference and countertransference from relatively covert and subtle transference and countertransference. Because of the amount of time and effort necessary for diagnosing transference and countertransference, decode only what can be readily decoded, leaving more difficult material to inter-session work. However, if transference and countertransference are contributing in a significant way to a therapeutic impasse, no matter how covert or subtle, use as much time and effort as necessary to diagnose them during sessions.
- Think of TRIs and CTRIs as usable if they refer to the present and to the therapeutic situation. The more demanding criteria of interpreting the here-and-now only in combination with the there-and-then need not be met.
- Remember that risk of harm is lowered if the frequency of TRIs and CTRIs is moderate, in some cases low.
- Remember that TRIs and CTRIs used too often or prior to dealing with client-selected issues can cause clients to regard therapists as persons against whom they have to be defended. Similarly, both clients and therapists can use interpretative work as a way of getting out of exploring clients' non-transferential issues.

- Avoid looking at the immediate effects of TRIs and CTRIs and judging them to be harmful because they have an inhibitory effect, for an initial effect is often replaced by progress over the course of the entire session.
- Keep in mind that the vast majority of clients want to work on the non-transferential and non-countertransferential issues that they have identified for themselves. At the same time, remember that transference and countertransference may actually be related to clients' problems as they have identified them. It is unwise to lose out on the powerful effect that processing the here-and-now can have on outcome. Furthermore, TRIs and CTRIs that connect clients' presenting problems or core conflicts with transference and countertransference have significant potential when used with appropriate clients.
- Examine clients' resistance to TRIs and CTRIs. It may be due to their inability to use interpretations. Or it may be due to a particular TRI's or CTRI's inaccuracy either on a denotative, overt level or on a meta-communicative, covert level.
- Weigh theoretical pros and cons and scientific information against the needs of individual clients at given times in the history of their therapeutic work.
- Most importantly, keep uppermost in mind that though successful outcome can be achieved without interpreting transference and countertransference, doing so with appropriate clients at the right "teachable" moments can strengthen the therapeutic alliance, enhance the working alliance, and reveal to clients the power of articulating what is going on between them and others. Once clients can put into words what they know by instinct is happening in their lives, they can fashion their feared, hated, sad, or unrealistic relationships into realistic, wholesome, sustaining, and supportive ones.

# CHAPTER EIGHT

# WORDING TRANSFERENCE AND COUNTERTRANSFERENCE INTERPRETATIONS

## Introduction

In order to appreciate specific guidelines for wording transference and countertransference interpretations (TRIs and CTRIs), readers first need to define these interventions. They need to hold them to the light of the theoretical bases on which they depend as well as place them within the context of non-analytic therapy. Readers also need to become familiar with an attitude that has been found to precede and accompany effective TRIs and CTRIs: an openness to simply observing each client's unique phenomenology and the therapist's own distinctive responses to it.

## A Transference Interpretation

A transference interpretation (TRI) is a comment or question voiced by the therapist to call the client's attention to an apparent problem within the client-therapist relationship that appears to be the result of transference. The therapist experiences a conflict between what is transpiring in the therapeutic setting and the way the client and therapist need to interact so that their collaborative work is fruitful. (1)

In the non-analytic tradition, a TRI may simply state the transference-based problem, as in, "You seem frustrated with me because of my limit-setting." Alternately, the TRI may link the therapy situation to a current or past conflictual relationship that the client has described or somehow alluded to (Pearson, 1995), a relationship being transferred to the therapy session. The therapist may say, for example, "You seem frustrated with me because I set limits similar to those your teachers set."

A TRI that directly refers to displaced material, Schafer (1977) says succinctly, is "a creative re-description that implicitly has the structure of a simile. It says 'This is like that.' It adds new actions to the life [clients] have already lived" (57). It helps them see pre- or extra-therapeutic experiences as sources of unquestioned beliefs and unchallenged emotions that cause interpersonal problems. It suggests that the client may be imposing presuppositions, without question, on new experience (Cooper, 1987). The following TRI, for instance, would help a client question the belief that all adults make unreasonable demands: "I wonder if you see my request that you pay before your session as your teachers requiring you finish labor-intensive assignments before you eat lunch."

Indeed, a TRI suggests that the therapeutic relationship has become a re-enactment of clients' previous or current, unresolved conflictual experiences outside of therapy. It is an implicit acknowledgment of the powerful impact that people not actually in the therapy room and events connected to them can exert on feelings and attitudes arising in therapy. It alludes to here-and-now cognition and emotion based on there-and-then experience. It identifies clients' unconscious expectations of others and asks them to evaluate their appropriateness. Said succinctly, a TRI encourages clients to subject potentially harmful beliefs and emotions to the criterion of factual evidence. Clients may need to ask, for example, "Are others' requests actually unreasonable demands?" "Could not their demands be reasonable even though I feel resentful?" (2)

Even a TRI that does not directly refer to displaced material but exposes a conflict in the client-therapist relationship that has arisen because of transference encourages clients to discover whether their interpersonal schemas are maladaptive or adaptive. "Do I need to hold more realistic expectations of myself and others?" clients may need to ask.

Clients' expectations tend to rest on both conscious beliefs for which there is usually some objective evidence and unconscious assumptions to which clients have been holding fast, often against objective evidence to the contrary. The belief that those in authority have power to make demands, for example, has objective validity. The assumption that one person in authority will make unreasonable demands because another like her has done so, however, lacks that objective validity. Nevertheless, in spite of unconscious "certainties" never being personally validated, clients tend to accept them as principles of knowing and guidelines for interpersonal relationships (Schafer, 1977). To use the previous example, clients perceive their therapist as a person in authority and experience his or her request for prompt payment as unreasonable.

Consequently, clients need to look at how they are unconsciously constructing the therapeutic relationship in accordance with their unconscious principles of knowing. If they do not do so on their own, therapists need to help them by interpreting the transference that betrays the assumptions. "I wonder if you see my asking you to pay your fee as an unreasonable demand similar to those made by your teachers," a therapist might say.

Put in a slightly different light, a TRI reminds clients that transferential wishes, feelings, and cognitions connected with their present relational conflicts exist within their own psyche and need to be recognized as such. They may or may not reflect objective reality. Thus a TRI is a means of performing one of therapists' fundamental tasks: "to help clients recognize that current interpersonal conflicts are, in actuality, intrapsychic conflicts" (Gill, 1982, 21).

Of course, many TRIs also refer to the interpersonal nature of clients' conflicts. "I believe I have done something to anger you," a therapist might add to recognize that he or she is an active, though unwitting, participant in transferential aspects of the therapy process (Cooper, 1987).

Similarly, many TRIs clearly link previous life experiences with emotions and cognitions arising in the current therapist-client relationship (Cooper, 1987). "Could you be angry with me because I made you wait today, just as your mother made you wait for supper?" a therapist might say. Other TRIs refer to current experiences outside of therapy, as in "Could it be that my upcoming vacation feels like the abandonment you are experiencing because of your friend's death?"

Stop to recall a person in your early life with whom you had a significant negative experience. Let yourself re-experience that event in some detail. Then ask yourself if at other times in your life, you unconsciously expected others to treat you in ways similar to that person.

When therapists interpret transference as a new here-and-now enactment of an old conflict and ask clients to evaluate what they are doing, therapists bring to clients' consciousness all aspects of the new experience: its past origins, its present operations, and its future implications. They invite clients to take a trip back in history for the sake of insight (Cooper, 1987) and future interpersonal relationships. Should they be based solely on long-held assumptions or should they also be allowed to develop in accordance with the unique facts that define them?

Unlike a psychoanalytic TRI, which suggests that clients process intrapsychically the information the interpretation provides, a non-analytic TRI is an invitation to clients to process the information collaboratively. A non-analytic TRI encourages clients to talk about the dynamics of their session with their therapist in order to arrive at insight in a relatively short time, as befits most session-limited non-analytic treatment.

A non-analytic TRI is often a question like, "Could it be that you are angry with me because I remind you of your mother?" Even if it is a declarative statement like, "I think you are angry with me because I acted like your mother," a non-analytic TRI invites verbal response because of its open-ended intonation. There may be no clear, immediate agreement or disagreement on the part of the client to whom a TRI is voiced, but as a general rule when clients hear TRIs that strike them as accurate, they tend to elaborate on the material. When TRIs appear inaccurate, they do not.

Hence, Meissner (1996), agreeing with Jacobson (1993) and Treurniet (1993), writes, "When the interpretive process is working well, therapist and [client] are engaged in the exploration of hypotheses [regarding their relationship] arrived at by a collaborative process, based on the [client's] intrapsychic content" (257).

*At the beginning of the session, the cognitive-behavioral oriented-therapist drew her client's attention to the fact that she had not paid her fee for the third week in a row. Though the client acknowledged this and promised to send a check the following day, she responded curtly to several of her therapist's subsequent reflections on her accomplishments that week. Recalling the client's stories about her overly critical father, the therapist finally said, "Could it be that you are annoyed with me today because at the beginning of our session I reminded you of your bill? Perhaps I sounded like your father when he chastised you for your unfinished schoolwork."*

*Responding to this countertransference interpretation, the client admitted that she was angry with her therapist. She refused to admit, however, that she was displacing feelings toward her father, at least not during that session and the one immediately following. In time, though, when the therapist again made a tentative connection between the therapist's remarks, the client's behavior, and its possible relationship with how her father treated her, she conceded. Afterwards the therapist and client were able to explore together the deep pain the client had suffered—and was still suffering—because of her father's rebukes.*

Thus by making conscious an unconscious memory, a TRI helped a client free herself from *having* to relate in the present as she had in the past.

## A Countertransference Interpretation

A countertransference interpretation (CTRI) is a comment or question voiced by the therapist to call attention to a problem that the therapist is experiencing which seems to be linked to displaced material. It may be being displaced by the client, the therapist, or both. The therapist shares that he or she is experiencing a conflict between what is transpiring in the therapeutic setting and the way the client and therapist need to interact in order to make their collaborative work fruitful.

At times the CTRIs links the feelings, thoughts, and behaviors of the therapist to phenomena transferred to the therapy session by the client. "I feel attacked by the remark you just made, and I wonder whether you are unconsciously trying to show me how your mother used to attack," a therapist might say. At other times the CTRI links the therapist's problem directly to his or her own displaced material. "I feel demeaned by the comment you made, just as I sometimes felt demeaned by teachers. Can we talk about what's going on?" the therapist may say. At still other times the CTRI suggests that the therapist's countertransferential response is linked both to the client's transferential behavior and to the therapist's own personality, history, or current extra-therapeutic life. "I wonder if my sleepiness is due solely to not getting enough sleep last night or whether something going on in here is putting me to sleep," the therapist may say.

In any case, the CTRI is an invitation to clients to identify distortions, misinterpretations, and unfair attributions that their therapist might be unconsciously making, with the hope that this will increase clients' insight into both their intrapsychic conflicts and their interpersonal problems. The CTRI is not an invitation to explore the *therapist's* problem as such. It is meant to facilitate an exploration of the *client's* conflict.

As with non-analytic TRIs, a non-analytic CTRI may name only the therapists' feelings, thoughts, and behaviors that the therapist suspects are being elicited by the client's transference. Especially when previous CTRIs have done so, a CTRI does not have to refer directly to the client's transferred material. "I am frightened by your yelling in anger when I ask you to pay your bill," for example, is a revelation of the therapist's reaction to what the client does when reminded of similar conflicts. Similarly, a CTRI may simply refer to what therapists themselves are doing in sessions and question whether transference or countertransference is at work. "I feel so angry today and am not entirely sure why. Is something negative going on in here today as a result of some unfinished business?" a therapist might say. Though it does not do so explicitly, this kind of CTRI is still intended to help clients identify what *they* are contributing to the client-therapist interaction.

Finally, it is helpful to consider Racker's (1953) distinction between concordant and complementary CTRIs. Concordant CTRIs tell clients that their therapist is identifying with them, as in "I feel so sad as I listen to you and wonder if you are not only angry with your brother but also sad because of him." Thus the therapist is revealing that the client has transferred unacknowledged feelings to the therapist.

Complementary CTRIs, on the other hand, tell clients that their therapist is identifying with those affected by their client's words and actions, as in "I experience humiliation in listening to your report of how you dealt with your son. Is it possible that your son felt humiliated when you scolded him?" Therapists are sharing their understanding of what significant others might feel when interacting with their clients.

*The client elaborated on a pleasure trip he had just made, providing comical anecdotes interspersed with interesting descriptions. Though she was at first intrigued by her client's account, the Rogerian-oriented therapist soon noticed herself becoming bored and irritated. The incongruity between his enthusiasm and her negative response was striking.*

*She began to recall previously confronting her client about taking time off work in light of his family obligations, for his goal was to have fun without neglecting familial responsibilities. The therapist also wondered if her irritation might be also due to her going out of her way to accommodate her client. She had rescheduled an appointment for his convenience, she recalled, which had extended her work week.*

*The therapist hoped that by using a CTRI linking the client's actions to her own irritation, she could help him address an issue he had identified earlier. In the course of that she might also process her own negative feelings, but that was not her primary goal. She had noted her complex countertransference but would focus only on an aspect of it clearly related to her client's goal*

Eventually the therapist interrupted the client and said, "I'm feeling irritated by this account of your trip. Could it be that your detailed account is preventing me from addressing how that trip might have imposed a hardship on your family? Your goal, you recall, is to balance fun with familial responsibilities."

Thus the therapist used her own emotional response to her client to help him look at his behavior and its impact on therapy, with the hope that he would also gain insight into how his in-therapy behavior related to the attainment of his goals.

## The Right Attitude

Therapists who choose to share their hypotheses about transference and countertransference with clients increase their chances of being effective if they agree to simply observe and wonder. "It is . . . observation itself, its meaning sought without preconception, which enables the interpretation to follow in such subtle form that it may lie simply in the answer given by the [client]" (Schwaber, 1990, 234-5). By observing and wondering, therapists say to their client, "Let's together determine what is going on between us."

"To observe and wonder is not to be ahead of clients in ascertaining impersonal and personal reality. It is to give up an agenda for understanding new and unique phenomena, [saying in effect] 'I know less rather than more'" (Schwaber, 1990, 237).

When therapists simply observe and wonder, they refrain from superimposing their preferred ways of thinking on clients' transferred material. They follow the lead of Winnicott (1960), who said whimsically, yet insightfully, some 20 years earlier: "I interpret mainly to let the [client] know the limits of my understanding" (711).

Therapists who simply observe and wonder remember that both transference and "countertransference [are sources] of data but not [sources] of evidence" (Smith, 2000, 105). They suggest complex realities but do not provide proof. Even if based on what appears to be relatively conclusive evidence, transference—and even more so countertransference—are vulnerable to bias. Interpretations of them, conscious derivatives of unconscious phenomena, cannot be used to describe them definitively. Neither therapist nor client is truly objective in spite of sometimes feeling strongly that he or she is. Neither is without pathology, anxiety, or vulnerability to defense mechanisms (Racker, 1972). Both are holders of partial truth that can be known in its fullness only when parts are shared.

Thus therapists who wonder are open to rejection or revision no less than confirmation of their hypotheses regarding transference and countertransference.

in spite of sometimes feeling strongly that he or she is. Neither is without pathology, anxiety, or vulnerability to defense mechanisms (Racker, 1972). Both are holders of partial truth that can be known in its fullness only when parts are shared.

Thus therapists who wonder are open to rejection or revision no less than confirmation of their hypotheses regarding transference and countertransference. They resist their tendency to become attached to their interpretations and forget that they are only hypotheses (Cooper, 1993). They await something definitive—truth that develops only with the active cooperation of clients (Bezoari et al., 1994)—rather than dispense to clients truths that they, therapists, have already gleaned (Cooper, 1993).

In fact, therapists who observe and wonder go one step further. They assign secondary importance to their knowledge in order to know clients by what they reveal (Smith, 2000). They acknowledge the working primacy of the truth that the client holds. "It is the [client] and only the [client] who has the answers" (Winnicott, 1960, 711), however key to the client's discovery might be the therapist's intuition and insight.

Furthermore, for therapists to observe and wonder is for them to simply watch the past becoming dynamically present in therapy through transference and countertransference. It is to understand gradually how the past is being re-experienced in the present and to share that understanding with clients (Casement, 1991). It is to be open to what might be the actuality behind the appearance and the reality beneath the surface. It is to acknowledge that, because material in the unconscious is highly undifferentiated, it is extremely difficult to determine exactly what and how much clients, versus therapists, are contributing. It is to wait and see whether transferential "truth" actually resonates in the countertransference. For it takes the psyches of both therapist and client to verify what is actually occurring.

# Qualities of Effective TRIs and CTRIs

Effective transference and countertransference interpretations are worded in such a way that they meet the following criteria.

## Calming

Though effective TRIs usually convey disturbing information, they are calming (Strachey, 1934) for three reasons. First, they recognize the value of what might otherwise be considered destructive subjective feeling states, as in "You seem to be angry with me. Can we look at how that anger may be related to what you experience toward your spouse?" TRIs indicate that, far from being unmanageable, affect can be used to acquire insight into a problematic interpersonal dynamic. TRIs allow painful reality to finally overcome clients' efforts to repress it. Thus TRIs bring relief, even comfort, as hey reveal what clients unconsciously "know" but prefer to deny in spite of the psychic energy that it takes to deny reality (Lear, 1993).

Second, because TRIs are voiced by therapists who are noticeably calm, they signal that clients are in a safe environment. Therapists are holding their countertransferential response up to the light of scrutiny without "falling apart," collapsing, or retaliating (Winnicott, 1960; Casement, 1991). Hearing, for example, "I wonder if your yelling at me is a way of telling me you were angry with your father. Am I right about that?" clients can deny, confirm, question, revise, or reject the TRI—all with impunity.

Third, effective TRIs reveal that therapists have simply received a communication; they are not determined to correct a client's inappropriate behavior (Casement, 1991). Clients can remain calm, for example, when therapists say, "In yelling at me you may be unconsciously trying to show me what it was like to be a child in your family. If so, can we talk about that?"

Bollas (1987) suggests that therapists introduce TRIs with such calming phrases as "What occurs to me," "I have an idea," "I'm curious about what you think," "I'd like to share a thought with you," or "You may not agree with me but . . ." (206). Beginning TRIs in such a way that clients feel calm is the surest way that therapists have of not getting drawn into client-initiated re-enactments. In the case of rage, in particular, therapists can be unwittingly seduced into continuing an intense transferred feeling through their interpretations.

| Write phrases that calm *you* when you confront others or they confront you. |
|---|
| |

In order to make TRIs calming, therapists might also need to take a moment between hearing and speaking during which they monitor for the potential re-enactment that may be concealed within the first interpretation that comes to mind. A short pause between what clients and therapists say can serve as an indication that therapists are truly "holding" what their clients are expressing. Therapists are not so eager to process disturbing feelings that they cannot hold them calmly as a first step in the interpretative process. (3)

Like TRIs, CTRIs should calm both clients and therapists. Therapists must even report feeling insulted in such a way that they remain tranquil in spite of their unpleasant experience and the paranoid anxiety that might accompany it (Little, 1951). They can survive being treated badly (Winnicott, 1971) when transference is negative. Similarly, they can manage positive transference, such as being idolized. They need not let it stop them from demanding hard work from both themselves and their client. Occasionally, therapists may need to refrain from naming an emotion in order to remain calm. Instead of saying, "I feel demeaned by your last remark and recall how you said your mother demeaned you," for example, they might simply reflect upon what has just occurred. They might simply say, "I am experiencing a communication from you that's coming in the only way you know—by behaving towards me as your mother behaved towards you." Having established a calm atmosphere, therapists can then use the precise word for their experience without sacrificing tranquility. Similarly, therapists may need to preface CTRIs by an explanatory remark in order to remain calm. "I get the impression that you have often had the experience of being put in the wrong," a therapist might say before adding, "I think that that's why you have been putting me in a similar position today and making me feel blamed" (Casement, 1991, 147).

Of course, metalanguage markers must be equally calming for TRIs and CTRIs to be effective. Therapists must convey calm through such secondary features as tenor, volume, tone, and pitch. In some cases, they must even add a reassuring look or respectful gesture.

## Emotionally Immediate

Strachey (1934) states emphatically that if TRIs are to be mutative at the same time that they are calming, they must be emotionally immediate, that is, charged with emotion. TRIs must clearly identify the affect underlying clients' transference conflict, however uncomfortable that naming may be for both client and therapist. Furthermore, for TRIs to be mutative, they must be given as closely as possible to clients' emotional experiences. (4)

It may seem contradictory for an interpretation to be both calming and charged with emotion, but these qualities are not actually mutually exclusive. Emotions can be expressed in varying shades of intensity, all the way from hardly conveying the emotion to subsuming content by pure volume and strident tonality. The challenge is to find a balance between accurate reflection of emotions and their containment within the boundaries of the rational mind. It helps if therapists think in terms of mild to moderate, rather than strong, levels of affect, Kiesler (1982b) writes.

Winnicott (1971) enjoins therapists to examine and sift ideas and feelings that come to mind before they speak. After reflecting, they can say, for example, "You seem to hate me" in such a way that there is no doubt that the therapist has simply observed and recorded the primary feeling of the client toward the therapist. The therapist has not internalized it or necessarily found it justifiable.

Crowley (1988) uses an especially apt metaphor to describe the challenge of balancing emotional immediacy with calm: "it is tremendously important for [therapists] to burrow through the exaggerated parts of [their] reactions to the healthy rational substratum . . ." (87). The anger that therapists experience, for example, may be largely inappropriate, and they must recognize that. At the same time, they must use the anger to hypothesize about what the client did to provoke it and why. They can then meet the criteria of immediacy and calming by using a TRI like, "You appear to be angry with me right now because I, like your father, said that your behavior is unacceptable. Can we talk about what you are feeling?"

Regarding countertransference, Maroda (1995) suggests that therapists offer emotionally immediate CTRIs to appropriate clients under most conditions. CTRIs are most effective not because they are intellectual statements but because they are revelations of genuine emotion. She writes that "Ouwe!" can be more effective than "I am hurt by your remark!" Similarly, "I think your wife's comment is very abusive. I can't believe that you didn't get angry with her!" can be more effective than "I'm disturbed by your not being angry with your wife." However, Maroda (1995) also warns that in formulating CTRIs therapists must express feeling without losing control. CTRIs, like TRIs, should be accompanied by mild to moderate levels of affect, Kiesler (1982b) instructs clinicians.

Therapists must also time emotionally immediate CTRIs carefully. Using them when clients are already highly aroused can overwhelm them. Using CTRIs when clients are already very anxious can disrupt their ability to use the interpreted material profitably.

## Ego-Based and Neutral

Volkan (1995) states that TRIs must come "from the side of the ego" (213), especially when directed to significantly regressed clients. They must not come from the side of the id in that they simply accept reality as it appears to be or as one would like it to be or to demand that reality conform to one's impulsive and instinctual desires. In contrast to an id-based interpretation like "You are angry because I kept you waiting," an ego-based TRI would be "You may be angry because I kept you waiting." The wording of this second TRI implies that a strong reaction, while accurately reflecting a client's affect, is unlikely to be the totality of the client's state of mind and related communication. (5)

Neither must TRIs come from the side of the superego in that they pass irrefutable judgment on clients' versions of reality. Instead of teaching yet another version of the truth as understood by the therapist, TRIs must be neutral with regard to the truth. For instance, a therapist should use an ego-based TRI like, "Your anger with me may be something even you don't feel good about" instead of its superego-based counterpart: "I think you are angry because you can't tolerate the faults in you that you see in me." The ego-based TRI implies that emotions have neither immoral overtones nor morally unacceptable meanings.

| |
|---|
| Rewrite the following superego-based TRI to make it ego-based: "I think that you are unconsciously punishing yourself, as your father often did, because you feel so badly about what you did."(6) |
| |
| |
| |

Ego-based TRIs—and one might add CTRIs—invite clients to observe and face their own truths (Schwaber, 1990). They encourage clients to examine what seems to be happening: to verify perceptions, check out impressions, and elaborate on deductions. They further the client's work of reality testing by facilitating a process within which a coherent truth can gradually emerge. They are means whereby clients gain insights that make sense of their transferential experience (Casement, 1991) and their therapists' countertransference.

In some cases, TRIs and CTRIs can also meet the criterion of being ego-based and neutral in that they encourage clients to process specific defenses being used by the ego, defenses that should be dealt with prior to addressing primitive urges and impulses (Freud, 1926). Indeed, with many clients, therapeutic work needs to focus less on their negative emotions than on the reasons for them, that is, the defensive functions of the emotions. An interpretation that identifies the insecurity underlying arrogance, for instance, directs attention to where therapeutic work should be done. A TRI like "When you feel threatened, you try to protect yourself. Then I experience you as being arrogant and overlook the possibility that you may be trying to defend yourself from feeling small" opens the door to an examination of the defense rather than the emotion and reduces the combative atmosphere created by the client's arrogance. (7)

The ego-based and neutral criterion leads to an important corollary: it is often more helpful for therapists to use what they "know" and to find a way of approaching this through "not yet knowing" than it is to simply reflect what clients are saying. An example would be, "You seem to be envious of me as was your younger brother of you, but I sense you don't want to be." Clients who hear this are likely to deduce that their therapist is siding with a reality-focused ego rather than a guilt-assigning superego.

For their part, CTRIs should simply state what therapists are feeling and thinking about their clients. They should not encourage a heightened emotional response in clients. "I am afraid of you today because of your shouting," for example, simply reports the experience of the therapist, provided, of course, that its tone, volume, and intonation are modulated and respectful. Similarly, CTRIs should not include overt or covert justifications of what therapists are experiencing in relation to their clients. "I am angry with you today" said in the right way should imply neither that the client is guilty nor the therapist justified. The therapist's emotion simply deserves to be looked at. It is to be condemned by neither client nor therapist (Little, 1951). To make this clear, therapists might add, "Can we take a look at what I am feeling and try to understand it?" or "Would it be all right to try to see where my anger is coming from?"

| Stop to write sentences that fit your style of communicating with clients (or significant others if you are not yet a therapist). |
| --- |
| |
| |
| |
| |

Schafer (1983) writes that, in contrast to unquestionable pronouncements or indisputable moral judgments, TRIs and CTRIs are to be expository as befits the therapist's clinical role. They are to be clarifying, explicating, or enlightening observations. They are to come across as objective in that therapists voice them without defensiveness, Gill (1982) adds. They are to give clients the "okay" to feel and express feelings, even to re-experience the earlier times when they were felt. "You may be angry with me" or "You appear to be angry with me" or "I believe you are angry with me" are much less likely to carry condemnatory or judgmental overtones than "You are angry with me." Similarly, "I seem to be angry with you" or "I'm finding it hard not be angry with you" sound more ego-based than "I am angry with you."

Of course, the requirement to keep TRIs and CTRIs ego-based and neutral depends on an accepting tone, courteous tenor, modulated volume and speed, calming pitch, and respectful inflection, which combine to create an appropriate mood and interpersonal atmosphere. As Pick (1997) asserts quite accurately, some clients only listen to the "mood"; they do not even hear the words. Hinshelwood (1999) corroborates, observing that very disturbed clients acutely scan interpretations to assess what is happening in their therapist's mind: Is it retaliation? Is it resentment? Is it forgiveness?

Indeed, while almost anything can be said in an accepting atmosphere, even the most sensitively worded message will meet with resistance in one that is negative. It is "important to remember that some [clients] are acutely sensitive to the hidden meaning in what the [therapists] says" (Casement, 1991, 131). (8)

## Precise, Clear, and Concrete

Rather than being abstract or relying on implications, effective TRIs and CTRIs are precise and clear about the distortions that clients or therapists are making or the specific actions that have impacted therapy (Kiesler, 1982b). Effective TRIs and CTRIs are detailed and specific (Strachey, 1934). They befit the therapist's discerning, clinical role in that they can be challenged up-front (Schafer, 1983).

TRIs that clearly identify transferential phenomena provide clients with precise information about how their behavior contributes to interpersonal problems. They awaken unconscious resonances and permeate intrapsychic boundaries (Lear, 1993). "You seem angry with me because I said your behavior is inappropriate, as did your teacher" is clear, concrete, and direct because it specifies the client's behavior as an interpersonal problem. Even more specific are, "You seem to dislike me now that I have suggested, as did your mother, that you also are to blame" and "It seems as if you are afraid to tell me that you are angry with me. Instead, you just come late. Is this true?"

In contrast, if clients hear a TRI like, "Could it be that you are disturbed because of my remark?" or "You seem to be getting upset about what I'm saying," they may be left with an ambiguous message. They may be unsure about what "my remark" or "what I'm saying" means. Vague, imprecise TRIs can also give clients a chance to thwart their therapist's attempts to bring unpleasant unconscious material to consciousness (Strachey, 1934).

Like TRIs, CTRIs should bear correspondence to historical facts or to specific features of clients' scripts (Joyce & Piper, 1993). Ideally, CTRIs should refer, directly or indirectly, to clients' presenting problems, major themes of their work, and the metaphors that they use repeatedly. "I am angry right now because of not getting any real information today. Could it be that your spouse also finds it hard when you don't share with her?" would be an example.

If possible, CTRIs should include clear references to what is happening in therapy in the here-and-now. They should identify specific affective reactions that therapists have just experienced or concrete behaviors they have just performed. At the least, CTRIs should identify events that clients will recall as having occurred in the therapeutic setting (Strachey, 1934; Swift & Wonderlich, 1990; Stolorow, 1993; Stone, 1984; Strupp, 1989; Casement, 1991; Piper et al., 1993). "I am aware of being frustrated with your silence today," a therapist might say. Or "I looked at my watch so often today, perhaps out of a desire to disconnect from you."

| Stop to write other CTRI's that you yourself might use. |
| --- |
| |
| |
| |
| |

## Tentative

At first it might seem as if the criteria of clarity, precision, and concreteness, on one hand, and tentativeness, on the other, are mutually exclusive. But both criteria can and do apply to effective TRIs and CTRIs. They must convey specific information as well as indicate that they can be revised, even rejected. Rather than being conclusions made by therapists, TRIs and CTRIs are invitations to clients to collaborate in discerning the validity or invalidity of therapists' observations. Tentative TRIs and CTRIs are clearly "meant to be played with, kicked around, mulled over, and torn to pieces rather than regarded as official versions of the truth" (Bollas, 1983, 7).

If therapists are always certain of what they say, clients have to contend with a dogmatic individual who claims to know more than what is actually knowable (Field, 1989). They feel pressured to submit to a purely receptive and acquiescent style of working (Bacal, 1990) rather than free to interact with their therapist to explore different potential meanings (Winnicott, 1971).

When therapists use tentative TRIs and CTRIs, they bring a subjective state of mind into play by offering to clients "a scrap of material and a chance to elaborate on it" (Bollas, 1987, 206). Therapists are open to questioning, clarification, and revision. They are listening for evidence or consensual reality that supports their own or their clients' perceptions and judgments (Schafer, 1983).

They are hoping that both they and their clients can gradually understand their displaced perceptions and feelings.

"Could it be that . . . ," "I wonder if . . . ," "Perhaps it's that I don't know whether you will agree with me, but . . . ," "What occurs to me," "I have an idea," and "I don't know if you are going to like what occurs to me, but . . ." all signal the tentativeness of the interpretation and invite clients to respond in agreement, disagreement, or partial agreement (Bollas, 1987). They introduce TRIs and CTRIs that are more communicative than informative (Brodbeck, 1995) and more probabilistic than certain (Schafer, 1983).

It is especially important, Bollas (1987) contends, for therapists to acknowledge the difficulty of putting into words what they believe clients are feeling toward them. When therapists struggle openly to find the right words for what their clients experience, they model how to deal with what they somehow "know" but cannot easily describe or with what they suspect but may never have known. Therapists counteract that certainty with which clients have often been judged and with which they judge themselves. They invite clients to collaborate with them in an effort to discover the complexities of the human person, especially in relationship to others. By using tentative TRIs and CTRIs, therapists underscore the wisdom of passing subjective perceptions back and forth until only those that withstand scrutiny survive. By using tentative rather than irrefutable TRIs and CTRIs, therapists make a fundamental distinction between interpreting "countertransference as *one* indicator of what *might* be going on in a complex field and using it as the complete explanation of what is transpiring" (Herron & Rouslin, 1982, 146).

Tentative phraseology is even more appropriate for the countertransferential unthought "known": what therapists feel but do not understand because it is being transferred from extremely primitive parts of the client's unconscious mind (Bollas, 1987, 232). Yet this material is extremely valuable because, though the core of its significance has yet to be discovered, both therapist and client recognize it as meaningful communication. "Could it be that my frustration today is related to some kind of message you are giving me? I can't put my finger on what is causing this feeling," the therapist might say, for example. Besides reducing defensiveness, such wording allows therapist and client to "play with" meaning and significance in a relaxed and respectful way (Winnicott, 1965), kicking ideas back and forth until meaning becomes lucid and significance, compelling. (9)

## Pertinent

Closely related to criteria for TRIs and CTRIs to be clear, precise, and concrete is the requirement that they refer, either directly or indirectly, to phenomena pertinent to the issues that clients have identified and the goals they have set. The criterion of pertinence also pertains to clients getting exactly what they need during a given session. Stereotypic interpretations—those used easily, those foremost in thinking—are better off delayed, for when clients are given time, they lead therapists to insight that is more specific and often quite new (Casement, 1991).

While TRIs and CTRIs may refer to past figures, they are now considered more pertinent if they address material related to those problematic core conflicts presently occurring both outside and within the therapeutic setting. Not focusing on the present, Gill (1982) warns, can make clients feel that therapists are examining relatively non-significant past relationships at the expense of their presenting problems. By interpreting the here-and-now, by contrast, therapists imply that clients' presenting problems are more important than their past difficulties.

As noted in Chapter One, most contemporary non-analytic theorists find it more important to work with clients' reactions to their therapists than for clients to recognize them as transferred. In addition, because most intrapersonal issues involve others, TRIs are said to be most effective if they are "pertinent to unresolved impediments to congruous and continuous relationships with people in the present" (Wolstein, 1996, 505), both the therapist and people outside therapy. What happens in therapy sheds light on problems that clients have already identified, intrapsychic as well as interpsychic, for even personal problems tend to arise from interpersonal conflict (Wolstein, 1996).

The criterion of pertinence—meaning here-and-now, in-session occurring—is based on the fact that therapists are not always able to discern the true source of clients' and therapists' feelings toward each other although both parties perceive those feelings. Moreover, feelings usually precede thoughts. In time, therapists may identify previous phenomena, but initially they are likely to be aware only of their feelings and their suspicion that those feelings cannot be accounted for solely by what is happening in the session.

Indeed, the criterion of pertinence is met by here-and-now, in-session occurring TRIs and CTRIs because therapists can validly suspect displacement from the past or from outside therapy simply when they notice their sudden, strong, or unusual affective and somatic reactions to the therapeutic situation. It is unrealistic to expect therapists to be certain of the fact that transference or countertransference is occurring, let alone certain about the source of displaced feelings and attitudes. As a consequence, the criterion of pertinence does not require therapists to tie "then" and "there" happenings to "here" and "now" incidents. If they are actually linked, clients will link them, mentally if not verbally. Or therapists themselves will obtain further data to link the then-and-there and the here-and-now in subsequent interpretations.

## Inclusive

Though the criterion of pertinence allows TRIs and CTRIs to refer only to the present, there is a place for inclusive interpretations that link the present with the past or the therapeutic interaction with that which occurs outside it. When it is relatively clear that therapeutic events are being triggered by non-therapeutic experience therapists may say, for example, "I wonder whether my being judgmental toward you today is partly the result of your finding various reasons not come to therapy for more than a month." Or they may remark, "Is my being judgmental toward you today solely the result of my having a hard day?" (10)

In some circumstances, if TRIs and CTRIs are not inclusive, clients may feel more comfortable but draw erroneous conclusions. Simple here-and-now TRIs and CTRIs may imply that therapists are afraid of their feelings. As a consequence, clients may suppress their strong feelings for fear of their therapists not being able to cope with them. Similarly, here-and-now TRIs and CTRIs may lead clients to think that their therapist's examination of the therapeutic relationship is being done at the expense of their presenting problems or other very real concerns (Bauer & Mills, 1989).

One way to meet the criterion of inclusivity is to start with an observation that the client has made about the past and follow the direction of the transference to where the past is spilling over into the present. For example, "When you were dependent upon your mother, she went away and left you. Because you were feeling dependent on me before I took a vacation, you may now experience me as the mother who left you when you most needed her." By wording TRIs this way, therapists are offering insight into the client's past distress while keeping the focus on the present, the time of expressed transferential feelings.

Similarly, clients can benefit from therapists' introducing material from a previous session while focusing on the session at hand. "Last week you spoke of John, who is unkind to you. I wonder if today you are also finding me unkind," for example.

In fact, Gill (1982) recommends routinely including *also* or *in addition* in inclusive TRIs and CTRIs, for these words clearly link "there" with "here" and "then" with "now." Thus clients are "helped to learn the ancient and deep source of the re-experienced impulses. Thus remembering and re-experiencing become organically blended" (Kahn, 1997, 59). (11)

## Brief and Simple

As valuable as inclusivity is, however, it must not destroy the brevity and simplicity of TRIs and CTRIs. Though complex in that they link key events, TRIs and CTRIs should not require such extensive cognitive work that they require clients to dissociate from the feelings that their transference and their therapist's countertransference are revealing.

Matte Blanco (1975) rightfully argues that TRIs and CTRIs should be simple because transference and countertransference, products of the unconscious, are relatively simple. The unconscious considers only one characteristic of objects, disregarding all others and making this feature equal to the whole. While this process is certainly not simple in the strict sense, it bears the stamp of deduction and simplification and consequently puts the client's mind in a simple mode. It makes the client comfortable with interpretations in that same mode.

Swift and Wonderlich (1990) recount that Harry Stack Sullivan purportedly said that interpretations should not be longer than seven words. They should be short (Sullivan, 1954; Strupp, 1989), simple (Schafer, 1983), and to the point (Joyce & Piper, 1993). Thus for the sake of brevity, therapists might have to divide TRIs and CTRIs into two successive TRIs and CTRIs, with the first addressing just the emotional or cognitive-emotional nature of the client-therapist relationship and the second adding the extra-therapeutic or pre-therapeutic aspect (Roth, 2001). For example, after processing with the client, "I wonder if you are turning me off because I have hurt you," a therapist could add, "It could be that you feel hurt when your wife fails to appreciate your help, as you mentioned earlier."

| |
|---|
| Stop to shorten a longer TRI by dividing it into a TRI that address an in-session phenomenon and a second that links it with an out-of-session phenomenon. |
| (1) |
| (2) |
| |
| |

A second way to ensure brevity is to focus on just one aspect of the transference: how clients' experience of the therapist relates to their organizing activity, for example (Gelso & Hayes, 1998). Therapists might simply say, "You can't trust me because your sister betrayed you. You use what she did to you as a model of how other women will act."

Similarly, to keep CTRIs simple and brief, therapists might focus on just one affect or one behavior. "I am impatient today," is preferable to, "Even though I want to be patient today, I am feeling impatient." So is, "Your not coming on time frustrates me," preferable to, "Your not coming on time and presenting a hard-to-believe excuse frustrates me."

## Respectful

Respectful TRIs and CTRIs leave clients feeling accepted, affirmed, and esteemed even though they have developed dysfunctional relationship patterns. Far from feeling demeaned, clients feel respected for their approach to life and their struggles to change (Kiesler, 1982b). Far from feeling attacked in isolation, clients feel included as collaborators in a process designed to gain them respect.

Respect is not easy, however, when clients express both pronounced and pervasive negative transference and are resistant to looking at it. It is hard for therapists not to unwittingly resort to bullying clients, most often through an attacking style of interpreting rationalized as being aimed at "dealing with resistance." To counteract this and make sure that TRIs and CTRIs are respectful, therapists are wise to remind themselves that pathology is not only a defense but also a form of communication without which some clients cannot get along (Casement, 1991). "It seems hard for you not to be angry with me," a therapist might say. "You seem intent on helping me know how awful someone's anger can feel," the therapist might add in order to remind both herself and her client that harsh treatment of others is more often intended to communicate distress than punish others.

## Humility-Informed

Making TRIs and CTRIs humility-informed is related to making them ego-based. Truly humble therapists who share their interpretations do not imply that they are superior to their clients in insight or intelligence (Bollas, 1983). They accept, rather than deny, their weaknesses and limitations. They are skeptical about their own objectivity and how well they perceive their clients' reality (Gill, 1982). They offer equal partnership in a process that creates or "restores mutuality in the 'affective response' of one to the other" (Winnicott, 1960, 117).

TRIs and CTRIs prefaced by such humility-informed phrases as "This may sound crazy, but..," and "I could be way off base, but . . ." enable clients to feel secure. They can survive revealing—and hearing their therapist reveal—their personal weaknesses because their therapist also acknowledges limitations and learns from mistakes (Casement, 1991). Indeed, their therapist is willing to learn from his or her clients.

The criterion of interpretations needing to be humility-informed also calls for therapists to be wary of minimizing their countertransferential reactions. As a general rule, they must not deny the truth, telling themselves that the distress that they are experiencing is too insignificant to mention. Racker (1953), among others, warned against failing to interpret countertransference because it does not seem worthy of attention.

## Externally Consistent

Finally, TRIs and CTRIs must be externally consistent: sensitively time and accompanied by appropriate tone, volume, gestures, and other meta-verbal characteristics. During the course of non-analytic therapy, however, as therapists are eager to accomplish goals, they may use TRIs and CTRIs too soon, too frequently, or too enthusiastically. Just as moderation is always the best rule, so is careful monitoring of clients' level of anxiety or comfort and therapists' own tendency to use TRIs and CTRIs simply to express negativity or to accomplish their own goals rather than patiently seek the well-being of their clients.

It is Blum (1986b) who has warned therapists most succinctly. Even where interpretation is correct in content, the countertransference [or transference] may be conveyed through inappropriate timing, tact, or tone, and in the subtle nuances of preferential attention or lack of interest (321). Thus a TRI or CTRI can be ineffective or even harmful. (12)

# Final Thought

Admittedly, attempting to meet eleven criteria for wording TRIs and CTRIs is a challenging undertaking. Beginners certainly want to remember that the more they actually use TRIs and CTRIs without being harsh critics of themselves for making minor errors in wording, the more adept they will become. In addition, they will be more relaxed if they simply observe and wonder about the interpretative task they are performing.

# Endnotes

(1) Readers will note that TRIs and CTRIs are being defined in accordance with the operational definitions of transference and countertransference given in Chapters One and Two. It is especially important to note that TRIs and CTRIs need not refer directly to the unresolved conflictual relationships being transferred to the therapy relationship. Rather, they can simply identify a therapist-client conflict that is available for immediate and concrete examination. Later, if it is in the interest of the client, the therapist and client can explore the original experiences that laid the groundwork for the therapist-client conflict.

(2) Therapists should also be wary of their own tendency to see evidence of what they are expecting to find, for it is human to relate to something familiar as if it were universal and ubiquitous. "We do not have to be so quick to use old insights when we can learn to tolerate longer exposure to what we do not yet understand. And, when we do think we recognize something familiar from a [client], we need still to be receptive to that which is different and new" (Casement, 1991, 29).

(3) One might argue that if clients are not calm, TRIs should be reflective of that state. If therapists attempt to calm disturbed clients immediately, they give them the message that their disturbing feelings are not acceptable. While this point is well taken, responding to heightened, unprocessed emotional disturbance in kind is not as therapeutic as those who are disturbed would like to believe. It is not the harboring of disturbance that is healing but the recognition, containment, and interpretation of it. It is new and different thinking that both serves as a basis for remedial action and leads to an emotion's demise.

(4) Especially in the realm of sexual abuse, therapists must make TRIs emotionally immediate. If they wait too long to interpret material, clients can experience therapists as being afraid to face facts. Therapists can appear to be re-enacting like someone who turned a blind eye to what was happening (Casement, 1991). Timing of TRIs is crucial, however, because immediacy must be tempered by emotional readiness on the part of both clients and therapists. TRIs referring to sexual abuse, in particular, must not be spoken too soon, lest clients experience therapists as either voyeuristic or uneasy with the material.

(5) Neutrality is especially important when clients give their therapist negative feedback about a TRI, such as their feeling criticized because of it. "It is harmful . . . when [therapists] appear to ignore clients' accurate perception or interpret defensively in the face of it" (Casement, 1991, 131). Focusing first and only on the transference could strike clients not only as therapists' being defensive but also as their denying the elements of objective reality in their relationship. It could be detrimental to the working alliance to say to a client something like "I wonder if you see me as critical because I resemble your critical father" (Casement, 1991).

Instead, therapists might simply acknowledging the reality, saying, for example, "I can see how you could have heard what I said as critical." In some cases, therapists might also add, "I must have sounded critical." They would thereby be acknowledging the client's feelings but not admitting doing something that justifies those feelings.

(6) A possible rewrite would be: "I wonder whether you are suffering a great deal from punishing yourself." One might even add, "But it isn't clear what you are feeling guilty about" when clients' superego attacks are already so acute that it takes very little for them to hear TRIs as condemnations.

(7) In some instances, if positive therapeutic outcome is to be achieved, TRIs must focus not just on defenses or resistance. Therapists must also refer to client's wishes and fears (Winston et al., 1993). For example, if a client were speaking of a third party as especially supportive, the transferential message to the therapist could simply be a wish that the therapist were similar. The client could simply be signaling that there is a conflict between what is being experienced and what is hoped for and that this conflict needs attention (Casement, 1991). In such a case, the therapist should simply say, "Do you wish that I would be more supportive of you also?"

At times therapists should also refer to the fear or anxiety which causes the defense or resistance. They might say, "It seems as if you are extremely anxious about sharing with regard to your past. Could we look at what that anxiety is all about?" rather than "What is so hard to share?" or "You seem so unwilling to share." It is safe to focus on the anxiety before the content accounting for the resistance, Klein (1952) assures therapists not wanting to lose important content. The content associated with the anxiety will not recede permanently; it will return.

However, there are times when clients must be helped to cope with old, dangerous situations before they can even admit their fears (Greenson & Wexler, 1969). Thus a TRI such as, "You seem unable or unwilling to share with me today. I wonder what might be going on," would be a more effective than, "Could it be that you fear me today, that you see me as your abusive mother?"

(8) When clients use strong terms or exaggeration to describe others, they make therapists wonder if their clients are also referring to them, which makes it more difficult for therapists to remain ego-based and neutral. "My mother is a witch!" an adolescent might cry soon after a therapist sets limits to the client's behavior. To maintain neutrality and calm and yet keep the TRI emotionally immediate, the therapist might reply, "You put great emphasis on how your mother seems to you to be a witch. Are you experiencing someone—maybe me—as being mean to you?" In using phases like these, therapists play back clients' descriptions as clearly *their* perception, rather than both theirs and their therapist's. Thus therapists keep a balance between respecting clients' points of view as subjectively valid and questioning their objective validity, their being defenses against reality rather than facts. Therapists remain neutral at the same time that they note the forcefulness and immediacy of clients' feelings.

By contrast, if clients talk about their "shitty feelings" and therapists also refer to their "shitty feelings," clients might be relieved to hear their therapist accepts their viewpoint. But they might also hear in the interpretation, "Your feelings really are shitty" and consequently not examine feelings that they themselves may actually question. Indeed, further questioning seems unnecessary if clients' descriptions and perceptions have been accepted as accurate by their therapist. By contrast, "You have come to regard your feelings as shitty. How did this come about?" gives clients the psychological space within which to examine their feelings. Similarly, a TRI that invites further examination, such as "I think you expect me also to see your feelings as shitty," permits clients to hear a helpful reflection (Casement, 1991).

(9) It is also especially important for therapists to use tentative CTRIs when they attempt to share an instinct, Viederman (1974) explains, because it is an experience on the boundary between the somatic and the psychic. Vague, obscure, nameless, and barely outlined, an instinct demands tentative language of those who try to share it.

(10) In an attempt to be appropriately inclusive, a therapist might say, "I wonder if you resent my not being pleased with your progress. You would like me to say you have done enough to acquire a new habit even though you really haven't been consistent." Or a therapist might reflect, "Could it be that you fear my judgment so much that you exaggerate your progress? You see me as a more important judge of your conduct than you are?"

(11) The following inclusive CTRI serves as an additional example of movement from here-and-now to there-and-now. "My anger toward you may be similar to your wife's anger toward you, the anger you said you simply couldn't understand." So does, "Could it be that my getting distracted when you talk too long is reflective of what your wife does?"

(12) See Chapters Six and Seven for additional reasons and empirical data supportive of using TRIs and CTRIs in moderation.

# PART IV

## INTERPRETING TRANSFERENCE AND COUNTERTRANSFERENCE IN A NON-ANALYTIC SETTING

# CHAPTER NINE

# SUBTASKS OF THE INTERPRETATIVE PROCESS AND SELF-MONITORING

## Introduction

In order to identify, decode, and interpret transference and countertransference, therapists must involve their non-verbal right brain no less than their verbal left brain. For transference and countertransference, like most relational transactions, rely heavily on client-therapist cueing and responding that occur too rapidly for simultaneous verbal exchanges and conscious reflection (Lyons-Ruth, 2000). The right brain, the "center" of unconscious material must assist the left brain, the "center of conscious material.

Besides using both hemispheres, therapists will find it helpful to slow down their mental activity and break it into distinct but interwoven subtasks: taking in manifestations of transference and countertransference, holding them and allowing regression in order to experience them more fully, decoding them, and hypothesizing about them. Those who choose to interpret transferred material can then perform a fifth subtask: verifying hypotheses with clients.

All the while, therapists must monitor themselves closely in order to decide how well they are performing each subtask and when to move from one subtask to another. They must also integrate the subtasks in order to accomplish their main goal of interpreting transference and countertransference.

## First Subtask: Taking-In Transferred Material

Therapists perform the first subtask by making a conscious decision to continue to take in what they suspect they have already received on an unconscious level, namely manifestations of clients' transference, and responded to within their own unconscious mind, namely manifestations of their own countertransference. The first subtask requires therapists to deliberately open themselves up to what they sense is occurring on an unconscious level: conflictual contents of their clients' and their own unconscious minds attempting to enter their conscious minds.

Thus the first subtask is a matter of therapists trying to "be there" for clients and themselves in a new way (Heath, 1991). They endeavor to form a composite picture of conscious and unconscious information from which they and their clients can, in time, derive fuller meaning than that based solely on conscious communication.

As explained in Chapters One and Two, the mechanisms by which therapists receive unconscious material from their clients and themselves, namely transference and countertransference, operate first on an unconscious level. Without knowing it, therapists receive the affective, cognitive, and sensate messages their clients displace. Without intending it, therapists respond to subtle messages from the recesses of their own unconscious mind and transfer related material to their clients.

Then, when therapists perform the first subtask, they intentionally "make room" for displaced material in their conscious minds. They choose to increase their awareness of the feelings, attitudes, fantasies, dreams, images, thoughts, sensations, and behaviors that they and their clients are unconsciously transferring to each other (Bird, 1922). Therapists open themselves to a state of 'convergence' of past and present. They offer to clients their "entire availability": all the time and mental space they need in order to deal with their still unresolved conflicts (Grinberg, 1997). (1)

In performing the first subtask, therapists take seriously their professional responsibility to regard displaced material as central to therapeutic reality (Deutsch (1926). They become congruent with the painful, unconscious memories of their clients (Vanaerschot, 1997).

By deliberately increasing their awareness of what their clients are transferring, therapists also bring to consciousness their own countertransference. They take note of the roles they are unconsciously assigning clients as well as the transferential roles their clients are unconsciously assigning them. Therapists assigned the role of being a parent figure for a client working through early child-parent conflict, for example, deliberately "accept" an otherwise fleeting image of themselves as a controlling, self-indulgent parent. Similarly, if they themselves are assigning the role of unruly child to their client, therapists hold in focus the emotional satisfaction they have begun to experience from subjecting another to their will. They allow themselves to note the muscle tightness of one who is immobilizing, on a fantasy level, a struggling child.

Thus the first subtask is one of adding latent content to manifest content. Therapists combine clients' unconscious body language and meta-language with what they consciously say. Therapists also add their own unconscious perceptions and desires to conceptions and intentions of which they are already conscious, or at least suspect. Put in 21st century cognitive terms, therapists allow right brain learning to augment left brain learning. They open themselves to receive nonverbal communication that cannot be put into words.

## Second Subtask: Holding and Permitting Regression

Therapists perform the second subtask by holding the transference and countertransference they have received, often for more than one session (Bion, 1961), and permitting the regression that tends to occur in a deepened and broadened holding environment. They embrace the full impact of their clients' displaced—and usually negative—reality. "This is the clear, sharpened, whole message my client is giving me," therapists come to realize as they hold, over a period of time, various manifestations of transference (Smith, 2000).

From a 21st century perspective, therapists perform the second subtask by containing and autoregulating their own negative states long enough to act as affective regulators for their clients (Schore, 2003b). (2) Clients become aware of therapists successfully managing the distressful feelings, sensations, and thoughts they have transferred to them. Clients conclude that they can continue to reveal their unresolved conflicts without being overwhelmed by the distress, particularly the anxiety, that has kept those conflicts from reaching consciousness. Their therapists are sharing their "burdens." (3)

Casement (1991) describes this affect regulation as therapists refusing to follow their natural inclination to disengage from the distressful transferential communications their clients send. Rather, therapists avoid closure, tolerate ambiguity and uncertainty, and permit lack of differentiation in order to share their clients' meaningful, displaced relational experiences (Schore, 2003). They do not return prematurely what their clients project into them (Joseph, 1978). They renounce their own need for gratification.

In performing the second subtask, therapists refrain from taking refuge in words. They resist their impulse to shift into a left hemispheric dominant state and respond verbally to clients' verbal messages. Instead, they hold sensations evoked by unconscious communication (Stark, 1994) and sustain the countertransferential feelings that transference triggers. They stay in the right hemisphere, which has a "Wait and See" mode of processing (Federmeier & Kutas, 2002). Thus therapists do for clients what they were unable to do for themselves at the time of their original conflictual experiences: allow psychic pain to remain in their conscious mind. (4)

As they remain silent, therapists observe their clients' posture, gestures, and movements, take note of the tone syntax, and rhythm of their clients' speech. Said succinctly, therapists allow their own felt sense to act as a bodily-based perception of meaning (Bohart, 1993). (5) For the sake of understanding through experiencing, they permit themselves to contain their clients' unresolved conflicts in their own bodies (Kernberg, 1987). They endure the aggression, sexual desires, dependence, depression, and other disturbing feelings and sensation that their clients unconsciously put into them. In more cases than not, they let clients use projective identification to transform them into someone "bad," someone deserving of disrespect, even abuse (Gorney, 1979) and let themselves feel that negative label physiologically. (6)

The second subtask also requires therapists to re-experience the breath and depth of their own unresolved conflicts, phenomena that constitute a key element in any countertransference response (Kernberg, 1975). Therapists willingly suffer the painful countertransferential affect and sensations that reflect their clients' conflicts (Roth, 2001) and deliberately entertain the countertransferential phenomena that act as stimuli for these conflicts.

Ordinarily, therapists find the second subtask difficult for three reasons. First clients persist in displacing conflictual material because on some deep unconscious level they are unwilling to entertain the possibility of alternative perspectives. They want to hold onto the illusion that they and their therapists are one person and that, once their therapists are feeling precisely what they are feeling or what they want them to feel, they, the clients, will no longer suffer (Slochower, 1999).

On yet another deep unconscious level, therapists also want to hold onto the illusion that they can resolve clients' conflicts without holding the transference and countertransference in which they are revealed. In particular, they want to understand transference without experiencing it (Bonnet, 1991). They want to make therapeutic progress in spite of distancing themselves from painful displaced affect by asking questions or shifting their focus to routine observations (Schwaber, 1990). (7) However, clients take note of these false assumptions and respond by displacing their conflictual material yet again. (8)

Second, therapists experience significant anxiety as they hold their clients' and their own displaced material and they and their clients assign each other conflict-related roles. Clients' toxic material mobilizes therapists' toxic material (Dosamantes, 1992). Therapists' anxiety compounds clients' anxiety, which, in turn, exacerbates therapists' anxiety. (9)

Third, therapists experience regression—to one degree or another—as they provide a holding environment for their clients' and their own primitive affective states (Winnicott, 1949). They regress "in the service of countertransference" (Bigras, 1979, 312) as they contain their clients' distressful communication. They even risk experiencing disequilibrium within their right brain (Spence et al., 1996) that leads to deterioration in technical competence.

Already in the middle of the last century, Little (1951) described successful therapy as both a normal process of two conscious minds sharing information and a pathological process of conscious regression. Even earlier, Glover (1955) explained that therapy is fruitful because therapists allow themselves to regress temporarily to early-life stages. They permit themselves to enter a state of regression for the sake of broadening and deepening within themselves their clients' experience.

The use of *regression* in this context is, of course, an extension in meaning of a word originally reserved for an unconscious process. Strictly speaking, unconscious regression cannot become conscious. However, the process of willingly entering into a regressive state so resembles doing so unconsciously that no other terminology seems appropriate.

Racker (1953) connects conscious, intentional regression with therapists' acceptance of the fact that, though they are adults and professionals, they are still children and neurotics. When they set aside some of the secondary aspects of mature mental functioning and embrace primitive states, they feel neurotic. When they deliberately allow themselves not only to hold but also to deepen the hurt, anger, and fear inherent in the transferential roles their clients assign, therapists experience a strong urge to engage in retaliating, withdrawing, or other counterprojective processes.

Rather than doing so, however, therapists performing the second subtask subject themselves to the psychic forces that characterize transference and countertransference. They relinquish the personal values and goals that are often rationalized and hidden behind models of the mind (Schwaber, 1990). They intentionally allow disturbing images, fantasies, and memories to arise: pieces of internal, unconscious experience that are often contradictory, "crazy," and disturbing (Isakower, 1963). They undergo fragmentary experiences that they hope will shed light on or add clarity to perceptions of their senses and conceptions of their conscious mind.

Levin (1997) makes it clear, however, that therapists who are performing the second subtask must not permit conscious regression to impair their basic ego functions. In particular, therapists must not lose hold of the fact that what their clients are transferring to them still belongs to their clients (Deutsch, 1926). (10) Therapists must not become delusional and think, for instance, that they are in fact the sibling of a client assigning them the role of an abusive sibling. They must not believe that they are allowed to actually perform their transferential roles. (11) They must not suspend their ability to recognize and regulate the negative affect being projected into them.

Nor must therapists who allow themselves to regress suspend their ability to recognize their own countertransference and regulate its negative affect and disturbing sensations. (12) In fact, in performing the second subtask, therapists must dialogue with themselves often in order to balance affect and sensation with thoughts about what is occurring and what needs to be done with it (Kernberg, 1987). They must periodically decide whether to begin decoding what they have been holding or to continue to extend the holding environment for the sake of additional information. Furthermore, they must ultimately decide whether to process the displaced material they are experiencing intrapsychically, consult with others, interpret it to clients, or combine these methods of managing transference and countertransference. Said succinctly, because of the other key functions they must perform, therapists who permit conscious regression must not allow themselves to become thought-disordered in the strict sense of the word.

However, therapists who regress may—and often will—experience what may be termed a thought disturbance: things will appear false to their sense of self. They and their client will *feel* as if the therapist were a parent. They will accept, on a temporary basis, a parental definition that allows them to *want* to act in parental ways. In other words, when therapists permit themselves to regress in the course of containing displaced material, they will experience something that seems true on one level but false on another. Regressing to babyhood at the request of a client who wants to be a parent, for example, will seem strangely true from an affective standpoint but not true from a perceptual standpoint. Similarly, regressing to the toddler age will seem strangely true from a sensory standpoint but not true from a linguistic standpoint.

When therapists temporarily set aside some of the reality testing functions of their ego as they entertain the evidence of past phenomena, they give their clients a powerful non-verbal "message." They say, in effect, that they trust their clients enough to become vulnerable in their presence (Kantrowitz, 1997). They are allowing themselves to feel confused and stupid at best, depleted and "lost" at worst (Money-Kyrle, 1956), and anxious in any case (Wallerstein, 1990). They are choosing to remain in a "world" where things that are not right are the norm.

From the viewpoint of clients who have regressed because of transference, nothing benefits them more than this. They can trust one who has willingly descended into the depths of their transferential emotional state. They can trust a "kindred soul" who is also experiencing a loss of understanding and insight (Bion, 1961). They can trust a "partner" who is willing to learn their primitive "language" in spite of the regressive fear they are experiencing.
Indeed, clients communicate early, primitive material most important to them only when their unconscious mind is fused with the unconscious mind of their therapist (Isakower, 1963). Critical images, fantasies, and memories arise from both client and therapist only when their minds are fused in a state of temporary regression within the confines of therapy. Clients learn to observe the present while experiencing the past only when their therapists learn to experience the past while observing the present.

With this basic trust established, regression becomes for clients not only considerably less frightening but also enabling. It allows them to continue to convey a sense of early and complex experiences otherwise not communicable. In addition, conscious regression permits therapists to add key experiential data to information their clients consciously provide, which, in turn, gives therapists a relatively complete "message" they must set out to decode.

## Third Subtask: Decoding

Decoding, a left brain activity, is a matter of extracting the probable meaning of what clients and therapists are displacing from the past to the therapeutic setting. Decoding is a matter of deriving hidden significance from apparent meaning. Decoding "breaks the code" in which complex human communication is transmitted. It brings clarity to what therapists and clients really mean to share.

Decoding is a matter of discerning the significance of garbled messages related to the work needing to be accomplished in therapy. It is a matter of amending what is said with words by what is conveyed through association or communicated through body language.

Decoding is an essential element of all forms of psychotherapy because truth and its bedrock of facts are usually shrouded from both clients and therapists in spite of their earnest attempts to reveal them. With rare exceptions, material that clients and therapists transfer from other people to each other lies largely, if not completely, outside the awareness of their conscious minds. Buried deep within the recesses of the unconscious mind, it is inaccessible to the conscious mind except in subtle, camouflaged signs, such as unwarranted or overblown affective responses, mysterious dreams, fleeting flashbacks, enigmatic somatic responses, surrealistic fantasies, and urges to act that seem to have no basis in reality.

Indeed, these encoded signs account for impressions others receive without individuals intending to reveal themselves. Not wanting to be known as hating their guests, for example, hosts make every effort to show acceptance and tolerance. But when leaving, their guest may find themselves hearing a negative feeling word imbedded in such a superficially positive statement as, "We hate to see you go." In spite of themselves and the "front" they have presented, their hosts have allowed their personal reality to "drip from their pores," as Shakespeare penned centuries ago.

Similarly, in the clinical setting, much of what clients communicate is not really who they are and what they really mean to convey. For they have unconscious needs equally important to their wellbeing than solving their stated presenting problems. They hope to resolve age-old conflicts with others. They hope to be valued and held in esteem, even loved.

As a consequence, clients unconsciously convey information quite different from their verbal explanations of what they do and why they are in therapy. A client rushes in late, for example, and blames his lateness on traffic. But because of subtle discomfort in her own mind, his therapist suspects another message: "I am resentful." She wonders whether her client's lateness is solely the result of his having to battle traffic. She wonders whether he resents therapy or something his therapist said the previous session that made her resemble a disliked person from the client's past. In any case, as the therapist questions the intent of her client's explanation for coming late, she inaugurates the difficult process of decoding.

Decoding is difficult for yet another reason: therapists are unconsciously filtering reality through the lens of their own experience and expectations. What therapists believe they perceive is somewhat different from what clients are actually unconsciously communicating.

The unconscious message of clients cannot pass through the unconscious mind of their therapists without some distortion.

Hence, therapists must also subject their own feelings, attitudes, thoughts, and behavior to the decoding process. What appears to be a positive urge, for example, like wanting to extend the session of the client who comes late, might actually be harmful because of its accompanying detrimental meta-message: "You are so valuable that I will be generous with my own time. You do not need to say clearly that coming here is not working for you."

Decoding is necessarily a multi-step process because deciphering mysteriously encoded psychological material is laborious. It requires intensive cognitive work involving meticulous attention to detail as well as a willingness to evaluate vague intuitive possibilities. "Transference . . . has to be detected almost without assistance and with only the slightest clues . . . ," Freud (1905, 116) declared almost a century ago. Since then, that task and that of decoding countertransference have not become easier.

In order to decode transference and countertransference, therapists must first consider their clients' and their own choice of words, expressed affect, reported dreams, suspected fantasies, and behavior, including somatic reactions. Some manifestations will be direct contributions of the therapy participants; others, reactions to the contributions that the other participant has made (Smith, 2000).

Then, therapists must hold in abeyance apparent meaning while remaining open to interpersonal meanings beyond personal meanings. They must take note of tone of voice, volume, word emphasis, gestures that match or fail to match content, muscle movement that supports or contradicts speech, and countless other signs of human communication. They must consider their own feelings and whether or not they match those of their clients. They must acknowledge bodily discomfort, noting sensations and physical responses that either contradict or correspond to what clients are saying.

Therapists must also be open to how they might be contributing to the therapeutic experience of clients. They must be willing to distinguish what their clients are inducing in them from what they themselves are bringing to the therapeutic setting. Feelings of success during a session, for example, may be explained more by occurrences removed from the therapeutic setting than by the therapist's skill and client's progress. (13) Similarly, therapists' feelings of envy may be due more to their own lack of similar professional success than their client's boastful demeanor, though it may be both.

*"Why does this client irritate me so?" the therapist queried. Why am I not simply flattered that he has come to see me? He is intelligent, articulate, and seemingly ready and willing to get to the heart of his problems.*

*"Yet there seems to be something subtly boastful about him. At least he strikes me that way," the therapist came to realize. "Though he does so nonchalantly, he keeps drawing attention to the recognition he has received for his films."*

*In studying his own countertransference, the therapist had to admit that he was envious. He also desired to make a name for himself professionally but had not been very successful. The difference between their professional success was playing against his desire to be empathic at times and neutral at others. He was bringing to the sessions the pain of his failures.*

*"Rather than interpret this countertransference to my client," he thought, "it would be good for me to process these feelings with a colleague." If, in spite of that they continue, I may consider sharing them with my client. The effect he has on me may well be his unintended effect on others."*

# Fourth Subtask: Formulating Hypotheses

The process of formulating hypotheses consists of therapists providing for themselves tentative explanations for why the phenomena they have decoded are occurring: probable reasons for why certain aspects of the past are now protruding into the present.

Ideally, hypotheses are simple statements. A hypothesis about familial relationships, for example, might be, "I am feeling like a parent because my client has never resolved a conflict with her parent" or "My client is transferring to me jealously toward an older sibling." The simpler the formulation, the more clear-cut can be verification of the hypothesis.

In some cases, hypothesis formulation occurs not after but at the same time as decoding. A therapist may think, for example, that a client's anger, which includes anxiety, is being caused by prior experiences of rejection. Thus the hypothesis at the time is likely to be, "My client is both angry with me and anxious about my rejecting her."

In other cases, hypothesis formulation must follow decoding because material is so complex that efforts to decode it yield only an affective or cognitive label. The hypotheses that can be derived at that time are limited to "My client is angry" or "My client thinks that I am mean." Hence, therapists formulating a full hypothesis must sometimes continue to look for causal links. They continue to open themselves up to the experience of their clients in relation to themselves with the expectation that new and more specific material will shed light on what is already present. The client who relates a story about a verbally abusive bus driver that she encountered on the way to therapy, for example, may be unconsciously providing an explanation of an original experience of victimization. But she may also be saying that her therapist's "taking" her along a certain therapeutic path feels abusive to her. By continuing to listen carefully, her therapist will receive confirmation of one, if not both, of her hypotheses or at least know she must entertain others.

# Fifth Subtask: Verifying Hypotheses

For effective therapy to proceed, therapists must verify the hypotheses they have formulated. They may do so by themselves, with consultants, and/or with clients.

One would presume that, just as therapists are eager to confirm their hypotheses, they are also eager to disconfirm them. The facts seem to be, however, that disconfirmation is more difficult for therapists than confirmation for formulating hypotheses inaugurates a bias or fondness for what is conjectured and encourages a search for supportive evidence. Hence, to be effective, therapists must learn the discipline of being as objective as possible about their hypotheses.

One important way therapists have of accomplishing this is paying close attention to their own somatic response to their verbal attempts to explore transferred material. The body will invariably, though perhaps subtly, "agree" or "disagree" with what the mind concludes. Being physically energized, for example, usually suggests appropriate hypothesis verification, while experiencing repeated fatigue, uneasiness, or worry suggests the opposite. This is especially true of hypotheses related to how helpful therapists are being to clients.

*When her client came in for his session, the therapist felt a deep calm. She was able to remain appropriate focused on what he was saying and usually able to resist giving advice or talking in place of holding the material her client was presenting. "He is given to intellectualizing," she reminded herself frequently. "He does not need me to offer additional intellectualization. Nevertheless, she hypothesized, "he is transferring to me an intellectualizing function once performed by a significant other."*

*On occasion, however, the therapist did talk instead of listening. She "grabbed" her client's thoughts and feelings and carried them swiftly to her mind, responding cognitively. In no time, her body gave evidence of her interference. She lost the calm she originally possessed. Then, consciously returning to a non-verbal stance, she once again became calm and tranquil.*

*Thus her bodily reaction had verified her hypothesis: "He needs me to allow him to feel," she decided to keep reminding herself. "He does not need me to help him intellectualize."*

Supervisors and consultants are also invaluable during the verification process. In addition, especially in cases involving significant countertransference, therapists are wise to interpret transference and countertransference to clients, asking them, in effect, to help them attain accuracy.

By interpreting transference and countertransference, therapists also enable clients to know experientially the benefits of identifying what actually is rather than engaging in fantasy. For only reality can serve as a solid basis for changing—rather than learning to live with—what has brought the clients to the therapeutic setting. Wishing for that which is not—and can never be—merely prolongs immature psychological states and reinforces ineffective interpersonal patterns.

## Overarching Meta-Task: Self-Monitoring

Self-monitoring consists of internal supervision for the sake of checking the quality of one's work. It involves watching oneself in order to verify thinking, observing in order to control affect, and evaluating in order to determine what behavior to continue or discontinue.

During therapy sessions, therapists self-monitor for the sake of autoregulating the stressful countertransferential alterations that their client's transferential communications evoke. They attend to their own functioning even as they and their client engage in mutual exploration of issues of which they are conscious and communicate on an affective level (Perna, 1997). They maintain a "binocular vision" (Holmes, 1992), distinguishing what they are feeling from what they are responding to. (14)

Self-monitoring during therapy begins with therapists noting how well they are observing clients. For choices regarding interventions intended to further the treatment plan must be made on the basis of how they impact clients. Therapists also note their own wellbeing, for clients' thriving is partially dependent on therapists' sense of how well they are bonding with clients. By extension, therapists make calculated observations of their interactions with the particular client before them in order to judge whether their sense of self-efficacy is based on those particular interactions rather than the client's own innate capacity or already developed skills. "Is the direction I am going increasing my client's insight?" therapists ask themselves, "or is she able to continue satisfactorily without my interpretation?"

In one sense, therapists must self-monitor continuously because of powerful forces like transference and countertransference pervading the entire therapeutic process. In the intimacy and regularity of the therapeutic setting, reenactment of unfinished "business" takes place over and over again without the conscious intent of either party.

In another sense, however, therapists must engage in self-monitoring periodically rather than continuously. Transference and countertransference must have enough "room" to display themselves—even to develop—during the therapeutic process but not so much "room" that they enable full-blown acting-out or acting-in. (15) If, through transference, clients assign therapists the role of hateful parent, for example, therapists must permit themselves to experience hatred of their clients to the degree that its contributory "causes" become identifiable. Therapists may not, however, go so far as to say something hateful to clients or even to let their neutral statements carry hateful nuances. (16)

Similarly, if clients displace positive feelings toward them—see them as a mother figure, for instance—at the beginning of therapy, therapists must ordinarily allow the transference to continue until the therapeutic alliance is firmly in place. But they must not allow their clients to become dependent on them to the point of needing to call frequently between sessions, being unable to disagree when they feel dismissed, or finding themselves unable to provide honest feedback when they feel patronized.

Thus self-monitoring is especially important during the first subtask when therapists consciously take in the transference whereby they suspect the roles they are being asked to play and the ways they are inclined to play commensurate roles in the process of countertransference (Hinshelwood, 1999). For therapists need to decide whether or to what extent they might perform those roles as a means of furthering the therapeutic and working alliances. Clients who are fearful of authority figures, for example, might benefit from time-limited signs of maternal acceptance or paternal approval. (17)

Self-monitoring during the first subtask also enables therapists to gauge to what extent they are unconsciously projecting their own unresolved conflicts onto their clients. Without this internal supervision, even experienced therapists are prone to simply re-enact their clients' maladaptive interpersonal experiences in countertransferential behaviors (Dreher & others (2001). As a result, clients never realize the contributions they are making to their unresolved conflicts and determine how they might act differently (Weiss & Sampson, 1986). (18)

Self-monitoring is also crucial during the second subtask when therapists contain transferred material and permit appropriate regression. Therapists must stay with clients on a psychobiological level in order to engage in necessary experiential learning but not go so far as to lose their ability to stand apart and take note of their participation in realms of transference and countertransference (Racker, 1972;Gorkin, 1997; Gelso & Hayes, 1998). They must remain disengaged enough to ask questions like, "How am I being manipulated to play the role of a demeaned person?" and "What is my client trying to have me experience?"

Self-monitoring becomes especially important when therapists permit conscious regression. They must become vulnerable to the workings of displaced material at a sufficiently deep, but not too deep, a level (Winnicott, 1965). They must be partially aware of the process they are undergoing in order to discontinue it at any time. They must periodically employ their observing ego to "keep track of the pressure to become trackless" (Schafer, 1997). They must 'swim' in the sea of clients' transference but not "drown" in their own countertransference (Racker, 1972).

Furthermore, only if therapists monitor their own regression can they be aware of the regression their clients are undergoing. Because of non-analytic therapy's customary time restrictions, therapists must ordinarily stop their clients from experiencing a full-blown neurosis. But they can permit clients to engage in mild-to-moderate regression in the safety of the therapeutic environment. For most clients—as well as their therapists—benefit greatly from carefully regulated exposure to pain that so overwhelmed it could not be processed.

Self-monitoring remains necessary during the third subtask when therapists direct their attention to decoding transference and countertransference, for these phenomena are operative even as therapists are trying to derive meaning from them. Therapists must stand back to decode and yet remain available to their clients so that the length and intensity of the decoding process do not weaken or destroy the therapeutic bond. Clients want to be accepted unconditionally, to be listened to intently, and to be followed closely. They do not want their therapist to engage in the difficult cognitive task of decoding for what seems to them to be too long a time. On the other hand, therapists need to self-monitor to see if they are allowing themselves enough time to decode accurately.

Self-monitoring during the fourth subtask, hypotheses-forming, is also necessary, for therapists must decide whether they are spending a sufficient amount of time and effort to hypothesize reasonably well. Though they may not be sure of what is transpiring, they must come up with at least probable explanations.

Self-monitoring continues to be crucial during the fifth subtask when therapists are verifying hypotheses. Therapists clearly need to test hypotheses, but they also need to balance this cognitive work with keeping an emotional connection with their clients. At the same time, therapists must continue to receive and hold new material that will allow them to revise inaccurate hypotheses.

Finally, therapists must self-monitor during all five subtasks in order to be able to move quickly and smoothly from one subtask to another. At times, therapists must decode what they have uncovered in order to know what more they—and sometimes their clients—need to discover. Similarly, therapists may need to experience more in order to verify what they think they understand. At other times, they must gather new information in the light of their hypotheses proving inaccurate. At still other times, when they suspect inaccuracy, therapists must stop decoding and "test" their hypotheses. Put simply, successful therapy lies heavily on therapists' self-monitoring of their decisions related to focus: what to focus on, whom to focus on, where to focus, and even how to focus (Hubble, 1999). (19)

# Further Directions

This chapter barely touches on the subtasks of decoding transference and countertransference, formulating hypotheses, and verifying the hypotheses. If therapists study their fundamental dynamics, however, they will learn enough about them to profit from related chapters. Chapter Four explores transferred material thematically. Chapter Five focuses on the most common categories of transferential and countertransferential manifestations that require decoding. Chapter Eight describes transference and countertransference interpretations in detail and provides guidelines for wording and using them.

# Endnotes

(1) The deliberate reception of transference begins a process whereby therapists acquire the intuitive empathy necessary for the therapeutic alliance.

(2) The clinician's primary function is as an affect regulator for the client's primitive, traumatic states, including those that are walled off by dissociation. (Schore, 2003a, 246). Dissociation, the blocking of the path between the limbic system and the cortex, is an early appearing, very primitive defense against traumatic affects that are stored subcortically in the right hemisphere.

(3) Wilkinson (2003) calls such a safe holding environment the most potent vehicle for healing.

(4) Bion (1967) suggests that containing is required because the client's mother's capacity to contain the client's distressing emotions was insufficient. They were therefore returned to the client little changed and difficult to integrate. The mother was unable or

unwilling to provide a model for the client's containment of his or her own feelings; this the therapist must do.

(5) As Gilboa and Revelle (1994) explain, "The longer the period during which a person is influenced by physiological and cognitive processes activated by emotion the higher the probability that this experience will be subjectively perceived as important and meaningful"(135).

(6) Because early relational trauma is stored in the right hemisphere, therapists choose to engage in right brain-to-right brain emotional communication. They refrain from using their left brain to put their experience in words. Instead, they tolerate uncertainty, for it is fundamental to a healthy growth process. Even though it is anxiety producing, it is an opportunity for change (Schore, 2003a). It is an opportunity for clients to create something out of themselves (Balint, 1968). By contrast, if therapists block their own negative somatic markers by shifting out of their right brain into their left brain, they cut off their empathic connection to their own pain and therefore to their clients' pain. If therapists speak quickly, their clients are likely to perceive them as critical (Ryle, 1994).

(7) The challenge of projective identification for therapists is to reveal to clients in a non-threatening way that they have received their unwanted traits. This is extremely difficult for clients to receive, however, for those using projective identification are already in dread of what they had to project in the first place (Kernberg, 1987). Then, in using projective identification, which is a matter of action rather language, they have regressed to a preverbal time (Maroda, 1995). Only with great difficulty can they accept the feedback that they have put their own unwanted trait into their therapist and now attribute the trait solely to the therapist.

(8) These are false assumptions because only by holding clients' transference can therapists facilitate an expansion of clients' narrow personal psychological space and collaborate with them to fashion what is real, in contrast to what they want to be real (Slochower, 1999).

(9) By containing and eventually processing transference, however, therapists facilitate a detoxification process whereby clients' unwanted transference projections lose their potency. By the course of holding transference, therapists really know their clients well enough to help them make transference a resource under the control of their reality-testing ego. By holding transference, therapists and clients together strip displaced material of its dangerous, uncontrollable pathogenic elements and make it simply a memory residing in the unconscious mind (Grinberg, 1997).

(10) Dealing appropriately with projective identification is difficult for therapists because of a delay between clients' projection of unwanted traits and therapists' becoming conscious of what has happened. In the interval, therapists can easily act in accordance with the traits or at least be disturbed by the feelings they stimulate. They find it hard to hold or contain their clients' painful feelings and allow their clients' experience to fully impact them (Roth, 2001). They desire to defend against an awareness of the projection and its painful feelings and act them out in an effort to get rid of them.

(11) Indeed, initially therapists cannot prevent themselves from being what their clients unconsciously want them to be. At the same time, according to Ogden (1994), successful outcome depends on therapists' maintaining sufficient psychological distance from the projective identifications. Therapists must be open to receiving projective identifications—receive them, hold them, and identify with them—but not own them or enact them. Instead, they must enable clients to own them and eventually subject them to reality testing.

(12) Sometimes therapists label what is happening as pure projective identification when it is actually avoidance of responsibility for their own countertransference (Finell,

1986).

(13) If feelings of success during a session are due primarily to clients' transference, the therapist's work might entail helping them realize that their wanting to sustain a positive therapeutic relationships is making them reluctant to reveal facets of their lives likely to inspire disgust or dislike in their therapist. This, in turn, might result in wasted therapeutic effort. On the other hand, if feelings of success during a session are due primarily to therapists' displaced attitude, they may need to manage their feelings carefully in order to stay attuned to the feelings of their clients, which are often those of failure. Should therapists allow their good fortune to become as important or more important to them than their clients' feelings of deprivation or misfortune, clients may have yet another poignant experience of being compared to others and found wanting.

(14) In terms of the right brain, therapists shift up and down between its higher and lower levels: those connected to cognition and those connected to emotion (Schore, 2003b).

(15) When therapists unconsciously assume the roles that their clients have transferred, they experience in themselves strong, sometimes even intense, countertransference attitudes and feelings (Diamond, 1989). Therapists fear clients' anger. They are disturbed by clients' erotic, dependent, or sadistic feelings and frightened by clients' desires to merge with them or to humiliate them. They are anxious about clients who have become victims of abuse and worried about how much their clients can take (Pick, 1997; Wallerstein, 1990). At times therapists even worry about how much they themselves can take: how many times they can be asked to take with impunity roles of harsh authority figures, of deficient parental figures, of victimizing sibling figures, and on and on. Concurrently, they wonder how many times they can unconsciously dredge up their own memories of painful interpersonal relationships brought to mind by their clients' self-revelations.

(16) Neither may therapists end the session early simply because feelings of hatred have become too strong for comfort. For while this solution might be helpful in the short run, it is harmful in the long run in that it implies that hatred is too unmanageable to be contained in the therapeutic environment. If hatred cannot be contained in the therapeutic environment, by inference it cannot be contained anywhere. It must be staunchly repressed, which only increases its power.

(17) Self-monitoring adds conscious processing of countertransference to intuition and other unconscious mental operations (Arlow, 1985).

(18) Contrary to what common sense might suggest, the goal of psychotherapy is not for therapists to be better parents by undoing pathological repetition or repairing conflicts for clients. Rather, it is for therapists to create the conditions under which clients themselves can become increasing able to manage what once was—and still is—pathologically conflictual. The goal of therapy is for therapists to ensure sufficient security within which clients will feel safe enough to risk feeling unsafe again in order to work through the feelings that had been associated with earlier difficult experiences (Casement, 1991). The goal of therapy is for clients not to remain vulnerable and inappropriately dependent on external forces but to develop enough psychological strength to act in truly appropriate independent and interdependent ways.

(19) However central clients are to the therapy "product," therapists must remain the heart of the therapy "process."

# CHAPTER TEN

# APPROPRIATE CLIENTS, TIMING, AND FREQUENCY

## Introduction

Therapists increase their chances of using TRIs and CTRIs effectively when they keep in mind the characteristics of their clients, time the interventions carefully, and use them infrequently. Conversely, if they use TRIs and CTRIs indiscriminately, they may do harm.

## Appropriate Versus Inappropriate Clients for TRIs and CTRIs

Though recognizing clients who can benefit from TRIs and CTRIs is far from easy, two fundamental principles provide guidance. First, TRIs and CTRIs are appropriate only "within the omnipotence of the patient, which has to be challenged sensitively and very, very cautiously" (James, 1960, 289). TRIs and CTRIs are to be used with clients who are open to them, ready for them, and able to benefit from them.

Second, and more specifically, TRIs and CTRIs are generally appropriate with clients having at least moderate ego-strength and low-to-medium levels of affective arousal. Though clients with these characteristics may be temporarily hurt or angered by what they hear in an interpretation, they can use higher-level defense mechanisms to protect themselves from the worst of the pain. They can avoid, in particular, the use of the splitting defense that labels them as "all bad" and prevents them from using such cognitive abilities as discriminating, relativizing, and accommodating to disturbing information. At the same time, they can use their reality testing functions to distinguish what is intruding form the past from what is being experienced in the present. They can counteract the common tendency to confuse facts with feelings and can subject perception to rational scrutiny.

To say this, however, is not to imply that TRIs and CTRIs are appropriate in any and all sessions of these clients. For there will be times when highly aroused clients, albeit those with moderate ego-strength, simply need to be listened to and allowed to process their strong feelings in their own relatively defensive way. If that takes the entire session, therapists simply refrain from interpreting transference and countertransference.

Specific highly charged emotions that rule out TRIs and CTRIs include hostility, bitterness, (Pick, 1997), and paranoia accompanied by high levels of interpersonal sensitivity (Lasky, 1990). When clients are experiencing these strong interpersonal negative affects or attitudes, especially at a moderate-to-strong level, they are functioning in an autistic, infantile-omnipotent manner. Emotionally—and to some extent cognitively—they have temporarily regressed to an earlier developmental stage. They are already under too much debilitating stress to tolerate participative interventions like TRIs and CTRIs that seem invasive, blunt, and personal (Searles, 1975). At least for the time being, they must defend their reputation for righteousness through denial, rationalization, intellectualization, and other defense mechanisms.

In contrast, clients with at least moderate ego-strength sometimes do not need an entire session to lower a relatively high level of affective arousal and cognitive impairment. Because they are not in the habit of relying on primitive defenses—especially splitting—or do so for only short periods of time, they routinely return to more discriminating cognitive functions, using less primitive defenses if need be. They thereby process their negative affect at least to the degree that their hostility is replaced by anger or irritation; their bitterness or regret, by disappointment; and their paranoia, by mild suspicion or wariness. They do not have to cling to a reputation of being all-good, for example, and be angry about being thought less of. They can rationalize what they did, admit the possibility of being somewhat in error, and be simply irritated both with themselves and those who have judged them.

On the other hand, clients with moderate ego-strength and generally low levels of affective arousal who bring to therapy embarrassing or highly sensitive identified problems may sometimes benefit from TRIs and CTRIs. Through exploring not only how they feel and think when talking with their therapist but also how their therapist feels and thinks, they may come to see that others are not actually despising them or looking down upon them. Rather, common humanity draws from others understanding and compassion. However, therapists are wise to take their repeated defensiveness, noticeable opposition, or prolonged passivity as indications that they are not ready for interpretations.

Similarly, when clients repeatedly or strongly reject material, more often than not they are indicating that their heightened arousal makes them unable to think well. They do not have the intellectual capability to manage the feelings that have been aroused. Especially if clients are highly internalizing and feel awkward, TRIs and CTRIs seem to intrude on their fragile mental capacities. TRIs and CTRIs feel invasive. For instance, clients who already feel deeply rejected by a significant other might hear such a TRI as "You are refusing to let me in on your pain" as simply critical of them. The interpretation indicates that they are being rejected because they are protecting themselves so staunchly from their therapist's efforts to help them. They must be accepted for doing so, these clients reason, for they cannot risk intimacy, which either reminds them of the intimacy that they have lost or has the potential to lead to more rejection. When this is the case, therapists are wise to engage in reflective listening and clarify presenting problems without referring directly to transference or countertransference—or at least make only discreet, indirect reference to them.

Even highly externalizing clients with moderate ego-strength need help with symptom reduction and skill building rather than with insight and relationship work when they are under great stress. Though they are in the habit of sharing their emotional life with others, they are feeling too vulnerable to do so at the time. Although they may benefit from a few, carefully timed TRIs and CTRIs, in general they need externalizing interventions like paraphrasing and summarizing to achieve a positive therapeutic outcome (Beutler, 2000).

Others who are generally unable to make good use of TRIs and CTRIs are clients who lack ego-strength or suffer other serious deficiencies, such as pervasive, high levels of affective arousal. They are emotionally unable to tolerate the honest feelings and thoughts of their therapist and cognitively unable to process them. These clients see others as basically identical to themselves and, as a consequence, cannot separate their own feelings from those of their therapist. Asking them to do so by using TRIs or CTRIs that focus on feelings may even harm them.

Similarly, clients with a strong need to merge with idealized others cannot usually tolerate working with limited, vulnerable therapists, as is sometimes revealed in their CTRIs. Clients with strong narcissistic tendencies, for example, need to bolster their sense of self-worth by being worthy of only obviously capable therapeutic partners. For this reason, Kernberg (1975) warns against challenging an idealizing transference, at least in the beginning phase of therapy. Instead, therapists might simply ask for clarification.

Most persons with dual diagnoses must also be added to the list of clients who do not ordinarily have sufficient ego functioning to work with TRIs and CTRIs. They include those with significant alcohol and drug dependence, those who habitually act out their feelings and impulses—especially those that are antisocial or suicidal—and those without the mental capacity to see connectedness (Crits-Christoph & Barber, 1991; Pollack & Horner, 1985; Davanloo 1990).

Clients with a borderline personality disorder present yet other problems with regard to TRIs and CTRIs. Because they are habitually inclined to act out their feelings and impulses— particularly if they are functioning at a lower level—they are likely to perceive TRIs and CTRIs as expected and deserved counter-assaults. They simply cannot appreciate them "as therapeutically meaningful [statements] offered in good faith, because such things are not expected from one's most immediate enemy" (Epstein 1977, 461),albeit one's most perfect friend minutes before—even if he or she is a therapist.

Kernberg (1975) explains that clients with a lower-level borderline personality disorder do not do well with TRIs and CTRIs because they either distort them or cannot put them to use. Their core self is simply parts of others, adds Searles (1979), especially in the early phase of therapy. Because of their excessive use of splitting and their self-observational, judgmental, rational, and other executive ego-function limitations, they do not have the ego-strength to handle TRIs and CTRIs (Lasky, 1990). More often than not, they experience heightened levels of affective arousal (Swift & Wonderlich, 1990) that interfere with the cognitive work necessary for processing interpretations.

Instead of using TRIs and CTRIs with clients with a lower-level borderline personality disorder, therapists may simply wish to clarify the way these clients use splitting and other defenses and thereby distort perceptions during their sessions. Rather than focusing on their clients' interpersonal patterns, therapists may simply need to slowly and indirectly resolve the resistances of these clients (Spotnitz, 1976).

If, on occasion, therapists interpret transference and countertransference to clients with a lower-level borderline personality disorder, their TRIs and CTRIs should ordinarily refer not to genetic material (Volkan, 1995) but to the here-and-now. They might say, for example, "It's hard for you to share your bad experiences" rather than "It's always been hard for you to trust others enough to share your bad experiences." This focus will enable therapists to supply corrective data in concrete detail as soon as they note their clients' perceptual distortions. Or therapists might say, "I wonder what has prevented you from saying almost nothing for half an hour" and add, "Is my questioning coming across as critical of you?"

At times, however, even highly disordered persons can benefit from TRIs and CTRIs. An example would be the autistic child client that Franch (1996) describes as unable to overcome two-dimensionality and relate to a world without meanings. Because the autistic child can experience neither inside nor outside, Franch approaches him almost exclusively from his countertransference. Using his own feelings, sensations, fantasies, and associations to get information about the client's state of being, assigning meaning to these data, and communicating it through CTRIs, Franch achieves a positive outcome. The child's "frozen" internal world gradually begins to "thaw," and his transference arises in response to his therapist's countertransference.

# Appropriate Timing and Frequency of TRIs and CTRIs

## Introduction

Aware of their responsibility to distinguish clients who can benefit from TRIs and CTRIs from those who cannot, therapists still face the major questions of when and how often or with what frequency (Piper et al., 1993) they should use interpretations. The following section addresses the appropriate timing and frequency of TRIs and CTRIs, while Chapter Eleven examines the appropriateness of TRIs and CTRIs during the major phases of therapy.

## Timing

Joyce and others (1995) state that timing depends on clients' "inviting" their therapists to interpret. Clients "invite" when they are in a state of readiness: they are able to give up their defenses, focus inwardly, and attribute increased personal significance to the content of the interpretation. They can profit from an interpretation and begin to process affect connected with it under these circumstances

As with many other principles, however, it may be easier to identify times when TRIs and CTRIs should not be used. Therapists would be unwise to use TRIs or CTRIs, for example, if moderately ego-strong clients were already dealing with significant past conflict. It would ordinarily be inappropriate to divert clients' attention to an unwholesome negative therapist-client relationship if they were already exploring a past unwholesome relationship that is being repeated in the present (Swift & Wonderlich, 1990). The clients have understood correctly if they have recognized a destructive pattern outside the therapeutic setting (Pearson, 1995). On the other hand, it would be appropriate for therapists to be on the lookout for transference data that persisted after the therapeutic work was apparently completed, for that unresolved conflictual material would indicate a need for additional work.

Similarly, therapists would be unwise to use TRIs and CTRIs when clients were already profitably focused on there-and-now present extra-therapeutic relationships, or there-and-then past extra-therapeutic relationships, or there-and-will-be extra-therapeutic relationships that are likely to develop. In all likelihood, these clients would already be in the process of identifying their dysfunctional patterns of relating, patterns like those appearing in the transference and countertransference.

Neither would therapists use TRIs and CTRIs when clients were already dealing with highly intrapsychic material, such as an experience of death, significant rejection or humiliation, and severe abuse. Simply listening respectfully and, perhaps, reflecting the client's pain would be much more effective in these cases.

However, if the manner in which the clients choose to share their experiences causes problematic negative reactions in therapists—reactions of which the clients are virtually unaware—therapists might consider using very carefully crafted and sensitively timed TRIs and CTRIs. They might say, for example, "Your shouting is scaring me into focusing on harm that might come to me, even though I want to focus on how awful the experience you are relating is for you."

In general, therapists should also refrain from using TRIs and CTRIs when clients are dealing with material too primitive for language, when they cannot "give voice" to what they were experiencing. If clients cannot give information, talk slowly enough to be understood, or speak coherently, TRIs exposing those phenomena would deepen clients' already disturbing experience. More effective in these cases would be attentive silence or short affective responses that prepare clients for a clearer focus on transferential and countertransferential affect. Clients might then feel comfortable with expressing subjective experience that is just partially known (Bollas, 1987). They might, in time, rely on the attunement of their therapist to bring partial awareness to fuller consciousness. They might then tolerate their therapist's CTRIs or direct expressions of subjective states that reduce the quality of the therapeutic interaction, given that such expressions would repair some damage in the relationship and thus preserve it in the long run.

Several additional guidelines—some seemingly contradictory—have guided clinicians well in determining when to use TRIs and CTRIs. First, these interpretations should not be used too soon. They should be used only when there is some evidence of the necessary comfort level associated with the therapeutic alliance. Otherwise, they encourage intellectualization and other defenses against resolving transferential conflict (Brenner, 1982). Restated, TRIs and CTRIs should be used after—not before—more supportive interventions (Gabbard, 1994). Clients must feel accepted and valued in their therapy before they can examine how they have contributed to interpersonal failures. CTRIs will be experienced as premature if clients are suffering from intense guilt related to not fulfilling their responsibilities. They will react with intensified guilt to any intimation that therapists are not finding sessions helpful. Clients in this condition cannot accept responsibility for their therapists' mental states, even if they are occurring in therapy (Searles, 1975).

Second, TRIs and CTRIs should be used to further—in some cases even to establish—the therapeutic alliance. They should be used to help clients discover that their unprocessed feelings toward their therapist—strongly positive or strongly negative—are creating an impasse in their therapeutic work. Used carefully, these interpretations can facilitate clients' trust and respectful acceptance of their therapist and thereby provide the energy needed to create a functional therapeutic alliance.

Third, TRIs and CTRIs should be considered when the therapeutic alliance or the working alliance is ruptured. When therapists have made a mistake—for example, when they are chagrined and notice their clients' corresponding distress—they might need to say something like, "You seem disappointed in me because of my insensitive remark. Can we talk about your feelings?"

Fourth, TRIs should not be used when therapists suspect that transference is actually a resistance to facing extra-therapeutic problems. Rather than focusing on the transference, therapists should address the problems being resisted (Brenner, 1982). Suspecting this situation, they might say, "You started our session by telling me how disappointed you are in your sister. Am I right in thinking that your disappointment in me is less important to you?"

Fifth, TRIs are to be used when therapists can correlate what clients are doing in therapy to their behavior outside therapy or to the issues and problems that clients have identified in their presenting problems. Especially in the case of erotic transference, therapists should avoid TRIs until the underlying linkages to past relationships and to current extratransference relationships approach conscious awareness (Gabbard, 1996).

Sixth, there are times when therapists may use TRIs before they are fully aware of their connection to extra-therapeutic phenomena. Provided they are relatively certain of TRIs basic meaning, therapists may interpret tentatively when they suspect that negative transference is revealing pervasive, harmful interpersonal patterns. Therapists might admit that they could be wrong but want to help clients avert major interpersonal mistakes if they are right.

## Frequency

A general, research-based rule is that TRIs should be used infrequently rather than frequently (Piper et al., 1991;Hoglend, 1993; Joyce & Piper, 1993) because other interventions are often equally appropriate or more appropriate. The same rule is even more applicable to CTRIs, which have an even greater potential than TRIs to divert attention unnecessarily from clients' presenting problems. TRIs and CTRIs should be alternated or interwoven with active listening, explorations, clarifications, confrontations, and other kinds of interpretations (Grunebaum, 1986). It is especially important to move back and forth between TRIs and supportive interventions, researchers Bond and colleagues (1998) discovered, for only in that way is a successful working alliance established for personality-disordered persons—findings which may be generalized to other kinds of clients.

Furthermore, neither TRIs nor CTRIs should be used in place of supportive interventions, especially when those interventions would be more effective. Therapists must always heed the cautionary words of H.S. Sullivan (1954): Since "the supply of interpretations is greater than the demand," the needs of a client must take precedence over a therapist's desire for insight.

However, the guideline of infrequency in no way diminishes the potential of TRIs and CTRIs to contribute to mediators of successful outcome. The therapeutic and working alliances in particular benefit significantly from the candor, immediacy, and honesty of these interventions.

# CHAPTER ELEVEN

# USING INTERPRETATIONS TO FORM THE ALLIANCES AND TERMINATE THERAPY

## Introduction

The answer to the question of how therapists can use transference and countertransference interpretations (TRIs and CTRIs) to form the therapeutic and working alliances rests on a working definition of these alliances and the major functions therapists must perform to make them viable. A similar answer regarding termination of therapy rests on the major functions therapists need to perform in order to manage what is often a disconcerting reality: a meaningful relationship is ending for both client and therapist.

## Interpretations and the Therapeutic Alliance

The therapeutic alliance is a personal, exclusive relationship fashioned within the clinical setting by therapist and client. It is a bond of sufficient depth, breadth, and longevity to support the goals that client and therapist identify and collaboratively pursue. It is a covenant of trust and respect that both energizes therapist and client and sets them off from others.

Challenges inherent in forming the therapeutic alliance come into sharp focus immediately, for it is not a given. It depends on what therapists and clients do or not do. Even when in place, it is subject to ruptures that must be repaired if goals are to be attained.

On one level, the therapeutic alliance is different from early parent-child bonding in that it is formal, limited, and codified. It is a convention: a contrived, designed relationship. Existing only within the context of the therapeutic arrangement, it is rule-bound, setting-bound, person-bound, and time-bound. Indeed, it derives its potency largely from the restrictions within which it operates. (1)

On another level, however, the therapeutic alliance is strikingly similar to the early relationship between child and parent described by Bowlby (1980) as positive attachment. Like that original liaison, the therapeutic alliance is elementary and primitive. In most instances, it is instinctive and natural. It simply happens when therapists, like early caregivers, respond in a consistent and timely fashion to the needs of clients. Neither party has to declare an intention to bond. Bonding simply happens because conditions are right, and reciprocal influences occur as the client's capacity for attachment combines with the therapist's responsive behaviors (Shore, 2001a).

The exclusivity, intimacy, and confidentiality that distinguish the therapeutic alliance from other relationships evoke a unique phenomenon: an affect-laden state and an experience of shared values. Clients feel profoundly accepted and respected as they enter into an energized state with professionals they can trust enough to allow them entrance into their private world of limitations, flaws, and perhaps even culpability.

The affective nature of the therapeutic alliance, however, does not exclude cognition. In fact, the therapeutic alliance is intentional: therapists and clients desire it, seek it, and consciously choose to form it. They agree on a fee, set appointments, and meet to share, plan, and evaluate what transpires. Therapists intend to provide a safe place for expressing feelings and probing assumptions, teaching new skills that will relieve pain and increase self-efficacy, and nurturing wholesome attitudes. (2) In parallel fashion, clients intend to trust their therapist with meaningful personal matters and collaborate with them to bring about change.

But the therapeutic alliance is also unintentional in that it is partly outside the realm of conscious willing. At times, despite conscious efforts and good intentions, therapist and client simply do not align.

Among the variables responsible for this failure are transferential and countertransferential actions and reactions (Danvanloo, 1990). Clients and/or therapists are unconsciously recalling and responding to situations even vaguely like therapy in which one person needed help and the other did not or could not meet that need. Perhaps, in fear and frustration, one or both even inflicted harm. Unaware of the wounds they are carrying, therapist and client collude to replay those scenarios with the hope of a better outcome.

Wallach and Strupp (1960) explain that like all affect-based bonds, the therapeutic alliance is highly vulnerable to the influence of what both clients and therapists transfer from past affective relationships to therapy. Clients may be unconsciously harboring hostility (Strupp, 1980), paranoia-saturated distrust, phobic needs for privacy or secrecy, or a retaliatory desire for dominance or absolute control (Anchin & Kiesler, 1982). For their part, therapists may be unconsciously trying to resolve their unconscious conflicts related to wanting "to do good" but not actually doing so, wanting to be needed but not being needed, or wanting to bring about change but not being able to accomplish it. They, too, may be unconsciously harboring retaliatory desires for control of their client and therapeutic success at all costs.

Thus challenges inherent in forming and maintaining the therapeutic alliance dictate two major functions of therapists, both of which can be performed, in part, by means of sensitively worded and skillfully used TRIs and CTRIs. Therapists must first engender trust, then infuse their clients and themselves with sufficient energy to sustain their relationship.

## First Function: Engendering Trust

Clients trust only those therapists who accept them as they are at the time, resonate with them, and give evidence of professional skills. Having fewer than three of these abilities may result in a temporary working relationship but not in a therapeutic alliance as such.

Therapists convey acceptance of their clients when they convey their conviction that clients can set goals and make progress toward attaining them no matter how unsuccessful they have been up to that time. Therapist say, in effect, that they believe that their clients can renounce, or at least temper, pronounced negative qualities that undermine change and make even experienced therapists want to withdraw (Lieberman et al., 1973). They believe their clients can learn new ways of perceiving their world and of relating to others. They are worth their therapeutic effort.

In some cases, TRIs like, "You seem very critical of me today. Can we talk about that?" provide evidence of therapists' acceptance of clients as they are even though they refer to what might be an undesirable reality. Therapists are inviting their clients to identify what they are experiencing so that they and their therapist can consider who or what should change for the sake of their relationship. (3) By implying a good reason for their client's attitude, in contrast to simple rejection of the client, therapists earn their client's trust.

In other cases, CTRIs give evidence of therapists' acceptance of their clients even as they suggest that something must change. (4)

*He was a blustery, opinionated 15-year-old, smart enough to argue his opinion effectively. But in the course of doing so he made his opponents, including at times his therapist, feel demeaned. At the same time, the client suffered from being made fun of at school. Those who did so he summarily dismissed as "jerks."*

*His therapist suspected that the demeaning experience he himself had undergone the first three sessions was close to what the client's peers experienced. He also hypothesized that their making fun of him was their way of retaliating.*

*The therapist waited, however, until the fourth session to offer a CTRI, using the three previous sessions to pay close attention to the youth's non-verbal messages when he recounted his experiences at school. He was not really sure of himself, even when he felt intellectually superior. He betrayed his nervousness even as he proclaimed the "facts." He glanced away in insecurity and self-consciousness as he flashed the information that flatly contradicted what his therapist had just said.*

*The therapist proceeded to share his feeling of being demeaned by saying, "Could it be that some of your peers feel as put down as I do when you contradict what they say?" When the client remained silent, the therapist added, " Could it be that though you don't intend to demean them, others feel demeaned?" The client then said he wasn't sure but he would think about it.*

*The next session, however, the client spoke of a date he had with a girl whose opinions he made every effort to respect, even though he had his own ideas. The work was by no means over, for the client needed to acquire the skill of offering additional opinions while respecting those just voiced, but at least he had begun to work on his way of communicating. Indeed, the client could trust a therapist who had not only accepted him as he was but also proved skillful in dealing with her countertransference and, consequently, his transference.*

Ironically, however, clients find their therapists even more trustworthy if they appear primarily skillful and capable but also deficient and wanting. They display a paradox of pervasive strength combined with periodic weakness: they are well-grounded but temporarily hurt and angered by interpersonal abuse (Tower, 1956; Hoffman & Gill, 1988). Far from being immune to negative experiences, they are weak when mistreated but strong when processing their experience of mistreatment. They model self-soothing as they receive and hold disturbing material.

It becomes easier to understand this paradoxical basis of trust when one recalls the theory of Kohut (1971). Trust depends on two universal needs arising early in life, the need for an idealized other who can calm and soothe and the need for a "twin" who can resonate with one's impairment and pain. Indeed, Klein (1952) added, infants become secure only when they are able to transform a good person into an ideal person.

According to Kohut (1971), first and foremost is the child's early need for an idealized other whose strength and calmness soothe. Before children can self-soothe, they must be soothed by another. In the therapeutic setting, this is also true.

One way that therapists can soothe is by simply receiving and containing what clients divulge (Winnicott, 1960) in spite of its disturbing, even disgusting or frightening, attributes. When therapists "hold" what clients reveal, "powerful affects [are] safely experienced and expressed without damage to either [the therapists] or [the clients]" (McDougall, 1978, 206). As therapists remain receptive and tranquil, clients are soothed and calmed. (5)

Another way therapists can sooth is by using TRI's and CTRI's to invite clients to subject negative transferential and countertransferential feelings and thoughts to constructive rational processes. Therapists might say, for example, "You appear to be angry with me as you correct what I say. Can you and I together look at the source of that anger?" Or, "I wonder why I feel so put down now. Is it due to your contradicting me or to something else?"

With TRIs and CTRIs like these in mind, Hoffman and Gill (1988) define therapeutic soothing as clients being understood and helped to change what disturbs them and, not infrequently, others. As their therapist interprets seemingly unmanageable negative communications, clients discover them to be actually manageable. As therapists calmly subject feelings and thoughts to evaluative processes, clients find their early experiences detoxified. Indeed, by participating in that detoxification process, clients enjoy—usually for the first time—freedom from the power of the past along with freedom to experience a unique present. Moreover, it is this very empowerment—not better parenting—that makes therapeutic change possible (Casement, 1991). (6)

Along with a need for one who can soothe is the child's need for a twin who can provide a sense of humanness, likeness to, and partnership with others (Kohut, 1971). Before experiencing oneness with others, a child in pain must come in direct contact with a similar other who also suffers. This, too, is necessary in therapy no less than in life.

When a therapist admits weaknesses and mistakes like failing to remain empathic, clients perceive that therapist to be a twin, a kindred soul with a shared humanity, Hoffman & Gill (1988) explain. The therapist, too, is limited and deficient and therefore able to identify with other fallible human beings. Indeed, for some clients, "it is only by witnessing [the therapist's] vulnerability and susceptibility . . . that they can gain a conviction that the [therapist] really understands what they went through . . ." (Hoffman and Gill, 1988, 59). "The experience of being understood is at least as important as the details of any insight that is conveyed" (Winnicott, 1988, 109), and therapists' sharing countertransference thoughts and feelings facilitates that experience.

It is common, however, for therapists to hesitate to interpret their negative countertransference.

*He seemed pleased with their first sessions, pleased that his therapist was Christian who, though not a member of his fundamentalist church, listened intently to language distinctive of his congregation. All seemed basically satisfactory to the therapist as well, except for a subtle feeling of uneasiness, a nagging suspicion of something being off-center, and an intermittent concern about her ability to measure up to her client's high expectations. The therapist's uneasiness was partially due to her "inability"—in the sense of unwillingness—to measure up to a religious group to which she had previously belonged. She had resented the judgment to which she was subjected because she was less fundamentalistic than the group, less intent on measuring up to their high standards. Rebelling against the group's one and only interpretation of what was moral, she had chosen to leave the group. She had freed herself once and for all, she believed. Having emancipated herself from fundamentalism, she could now help client, still a fundamentalist, meet the goals that he had set.*

*On an unconscious level, however, the therapist was bringing to her therapeutic work the unfinished business of her past group membership. While she consciously intended to accept her client's fundamentalism as his choice, she unconsciously desired to free her client from his fundamentalism as she had done herself. Hence, the vague uneasiness and subtle dissonance during his sessions.*

*Ignoring her countertransference, however, the therapist tried to understand a client both like her in her basic Christian beliefs and unlike her in his religious expression. She bent over backwards to be non-judgmental, sitting quietly as her client opened each session with a long prayer of submission to what his therapist would be led to reveal.*

*In addition, when the client referred to others who were meeting his needs in exciting ways outside of therapy, the therapist quelled her fears that she, by contrast, was not.*

*At the end of seven sessions, the client announced his satisfaction with progress and his intent to finish his work in a group setting. He praised God for his therapist, thanked her for her kindness, and promised to mail back her evaluation rather than complete it at the time.*

*When the evaluation arrived, however, the truth was revealed. The therapist had not, in the client's judgment, met his needs. He left therapy not because he was satisfied with his progress but because he felt unconnected. He had not bonded. He had not been able to trust his therapist enough to be honest. He had not set goals he really wanted to pursue.*

In contrast, the client could most likely have trusted a therapist who frankly disclosed her countertransference. "I feel uneasy in our sessions because what I am being expected to do with you is difficult for me," she might have said. Alternately, she may have chosen to interpret her client's transference by saying, "You mention other people giving you help. Are you trying to tell me that you wish I would give you more help?" She would thereby have resonated with her client's discouragement and paved the way for addressing his key therapeutic issue: experiencing his therapist as not actually helpful. (7)

Therapists also give evidence of their resonance with clients when they indicate through body language, eye contact, and empathic silence that they have created a holding environment. Should therapists find it difficult to do this, they can make use of such TRIs and CTRIs as, "I want to change the subject or do anything but stay with your feeling of being abused. You may have placed in me the powerful urges you yourself had when being abused." Therapists can then can simply listen to their client's response or wait in silence if there is none.

Finally, for the therapeutic alliance to form, therapists must also be able to trust their clients. They must be able to believe that their clients mean what they say when they ask for help to bring about change. They must be able to rely on their clients' intention to reveal, in due time, the truth of their lives though they initially withhold information, distort facts, and add self-enhancing details. They must be able to rely on their clients' commitment to the therapeutic process in spite of its difficulty and their willingness to change themselves.

When therapists cannot trust clients, it is likely that clients are transferring from past figures to therapists unwholesome attitudes that make truth-telling virtually impossible. Similarities between significant persons outside of therapy and the therapist, recognized even on an subliminal level, are stimulating transferential processes that cause the clients to perceive their present therapist as untrustworthy (Strupp et al., 1977). If so, therapists must somehow address both this transference and their own countertransference.

*He said that he wanted to join the military, as had his father. He would do anything it took to finish school with grades high enough to get accepted. He would consider no other goal.*

*But he continued to smoke pot, get drunk, and not complete assignments. As a consequence, much as his therapist tried, under these conditions she simply could not trust him.*

While the client in this example may have had an conduct disorder that precluded truth-telling, he may have simply transferred to his therapist an authority figure in his past that punished him for wavering from their "mutual" goal of joining the military. His transference may be obstructing his honest search for a more suitable life goal. If so, a TRI like, "I wonder if you see me as a harsh authority figure ready to explode if you waver from my plans for you," would gently expose this displacement and facilitate a trusting relationship. (8)

## Second Function: Infusing Energy

The second major function of therapists related to the therapeutic alliance is to infuse sufficient energy into themselves and their clients. Sufficient energy facilitates insight, the ability to see beyond the obvious, and creativity, the ability to make something new. Sufficient energy facilitates hope, the deepest need of clients.

Sufficient energy also makes possible movement toward change that is paced according to the strengths and weaknesses of both client and therapist. For if it is to endure, change must be adjusted to, accommodated to, and woven into the fabric of life, including the piece called therapy. Again, interpreting both positive and negative transference and countertransference can be an effective means of infusing energy.

Positive transference and countertransference would appear to be most welcome to therapists in their energizing role, for amicable past feelings felt in the present promote good will and collaborative efforts to attain therapeutic goals. Indeed, clinicians tend to hold that although positive transference distorts reality, it should simply be ignored unless it is clearly interfering with therapeutic work. (9)

However, positive displaced material can be insidiously prejudicial. Positive countertransference can blind therapists to subtle ways in which clients contribute to their own problems. It can make therapists hesitant to confront their clients' apparently benign, but actually malign, attitudes or behaviors (Boesky, 1982; Wolf, 1988). Especially during therapeutic goal formation, it can seduce therapists into unconsciously colluding with their clients to focus on changing others rather themselves. (10)

In contrast, most clinicians easily acknowledge the energy-robbing impact of negative countertransference on clients. Searching for unconditional acceptance, clients are keenly conscious of unfavorable judgments of them, however couched in benign phraseology. Most clinicians can also easily understand that therapists themselves can deal well with only so much negatively charged feelings and attitudes. In spite of their education and experience, they are not beyond losing significant energy when bombarded by negativity. Hence, the wisdom of using TRIs and CTRIs to draw attention to negative displaced phenomena.

*His therapist definitely felt relegated to second-class as a mentor when her client came in announcing that he was simply going to obey church authorities. In saying that, the client was implying that he had not done his homework of carefully weighing whose values—his own or others—would receive the most weight in his judgment system.*

*When his therapist expressed her concern, though not her frustration, in a carefully worded CTRI, her client smoothed things over, using distinctions in wording intended to placate the therapist. She was supposed to think that he had indeed done his homework.*

*However, the therapist began to wonder whether her countertransferential frustration was a reflection of his client's transference: his anger that his therapist had dared to venture into his church's systemic thinking, that she had actually challenged its wisdom. More likely than not, the client was demeaning his therapist in retaliation for her challenging the church's wisdom. The therapist also began to think that the client's fear of disagreeing openly with authority was the real issue.*

*When the therapist began to worry that she going to miss the mark and dissipate both participants' energy because they did not address this fear, she decided to interpret her countertransferential frustration. "I wonder whether my frustration today may be due to your not doing your homework as well as your attempts to diminish its importance," she said. "Perhaps it's not okay for you to be openly angry with me."* (11)

*"I could never stand up to my father," the client revealed in a small, timid voice. "I've never dared to get angry with others, especially if they are in authority."*

*The rest of the session proved fruitful, as energy returned to the therapeutic interaction and client and therapist finally began to address the client's childhood trauma.*

Finally, therapists energize clients by simply staying in the "fight" long enough to win the "battle." At times, to prevent their clients from taking a "flight into health" and quell in themselves an urgent and swift change mandate, therapists must work ardently and quickly with their own countertransferential feelings.

*She came to her first session timid and fearful. She needed to speak but hes-*

*itated to do so. Once she felt warmth, calm, and a welcoming attitude on the part of her therapist, however, she began to share a vague picture of her heavy and frightening burden. Her husband abused her, and she was pregnant. At the present time, his abuse was just verbal, for he wanted a healthy baby if they were to have one. But previously he had pushed her forcefully. He had shoved her against furniture, slammed her against doors, and thrown her on the floor.*

*But she truly loved the man, she professed. She believed he really meant to refrain from violence in the future. She wanted to stay with him and support him in his efforts to change.*

*Her therapist could not help but be aware of her own present fear, in combination with her strong countertransference. She still hated boys who had bullied her as a child and intensely disliked men who had humiliated her in college. She feared their power to hurt her again.*

*Ideally, the therapist realized, she would help her client to weigh carefully the present danger she might be in against her desire to stay with her husband. She would collaborate with her to sift the grains of fact from the shaft of good intentions and wishful thinking so that the client could clearly own her decision and be resolute in acting accordingly.*

*Rather than take time to address her strong countertransference, however, the therapist pushed ahead with her own agenda of convincing the client to leave her husband as soon as possible. She forcefully pointed out the fact of abuse and warned against ignoring or minimizing it. She offered to help her client make practical arrangements to move to a safe house even before their next session.*

*Her client listened intently, crying quietly even as she nodded in agreement. She appeared to know what she had to do as she took down phone numbers and directions and agreed to call her therapist for further help if needed. But when it came time to set the next appointment, she said she preferred to make it only after she was safe.*

*But she never called, for she and her therapist had failed to bond. She could not bond with one whose energy was directed so differently from hers.*

Failing to deal satisfactorily with her countertransference, the therapist had tried to transfer to her client the energy that she felt around her own solution. She had conveyed the message that she wanted to use her energy not to hold her client's distressful feelings and thoughts but to weaken her client's loyalty to an abusive person and her willingness to risk harm to her unborn child. How differently might the session have ended if the therapist had used a CTRI, such as, "Even though I'm worried by what you report, I want to stay with it so that we can really understand your situation and weigh both the dangers and your needs." She would have reflected her client's complex situation and modeled how to deal with real and present dangers as well as primitive and past-based fears. She would have partnered with her client to arrive at a decision that her client could have truly owned and implemented. (12)

Notice, by contrast, how a well-phrased CTRI focusing on a serious absence of therapeutic energy becomes a most effective intervention in the following vignette.

*She was smart, attractive, and loquacious with many of her peers. But she answered her therapist in one-word or short-phrase responses then glanced around uncomfortably. For a good half of the session her therapist tried to ignore her own uncomfortable feelings of being incompetent with this teen-age client. She asked question after question, waiting as long as she could for more information to come.*

*Finally the therapist decided to share her self-observations in a CTRI. "I have a high level of discomfort right now and wonder how much is coming from me and how much from what seems like lack of security and comfort on your part," the therapist said. "On a scale of one to five, with one being "Most Uncomfortable," rate your situation while I do the same?"*

*"It's a six," the client shot back. "I don't like talking to counselors who aren't young. How can they understand what I'm going through!"*

*"They can't," her therapist agreed, wisely using the third person plural to shift some focus from herself for the time being. "They need to be helped to understand. They need to be told the basics of what they don't get. What, for example, could you help me understand?"*

*"Well you have to see what a bitch my teacher really is," the client answered quickly. "She can't even accept an assignment one day late!"*

*"What a bummer," her therapist responded, after which her client disclosed how scared and discouraged she really was. Energy had been restored, and work could proceed.*

# Interpretations and the Working Alliance

The working alliance is a collaborative effort that permits therapists and clients to bring about change. It forms because clients are motivated to overcome their feelings of helplessness and participate in the therapeutic process (Epstein, 1977). It also forms because therapists are willing to perform at least two major functions, both of which can include the use of sensitively worded TRIs and CTRIs. First and obviously, therapists must help clients attain their goals. Second, therapists must address the negativity that clients experience when they realize that maintaining their gains requires making difficult personal changes.

## First Function: Facilitating Goal Attainment

At the heart of the working alliance is the therapeutic goal, usually identified in the client's presenting problem, and an explicit or implicit agreement to attain that goal. (13) The working alliance depends on both therapist and client providing sufficient ego strength and affective stability to expose and explore the client's interpersonal and intrapsychic patterns, especially if they are noticeably conflictual (Straker, 1968). Thus the working alliance depends on careful management of transferred material. (14)

In the analytic paradigm, therapeutic work is intrapsychic and reconstructive: it is designed to bring about fundamental characterological change and therefore focus directly on displaced material. In contrast, in the non-analytic paradigm, therapeutic work is primarily functional. Clients are expected to challenge their pathological assumptions and leave therapy with new attitudes, beliefs, and competencies without engaging in ego restructuring as such (Weiss & Sampson, 1986).

Does this mean that transferential and countertransferential phenomena will not challenge non-analytic therapists and clients? No, quite the opposite. While therapists will not ordinarily be directly working with major developmental injuries to the psyche of their clients, they will still need to address clients' present-day, displaced attitudes and feelings regarding changing how they—not others—think and act. Clients will have learned, in particular, that goal attainment involves making painful personal change and that maintaining goals is even harder than attaining them. They have reasons to want *others* to change and to dislike those whose intent is to help *them* change. (15) For their part, therapists have learned that "requiring" personal change of others is rife with fear of losing clients, frustration over half-hearted attempts, and disappointment in end results. In sum, it triggers memories of previous attempts to take an active role in the change-process of others.

## Second Function: Addressing Negativity

In the initial phase of the working alliance, clients and therapists have hope that they are partners who have identified their work and can accomplish it. Consequently, transference and countertransference are usually positive. But as the working alliance solidifies, unconscious signals to unconscious about a functional change. In order to begin the difficult work of personal change, clients must shift from venting, explaining, and exploring as their therapists shift from reflective listening, empathic responding, and tactful clarifying. Especially if clients believe that change can occur simply because they have expressed their emotional pain and identified their needs, the stark realization that significant therapeutic work is necessary is most unwelcome. Then, as therapists outline that work and break it down into concrete steps, transference usually intensifies and veers toward the negative. (16)

Ironically, however, the appearance of negative transference is a sign that real progress can begin. For until the arrival of that negativity, clients have unrealistically expected their therapist to be a loyal "parent" who would side with them against others, eliminate the need for painful personal change, and change others quickly. Indeed, their insurance classified their symptoms as problems that could be corrected within relatively few sessions. Thus clients have unconsciously equated therapy with infancy: a time when they wanted their needs to be met immediately, a time when caregivers obliged them as they floated about in realms of magical solutions and effortless improvement. If their therapist appears to meet their needs, transference is positive though they are not facing reality. If their therapist does not appear to meet their needs, transference becomes negative though realistic change can now be made.

While transference and countertransference were positive, therapists were also basking in the comfort of the early therapeutic relationship and enjoying interactions with toward those who felt good about them. Therapists unconsciously desired to protect their clients, and even themselves, from facing disconcerting realities. They did not want to see the blame that clients put on others as projection, for that would undermine the aura of trustworthiness created in the therapeutic alliance. They wanted to collude with clients to keep transference positive so that the pain of change would be mitigated. (17)

However, as time passes and therapists remind clients and themselves of session limitations, clients wonder whether they should avoid goal attainment by not putting much effort into a working alliance. They alternately wonder whether they should exert enormous effort so that change comes quickly. They also question whether they should reduce the gravity of their problems, even take "flight into health," so that they do not have to wait for the proverbial "second shoe" of termination to fall. They wonder whether they should control their fear of failure to attain their goal by focusing on extraneous material made to look urgent.

*"You're too young to understand," the elderly client blurted out as he negatively pierced the therapeutic environment. "When you get older, you'll know how difficult life is—how hard it is to get others to cooperate even if you're supposedly in control." Then, in response to his therapist's sincere request to be given more information, he responded, "You don't have the faintest idea of how things were during the Depression! None of you baby-boomers can even imagine how tough times were. And you never will!"*

*Heaviness in her chest drew the attention of the therapist from her client to herself. "Why must I look younger than I am," she complained to herself. "Why didn't I stop and work outside my field before getting my Master's" she berated herself as her client stood to leave, stating bluntly that she couldn't help him because she never experience the Depression.*

Though undoubtedly many variables were involved, therapeutic work might have continued if the therapist had shared her countertransference, saying perhaps, "I'm also feeling hopeless with regard to our work. Can we explore our feelings of hopelessness together?"

Clients may also be unconsciously motivated to act out in order to quell their fears of not attaining their goals. Then, as therapists give evidence of countertransferential anxiety and anger related to subtle hints of clinical failure, clients' negative transference blossoms. The working alliance is transformed from a collaborative effort into a combative struggle characterized by negative transference and corresponding countertransference.

*The adolescent client started off by protesting that she could not sit up because she was too tired. Even her mother, who ordinarily could control her for brief periods, could not get her to lessen her dramatic slouch for more than a few minutes.*

*Rather than use a CTRI, the therapist acted out her own negative countertransference by initiating a conversation with the adolescent's mother about how to impose negative reinforcement on her daughter when she came home intoxicated. The client sat up immediately and used foul language to show her disagreement.*

*Negative countertransference then burgeoned. The therapist declared her intolerance of that language in her therapy room and asked the mother to have the girl apologize. The youth abruptly stood up, stalked toward the door, opened it quickly, and slammed it in the face of her approaching parent. Her therapist could only watch.*

Again, while acknowledging many variables, one must at least consider how different the outcome might have been if the therapist had used a TRI like, "Could it be that you feel so much anger toward me that you need to control our session? If so, can we talk about it?"

For their part, therapists ordinarily become frustrated in the course of the working alliance if clients are not working diligently enough to meet their therapeutic goals while they themselves are expending considerable effort. Even if clients are working, therapists can lower their sense of professional self-efficacy by transferring past experiences of negative outcome to the present situation. They then experience significant anxiety as they doubt their clients' and their own ability to accomplish their therapeutic goals.

Based on their own interpersonal patterns, which are greatly molded by past experience, therapists are prone to enact negative countertransference in time-manipulation, over-involvement, or under-involvement. They unconsciously manipulate time, for example, by double scheduling: "forgetting" to write both clients' names in their appointment book. Or they keep clients waiting because they unconsciously dread those whose hour is to begin.

*The therapist never seemed to end the previous session on time. She always ran late, always had to apologize for keeping the eight-year-old and his highly educated father waiting, even for just a few minutes. Ostensibly, the clients that occupied the previous hour were often in crisis. It was hard to get the work done and get them out exactly on time.*

*There was more to it, the therapist came to realize, when she examined her negative countertransference related to the boy and his father. The latter was not only highly educated; he was also highly critical. She had come to dislike him and to dread the beginning of his son's session, a time when the father wanted to know in detail how well the therapy was progressing. There was good reason for her negative countertransference.*

In the case of relatively silent clients, therapists can resort to over-involvement. They fill the communication void by educating or asking serial questions, hoping to spur clients into speech. In the end, therapists work harder than clients and thereby weaken, if not destroy, the working alliance.

Therapists also tend to become over-involved when clients fail to complete their inter-session work. Following the common social rule that one does not draw attention to irresponsibility, therapists accept clients' lame excuses and overlook evidence in an effort to avoid embarrassing clients, if not engaging them in conflict. In time, however, therapists become resentful that they are working harder than their clients. Yet unless they confront their countertransferential anxiety and fear of clinical failure, they continue to do so.

Countertransferential over-involvement is common when therapists work with highly educated or respected clients. To quell their inferiority feelings, therapists unconsciously resort to "proving" their competence. They make extended educational efforts, truncate reflective listening, and move rapidly from problems to solutions to display their skill. They do not want to be seen as less skillful than those who have come to them—of with a great deal of skepticism regarding the therapist's profession—for help (18)

Countertransferential under-involvement, by contrast, is present when therapists' allow clients to remain superficially engaged and thus leave therapy virtually unchanged. Or therapists exaggerate therapeutic success, hoping to spare clients the angst of acknowledging their deficiencies. Alternately, therapists become aloof or sleepy, prolong their distractions, and allow—even provide—diversions from therapeutic tasks.

Should these inappropriate reactions occur, therapists would be wise to share their countertransference. They might say, for example, "My distractions are so frequent and strong today. Can we explore what is causing me not to be involved with you?" Or, "I want to protect you from facing personal responsibility. Where could that be coming from?"

## Interpretations and Termination

Termination may be second only to forming the therapeutic alliance as therapists' major challenge in therapy. For as much as beginnings bring for clients and therapists alike poignant recollections of the Mother Archetype, termination brings for them memories of the end of maternal care and concern. For clients, termination dashes hope of obtaining their therapist's love (Dewald, 1994). For therapists, it means no longer being needed by a particular client. Clients and therapists have to walk away from each other. Though by way of exception therapy will be re-undertaken, for the most part they must accept termination as the end of their relationship.

Moreover, termination increases awareness of adult independence, whether or not clients have truly replaced dependence with independence. Clients are expected to maintain their therapeutic gains, and therapists are not to involve themselves in that effort. Hence the major functions of therapists during termination: helping clients manage their reactions to ending therapy and processing their own thoughts and feelings.

# First Function: Helping Clients Manage Their Reactions to Termination

Several unwholesome transferential and countertransferential responses can occur as therapy draws to a close and clients and therapists transmit covert unconscious cues (Jacobs, 1986) about their separation anxiety. They can unconsciously "say" to each other, "Let us get this over with. Let us run from each other and lessen the impact of what is happening." Clients can then unconsciously set out to punish their therapists for their having to terminate. They can slip away or refuse to keep their appointments just at the time their continuance is vital for positive outcome (Little, 1951). Alternately, clients can make therapists suffer for leaving by neglecting to do homework or coming late for sessions (Schafer, 1997). They can reiterate old material instead of dealing with their anxiety (Little, 1951). Even worse, clients can shift back into their miserable pre-therapy roles (Schafer, 1997). In subtle though dramatic ways, clients can threaten to undermine all their success in therapy by permanently adopting dysfunctional ways of thinking and unhealthy patterns of behavior.

Yet another unwholesome reaction of clients to termination is their adopting a constricting preoccupation with therapeutic achievement. They limit life experience in general, try to control others, and avoid taking appropriate responsibility for their lives outside of therapy (Schafer, 1997). Alternately, they re-enact therapeutic conflicts with people outside of therapy (Dewald, 1994) to the degree that their families and colleagues wonder if the improvement they witnessed earlier was all imaginary or if therapy was for naught.

Thus a major function of therapists during termination is to help clients—especially those whose degree of transference involvement has been deep, intense, and convoluted—find ways to use the energy bound up in their negative feelings to solidify their gains. In doing so, therapists may find TRIs and CTRIs very useful (Dewald, 1994).

Perhaps the most difficult termination feelings are inconsolable abandonment and painful rejection. As in previous times, clients may unconsciously conclude that they are being abandoned either because they have been successful (Schafer, 1997) or they have failed (Jacobs, 1986).

Also motivational are feelings of painful aloneness and separation from someone who has proven valuable, feelings not unlike earlier times of endings and disconnection. Like former experiences of loss accompanied by ever increasing anxiety, termination is undesirable and therefore something to be avoided. Clients deny the importance to them of terminating yet scramble to find a replacement for therapy, perhaps by seeking the attention of medical personnel or quickly fall in love, often with inappropriate people (Dewald, 1994).

Alternately, clients who stubbornly refuse to mourn the loss of the therapeutic relationship replace mourning with dislike, even hate. It is easier to dislike someone who, because of therapy, knows too much, Blum (1997) explains, than to mourn the loss of a loved one. It is also easier to dislike the person connected with the termination, the person agreeing with or even initiating the termination for the ultimate good of the client, than to systematically mourn the loss of a therapist's unconditional acceptance and profound respect.

Clients' dislike of their therapists is more likely to develop into hate if clients have not yet resolved late-adolescence conflicts involving dependence and independence, self-identity, and meeting challenges of the real world (Dewald, 1994). These clients are prone to displace to their therapy the highly painful, tumultuous days when their relationships with parental figures were fraught with self-doubt and fear of an unknown future. In a word, it is this similarity to a time of actual or potential regression that makes termination such a major therapeutic challenge, as the following vignette illustrates.

*Because the client had met his goals, or so his therapist thought, a termination time was agreed upon. As the time approached, however, nothing seemed to go right. The client slipped back into his depression, protesting that he simply was not able to restructure his negative thoughts as he had previously learned to do. In addition, instead of refreshing his mind regarding restructuring work, he chose to vent almost continually.*

*Finally, his therapist knew he had to test his hypothesis that the depression was a substitute for some other feelings, perhaps anger and fear over ending his therapeutic relationship. He gently said, "I wonder if the thought of stopping your therapy with me reminds you of earlier separations from friends at college and the loneliness of returning to your rural home."*

*"I don't know," the client responded. "But I never was good at finding new friends. I always longed for the ones I left much more than they did. In fact, they soon got too busy to answer my letters. Then I began to wonder if I had ever really made friends."*

*"I wonder if you question the authenticity of our relationship also. Are you fearing that I will be so busy with new clients that I will forget you?" the therapist responded. "You won't remember me," the client retorted, "our relationship means nothing to you."*

*Client and therapist then began to process the deep pain the client had suffered and feared he would suffer again. The session and those following it were difficult, but his depression began to lift as he made use of the cognitive restructuring skills he had learned.*

## Second Function: Processing Personal Thoughts and Feelings

Therapists who do not want to terminate can convey unconscious countertransference messages to prolong therapy unnecessarily (Little, 1951). They can unconsciously attempt to meet their own affiliative and achievement needs as well as their desire for perfection by trying to keep their clients in therapy until every last problem has been addressed. (19)

Termination can also arouse in therapists countertransferential fear regarding financial stability, tempting them to focus on clients' remaining weaknesses rather than regard them as capable of changing on their own or at least with people other than their therapist.

On the other hand, countertransferential feelings of abandonment can cause therapists to rush toward termination, "get it over with," so to speak. Therapists can "push clients out the therapeutic door" rather than face the pain of losing a rich source of professional self-esteem.

By identifying and interpreting their countertransference, however, therapists can not only prevent harming clients but also model for them how to accept with grace and dignity the inevitable realities of life. Endings do mean surrendering a helping position. They mean separating from a meaningful relationship (Bird, 1922). At times, they mean accepting discouragement reminiscent of previous failures and defeat. They mean adding one more item to a list of failures and recognizing again painful personal and professional limitations.

Can these countertransferential reactions be shared with clients to their benefit? In some cases, no. In some, yes.

*The client was almost 15 minutes late for his session, the one he had requested to deal with termination issues. True, he had what sounded like a perfect reason: being called for orientation to his new job site. Yet, a countertransference response in his therapist suggested to her that she was being unconsciously devalued. She felt second-class: not as important as the people in her client's new job and undeserving of a full-hour termination session.*

*At first the therapist thought that her countertransferential feelings were unworthy of exploration. After all, her client began his session with an announcement of his new job, which directly related to one of his therapeutic goals. But when the client began to intellectualize, the therapist suspected avoidance of a key issue related to his other goal: his relationship with authority because of ill treatment by teachers.*

*So the therapist decided to share her negative countertransferential feelings, saying that she wondered if her feelings of diminishment might possibly be linked to the client's desire to demean authority figures as they had demeaned him. Her client listened intently, then responded that he wasn't sure if that were true, but he would think about it.*

Thus, by decoding, the therapist introduced doubt in the client's mind about whether he had finished processing his negative feelings toward authority figures. If indeed he had not, it was likely that he would be no more successful in his new job than in previous jobs.

# Endnotes

(1) In a strict sense, unlike parent-child bonding and other attachments outside the therapeutic session, the therapeutic alliance exists only during the actual therapeutic session. Although mental representations can and do reproduce in therapists and clients memories of actual sessions, it is only during therapeutic contact times that they experience the fullness of their bonded relationship. Should they meet at a party, for example, a

sense of awkwardness, strangeness, and artificiality replaces the trust, security, and authenticity of the bond. There is no mutual sense of deep connection and no fundamental message of exclusive concentration on what is transpiring between them as there is in their therapeutic session.

(2) Therapists intend to provide a safe place, in particular, when they set limits to what is allowed to transpire in the therapeutic setting. They limit clients' avoidance of emotions, excessive use of defense mechanisms, personal attacks on others, and monopolization of time by one client in couples or family therapy.

In addition, in the first session, therapists provide a safe place by limiting how much clients disclose so that the clients maintain a reasonable level of distress. When the therapeutic alliance is fragile at best, trustworthy therapists allow clients to share enough, but not too much, information; they permit clients to disclose personal material but not highly sensitive or greatly detailed intimate information. For, paradoxically, when clients disclose indiscriminately or share too much in their first session, they are usually responding to fear and anxiety rather than trust. They are unconsciously trying to counteract past fear-inducing experiences. They are replacing their heightened anxiety with information-sharing for its own sake. Unfortunately, however, their anxiety lowers only to rise again as clients become uncomfortably aware of having embarrassed and humiliated themselves in front of their therapist. Indeed, before feeling psychologically safe and secure, they have unwittingly stripped themselves of their defenses.

(3) Clients trust professionals who can put their finger on the exact nature of the distress either they or their therapist are experiencing.

(4) Examples of such CTRIs would be: "I'm feeling uptight in our session and wondering if I'm picking up on your difficulty with me as your therapist. Is there something about me that makes it hard for you to accept me?" or "You seem reluctant to talk to me. Can we talk about how I'm coming across to you?" or "Would you be willing to discuss how your past experience with someone my age makes it hard for you to see me as someone who can help you?"

(5) Winnicott (1960) associates this ability to receive and hold information tranquilly with the concept of reliability, which he regards as the most important therapeutic factor. No matter what archaic feelings and inexpressible "thoughts" clients communicate, reliable therapists are able to remain calm and tranquil. Rather than withdraw or retaliate, therapists contain them.

(6) The truly wholesome "corrective experience" is clients' discovering that they are not really powerless over pain; in fact, they can actually manage it (Hoffman & Gill, 1988).

(7) To emphasize clients' assessment of whether their therapist can actually help them attain their therapeutic goals, however, is not to identify the therapeutic alliance with goals and goal attainment. Rather, the therapeutic alliance is a matter of trust that enables a healing experience. While one of its foundations can be similarity, agreement, and concordance, its other, more sturdy foundation must be acknowledged dissimilarity and processed disagreement. "Conceiving of [the therapeutic] alliance as primarily the product of agreement," warn Cushman and Guilford (2000), "runs the risk of creating a fragile or false alliance that must by definition avoid disagreement or disagreeable feelings. Indeed, it seems that [an] alliance based solely on agreement reduces the concept to a consumer-satisfaction dynamic" (990). In contrast, if an alliance is truly founded on trust, it creates a climate wherein clients can confront their therapists with impunity.

(8) In contrast, focusing on the discrepancy between what the client said and what he actually did might have made him change in the present situation but not really understand his resistance. Unless his passive-aggressive pattern of anger expression was

brought into the open, he would be angry with and uncooperative with other authority figures.

(9) Most theorists say that bringing positive transference to clients' attention can make them too self-conscious to undertake bonding efforts. Similarly, most theorists hold that positive countertransference, also supportive of bonding, should not be addressed during the formation of the therapeutic alliance unless it impedes therapeutic progress.

(10) Additionally, positive transference can make clients unwilling to disagree with their therapists and uncritical of their well intentioned but deleterious suggestions. It can make clients refrain from honest disclosure for fear of being found wanting. It can encourage both therapists and clients to take minimal evidence as proof of therapeutic success

(11) To challenge passive-aggressive expressions of anger in an effort to energize therapists and clients, however, is not to recommend that therapists should categorically prohibit expressions of negative transference. Ironically, energy needed for the therapeutic alliance can also come precisely from what seems contradictory to positive bonding, namely challenges and limitations. For the therapeutic alliance rests on therapists' and clients' right to reject—no less than admit—each others' insights. As do children, clients need an adversary that will help them preserve their unique self and maintain distance from those who would destroy them (Wolf, 1988).

(12) Another explanation, combined with useful recommendations, comes from Goldin (1985). When clients exhibit strong transference resistance, he writes, they are unconsciously intending to relate with their therapist in such a way that infantile wishes come true or fears do not materialize. Though this pattern of bringing about a predetermined outcome in a relationship also occurs outside therapy and causes problems, these clients are not yet ready to deal with the problem. Their energy has been trapped, as it were, in infantile wishes or fears to such an extent that they do not have any power either to simply renounce those wishes or fears or to look at how they are defending themselves against that renunciation. Thus therapists have no other choice but to stay with those wishes and fears and process their countertransferential desire to move on immediately. They must move on only after containing and processing the material their clients are presenting.

(13) During most of the 20th century, that goal was to resolve some kind of psychological pain that had negatively affected the self-image, emotional well-being, cognitive functioning, or overall mental health of the client (Mann, 1973). More recently—with the emphasis on positive psychology—it is not uncommon for the goal to be the client's improved psychological functioning through skill-building, mood enhancement, increased awareness, cognitive restructuring, and appropriate forms of decision-making (Seligman, 1999).

(14) When transference data suggest that past or extra-therapeutic forces are at work during goal setting, a sensitively worded TRI referring to clients' immature attitudes and dysfunctional behaviors as they manifest themselves toward the therapist can make clients aware of behavioral patterns that might well be at the heart of their problems. Then, an ensuing exploration of the ways in which the therapeutic relationship is being negatively affected by those patterns can facilitate insight into how alternative attitudes and behaviors might create a more wholesome future. "I wonder if your annoyance with me for not understanding some technical terms might also get conveyed to your children. Could that account for why they don't always listen to you?" a therapist might say to a father whose goal is to change his children, not himself.

(15) Hence therapists need to confront clients regarding their tendency not to take at least partial responsibility for the distress that they are experiencing. Even as therapy

starts, clients need to learn that they are not being acted upon by a harmful universe as much as creating a world in which they can be harmed (Lear, 1993). They are not powerless, as regressive entitlement would have it (Boyer, 1961).

(16) Some will argue that expectations regarding change are not always matters of transference and countertransference. While this is true, as clients turn to another in an intrapsychic and interpersonal movement similar to the way they tried to cope in infancy, they activate memories of past dependent relationships with early caregivers. Similarly, efforts to work with clients in need remind therapists of earlier attempts in their own lives to collaborate, beginning with their own parental figures. Even then, it became apparent to therapists that caregivers were available for them only when they too were fed, refreshed by sleep, and renewed by absences. Now, as they are called upon to fill up a seemingly limitless cavern of neediness, therapists become increasing aware of their need to self-nurture.

(17) Ironically, however, keeping transference positive can actually result in premature termination. For clients instinctively know that they must tackle their resistance to facing the pain disguised by transference, experience that pain, grieve the past, and let the present be uniquely its own. Clients also know that the one to help them do their work—indeed insist that they do it—is their therapist, who must discern clients' unwitting contribution to interpersonal dilemmas. Indeed, therapists must confront even admirable traits of clients, for in some way they have played a part in their problems (Stein, 1981).

(18) Over-involved therapists under great countertransferential distress routinely fail to openly address their concerns through such direct interventions as CTRIs. They may be recalling prior experiences of "making matters worse," times when others have passively denied their obligations, become aggressive when someone tried to hold them accountable, or even ended a working relationship because of demands for productivity that struck them as excessive.

(19) In general, therapists are motivated to enter their profession because of their own unmet needs, both affiliative and achievement needs (Little, 1951; Cohen, 1952; Racker, 1953). Some therapists want to help others, by and large, as a means of helping themselves assuage the pain of not being loved and cared for enough. Others want to unconsciously meet early caregiving conditions: being accepted and respected by early caregivers whose own achievement needs surpassed their affiliative needs, caregivers whose message to their offspring was, in effect, that their value depended on their accomplishments. As adults, these therapists now attempt to live and work within a paradigm of personal value based more on interpersonal relationship than achievement.

# PART V

## A SPECIAL PROBLEM

# CHAPTER TWELVE

# TRANSFERENCE AND COUNTERTRANSFERENCE LOVE

## Introduction

Transference love and countertransference love deserve a separate chapter because, besides being prevalent and pervasive, they present significant challenges—even dangers—to therapists and clients, to the therapeutic process, and to positive outcome (Freud, 1915; Tower, 1956; Covington, 1996; Schaverien, 1997). Love that is originally non-erotic can become erotic simply because of human nature and the intimate design of the therapeutic setting, particularly the caring, concern, and self-disclosure that characterizes therapeutic interactions. During the course of therapy both clients and therapists can bring sexual desires, issues, and unresolved conflicts into their therapeutic work. Indeed, Mann (1999) warns that "erotic fantasies will almost certainly be activated in both [client] and therapist" (86).

Even more problematic, transference love can develop into eroticized transference and perversion transference, both of which are pathological. Similarly, countertransference love can become eroticized or perverse in spite of therapists' education, expertise, and determination not to act unethically.

Equally challenging is a related reality: non-pathological and pathological forms of transference and countertransference love are not mutually exclusive. As Westen (1988) explains within the context of cognitive psychology, the needs that generate these forms "are likely to call upon similar information-processing channels, so that in many cases they can be expected to arise in conjunction with one another" (30). In so far as therapists and clients see each other as persons with whom healing love can be shared, appropriate forms may exist alongside inappropriate forms that result from pathological conditions

(Gardner, 1999). They may defy separation. Even worse, they may take insidiously disguised forms.

When transference love is erotic to begin with or non-erotic transference love develops into some form of sexualized transference, it becomes "both a gold mine and a minefield" (Person, 1995). "The complex impact of intense transference on the [therapist] is perhaps nowhere more difficult than when such transference is dominated by erotic features" (Kernberg, 1994, 1139), such as sexual innuendoes or references to sexual fantasies.

Countertransference love that becomes sexualized is even more difficult for therapists to identify and manage. Lying largely within the recesses of the unconscious, it is subjected to denial and other powerful defenses. Even when therapists suspect this form of displaced love, they are prone to hide it from the eye of a consultant or colleague. "It's beneath my professional status and violates my ethical standards," therapists rationalize. "It's too embarrassing to admit to other professionals. They would only think badly of me."

Yet sexualized countertransference, like all countertransference, can motivate therapists to do what they would otherwise never consent to, as evidenced by scandalous sexual entanglements, even of Jung with his patient Sabina Spielrien (Tansey, 1994). "Sexual and loving feelings, in particular, are likely to impel us into action," Gabbard (1994, 1085) warns.

Indeed, neither male nor female therapists are immune from erotic countertransference desires. As late as the 1980's, 87% of male therapists and 53% of female therapists said that they had felt sexually attracted to their clients. Furthermore, according to surveys, up to 10% of male therapists act out sexually. Female therapists also act out sexually but in fewer numbers (Russell, 1993; Jehu, 1994; Garrett, 1994), perhaps because cultural norms strongly forbid such behavior or because male clients who develop an erotic transference are inclined to leave therapy once they become aware of it (Schaverien, 1997). They fear becoming dependent on an idealized therapist (Kernberg, 1994).

Dynamics that increase the likelihood of sexual transference and countertransference in therapy, such as abuse victims who seek or provide treatment, compound the problem. Childhood sexual abuse, in particular, predisposes victims to fuse sexuality and affection with the result that the therapeutic relationship, like virtually any positive relationship, takes on strong sexual overtones. Given that many sexual abuse victims eventually seek therapy, it is no wonder that 48% of 60 research participants who had formerly been clients reported a sexual transference to their therapists at some time during the course of their therapy (Dalenberg, 2000).

One can only conclude that clients' desire for a sexual relationship with their therapist in and of itself is not uncommon (Strean, 1983). It continues to arise even though it evokes guilt, embarrassment, and anxiety related to exposure, together with the possibility of rebuff and humiliation (Slochower, 1999). Therapists' desire for a sexual client-therapist relationship is similarly understandable though they know that acting on it is both unethical and illegal.

Still, there is the other side of the therapeutic coin: non-pathological forms of transference love and countertransference love are assets. Like all forms of positive displaced feelings and attitudes, these phenomena make it easier for the therapeutic alliance to form. They make possible direct confrontative interventions should the working alliance falter. They attenuate the pain of ending therapy and promote continued progress after termination. In brief, carefully managed non-erotic and simple erotic transference and countertransference love make a significant contribution to positive outcomes.

# Non-Erotic Transference Love

Freud (1912) taught that non-erotic transference love, like all transference, arises in the unconscious mind as an attempt to repeat early conflictual affiliative experiences, particularly those occurring when a child is about five or six. For most persons, those early attempts to meet their needs to love and be loved were both positive in the sense of meeting their basic expectations and negative in their failure to gratify deeper instinctual wishes. Many persons become conflictual about parental figures who were supposed to meet their unrelenting, primitive needs to love and be loved but met them neither fully nor consistently.

Freud (1912) explained that transference love, like all transference, is an attempt to avoid the painful affect that accompanies repressed memories of attempts to love and be loved. It is a case of repetition inundated by the hope that the person presently performing affiliative functions, namely, the therapist, will do so perfectly, or at least better than parental figures.

Thus Freud (1912) and later Covington (1996) explain that, because individuals' early affiliative needs are left unsatisfied, they feel compelled to approach every new empathic and understanding person as a potential candidate for becoming, at first, a nurturing mother figure and, in time, a protective father figure. They seek intimacy, which ordinarily includes bodily contact, with those they experience as warm and accepting.

In sum, transference love is normative. It is to be expected because the unconscious mind wants to experience sameness in setting and in the manner that it assigns persons specific functions (Rayner, 1995). The absence of transferential love, by contrast, is an aberration. Most clients can afford to repeat, their early affiliative or bonding experiences, both sexual and non-sexual. In fact, most feel compelled to. (1)

Indeed, for most clients the therapeutic setting is a natural, even fertile ground for the development of simple transference love. Clients bring with them to therapy expectations of being helped, guided, and supported as they try yet again to deal with the painful situation in which they find themselves. They have tried to resolve their problems by themselves or with others but have not been successful. They are now looking upon their therapist as a teacher and resource person, similar in several ways to those who, performing those functions in their childhood, helped them thrive or at least survive. They see their therapist as a person with whom they can enter into a simple, affiliative relationship.

As their therapist presses them for additional knowledge, however, clients can feel something more (Dalenberg, 2000). They experience a complex emotion: the pleasure of mutual love and the "pleasure in proximity, [the] desire for fuller knowledge of one another, [the] yearning for mutual identification and personality fusion" (Menninger, 1942, 272). Furthermore, if clients become aware of their therapist's caring countertransferential feelings, which is likely according to studies of the sensitivity of clients to therapists' moods and desires (Little, 1951; Dalenberg, 2000), it seems to clients as if their transferential love has been accepted. Consequently, they feel closer and closer to their therapists. They idealize them and respond with exaggerated deference and efforts to please (Dalenberg, 2000). They dare to reveal more and more of what they had previously withheld. They believe that they can be intimate with them in a fundamentally non-erotic way in order to bring about needed change, for their therapist has assured them—directly or indirectly—that what develops in therapy can be managed (Fox, 1998). All will go well.

Indeed, when all goes well, transference love assumes forms similar to love outside the therapeutic setting. Expectations of simply being accepted, nurtured, protected, and loved by a parental figure recede as expectations of working as a change agent within a context of positive emotional regard and reciprocal love emerge. Relatively immature, childish wishes and hopes give way to relatively mature adult realities.

At the same time, however, adolescent and adult development elicits sexual desire, which can cause non-erotic transference love to evolve into erotic transference, eroticized transference, or perversion transference (Bonasia, 2001).

## EROTIC TRANSFERENCE

Erotic transference is clients' normal sexual response toward persons outside therapy being transferred to their therapist. Except for being displaced, it is identical to love outside therapy. A non-pathological form of positive transference, erotic transference drives client and therapist into a relationship in which clients expect their therapist to cherish, respect, and love them as persons replete with sexual impulses, desires, and needs.

Erotic transference "occurs at the interface where mental and physiological experience come together" (Davies, 1994, 158-159). The greater the activation of erotic material in the unconscious, the closer client and therapist become at the level of fantasy (Mann, 1999).

Jung (1946) views erotic transference at an even more profound intrapsychic level. At a deeply unconscious level, erotic transference not only connects clients and therapists but also allows clients to find wholeness through reconciling the split-away parts of themselves that they are transferring to their therapist. Thus Ulanov (1984) regards erotic transference as a sign that clients want to be reconnected to a missing part of themselves, to some aspect of their own souls" (74).

Erotic love has as its foundation a willingness to share control of a relationship that blends love with other human feelings and aspirations. Neither fixed nor compulsive, it integrates both aggressive urges and sexuality with love and tenderness (Gabbard, 1989).

It brings with it ever-shifting feelings of love, shame, idealization, envy, and rage (Davies, 1994). Erotic transference is unlike lust, eroticised transference, and perversion transference in that, as a general rule, it develops gradually. When it first appears—perhaps in sexually-tinged overtones—erotic transference is marked by shame and embarrassment because clients recognize societal prohibitions against fulfilling their desires for their therapist (Gabbard, 1996). It then waxes and wanes and, as a norm, reaches its high point in the final stage of therapy (Etchegoyen, 1978), when it tends to manifest itself in strong urges to take advantage of opportunities to gratify sexual desires.

Freud (1912) writes that transference love begins as non-erotic in the strict sense of the word, but like all positive human relationships, it can be traced to an early erotic source: an intensely sensual mother-infant relationship. Thus when the mother-infant relationship is displaced to other people, it can be referred to as the maternal erotic transference, Wrye and Welles (1989) explain. All forms of love "are genetically linked with sexuality and have developed from purely sexual desires through a softening of their sexual aim" (5). In fact, Schaverien (1997) adds, "all human relations are in some way bound by eros [or love], and the early mother-infant bond is the first erotic relationship" (10).

Covington (1996) sees erotic transference as stemming from the infant's spontaneous, primitive need to feel wanted and loved and to experience that love physically. Part of the client's goal in the case of the erotic transference is to elicit the therapist's loving, accepting response so that the client can express love safely.

Freud (1912) explains that because "originally we knew only sexual objects, people who in our real life are merely admired or respected may still be sexual objects for our unconscious" (5-6). In therapy, a situation that "reinvokes the primal seduction or transformation of the infant by the mother" (Weatherill, 2000, 343), clients can come to see their therapist, a person they admire and respect, as a sexual object. Clients can desire sexual intimacy with their therapist. They can entertain fantasies of a sexual relationship. What was originally a maternal erotic transference can evolve into a form of transference that is basically genital (Wrye & Welles, 1989).

Seen in a slightly different light, clients who seek bodily contact with a mother figure can move from a desire for bodily oneness as a primitive form of contact to a desire for sexual union (Wrye & Welles, 1989). Efforts to meet the simple need for warm, pleasurable, physical contact pave the way for genital erotic transference. Pleasure that is primarily non-erotic gets fused with pleasure that is primarily erotic.

Clients unconsciously regard the resolution of their need for pleasure through sexuality as possible, even desirable, within the therapeutic relationship because of the intimacy of that setting and subtle but perceptible countertransferential love. As noted before, the exclusivity of the therapeutic setting can also bring out therapists' needs to love and be loved in more than platonic ways. Unilateral or mutual sexual attraction between them and clients can be the catalyst for transforming the therapeutic relationship. Therapists can imagine sexuality as a resolution of *their* need for affection. Then, under certain conditions, pathological forms of transference, namely eroticized or perverse transference, can arise.

## Eroticised Transference

In contrast to erotic transference, eroticised transference—also called erotisation—is a pathological displacement whereby actual expression of sexual desires is intended to heal painful, negative memories (Gabbard, 1994). (2) In the past, clients have experienced rejection and separation from those whose love they sought. Now, by acting out sexually, clients unconsciously hope to fulfill their desire for closeness and intimacy. As they and their therapist express their love physically, a sense of goodness will replace a sense of badness (Slochower, 1999), and their self-esteem will increase dramatically (Stacy, 1998). Inappropriate gratification of sexual desires will replace an appropriate quest for understanding and being understood (Freud, 1915). All other deep unconscious wishes will prove superfluous in the light of all-consuming sexual gratification.

In brief, eroticised transference represents a truncated form of love. In contrast to mature, seasoned love, eroticised transference consists of sexual components alone (Person, 1995). It makes sexual gratification the end-all of interpersonal relations.

Eroticised transference that appears in early stages of therapy is often precipitated by clients' lack of tolerance or by frustration (Eickhoff, 1998) and by a sense of losing control over the therapist and the therapeutic setting. Thus it serves as a defense both against fear of helplessness and feelings of powerlessness. By comparison, eroticised transference that arises at termination is usually a defense against working through the painful end of therapy and separation from a loved therapist.

According to Kernberg (1994), clients engaging in eroticised transference develop an intense, "impossible" sexualized love for an unavailable person: their therapist. Occasionally clients are able to generate marked rescue fantasies in their therapists and actually seduce them to meet their sexual needs. Most often, however, their therapists feel captured and bound rather than free to love. Experiencing a negative form of sexualized countertransference, their therapists wish to disconnect from an intensely needy, demanding client. Thus most clients come to realize how misguided or ineffectual their efforts to force love have really been. Their eroticised transference has resulted in a masochistic experience.

# Perversion Transference

Though perversion transference can be thought of as an extreme form of eroticised transference, it is more accurately conceptualized as a separate category. Even more pathological than eroticised transference, perversion transference is actually an erotic form of hate (Stoller, 1975). It is the hate once inflicted on the client by an abusive other and now projected onto the therapist as the client identifies with the abuser.

Signs of perversion transference are hostile provocation, sarcasm, rejection, emotional coldness, or intrusive forcefulness. "The pervert is not making love; he is making hate" (Kaplan, 1991, 40). The pervert is sadistically reducing the therapist to an inanimate object that can be used or abused and then discarded at will. And yet there is a highly sexualized quality to what is occurring. There may be no physical contact, but the client's penetrating and invasive words and actions make the therapist feel violated, humiliated, and exploited in his or her body. **(3)** The therapist's state of mind becomes aversive emotional confusion (Slochower, 1999).

Like eroticised transference, perversion transference is marked by obligation, compulsivity, fixation, and rigidity (Kaplan, 1991). Perverts have no choice. Their hatred is so deeply entrenched and so little understood that they cannot subject it to free choice. They must protect themselves against threatening disintegration or self-destruction (Springer, 1996).

Ironically, however, perversion transference may take an apparently opposite form: an attitude of extreme, unfailing kindness as clients "groom" their therapist (Gabbard, 1994). Clients may so normalize intimate exchanges that sexual material can be inserted almost without being noticed. At the same time, however, they may periodically reveal glimpses of abandoned children whose anger, anxiety, and sadness compels them to protect themselves against further abandonment by hating and seducing their therapist (Springer, 1996).

Gardner (1999) notes that clients engaged in perversion transference often become aggressive. They are attempting to gain mastery over painful humiliation, fear, and low self-esteem resultant from the abuse they once suffered, especially if it were sexual.

In some clients, the power imbalance of the therapeutic setting brings out discomfort and conflict over being dominated and a need to dominate or at least be equally powerful. In other clients, the therapist's omnipotent healer strivings uncover conflicts related to being healed by another, followed by an impulse to thwart that effort in any way imaginable (Searles, 1975). To the extent that clients have not resolved these conflicts, they fantasize using their therapists sexually as one way of denigrating them (Schaverien, 1997).

Conceptualizing perversion transference in a somewhat different way, Blum (1997) regards it as a sexualized defense against hate, hostility, humiliation, the desire to destroy, and the fear of being destroyed. It is a defense against the sadness, anger, and anxiety of having been deserted—and in that sense destroyed—

as a child. Clients are unconsciously hoping to seduce their therapists, instead of being seduced by them, and thus experience the satisfaction of revenge, Springer (1996) adds. In some cases, perversion transference even gives clients a sense of having eliminated, or at least become alienated from, the reality of the therapist. It puts an impersonal object—be it a fantasy, a gadget, or a pornographic image—between their desire for love and the person loved, the therapist (Khan, 1979).

Springer (1996) believes that at an even deeper level, perversion transference is a sexualized defense of the self: it stimulates a pseudo-wholeness and completeness. It protects against threatening disintegration through overwhelming excitation.

## Conditions under which Eroticized and Perversion Transference May Arise

The following are representative, pathological moderating conditions under which clients are prone to engage in eroticized or perversion transference:

- Clients with psychological injuries from early and intimate experiences with their mother fear intimacy, which reminds them of these early experiences (Chodorow, 1978). They desire but also fear intimate relationships, including one with their therapist, especially if their therapist's countertransference is noticeably positive. If their therapist enjoys working with them, looks forward to their coming, and sees their potential (Schaverien, 1997), these clients experience significant desires to act rather than feel.
- Clients with sexual abuse trauma experiences often fuse sexuality with affection. Especially if they are children and adolescents, almost any positive relationship takes on strong sexual overtones (Briere, 1996; Pearlman & Saakvitne, 1995; Dalenberg, 2000). These victims want to avoid remembering the pain of trauma. Yet they want to gain some kind of control over their traumatic experience (Kernberg, 1994). They, too, want to substitute action for remembering (Schafer, 1997). They want to either play the role of the aggressor themselves (Kernberg, 1994) or have the therapist play the role of a potential aggressor who chooses not to abuse them.
- Clients with a histrionic personality structure want to be able to attack an idealized other, partly because of guilt feelings (Kernberg, 1994). They want to punish their therapists for not returning their love even as they feel guilty for desiring that love. They want to seduce therapists into doing what is forbidden so that they also suffer from guilt. Sexualizing their relationship, they unconsciously assume, will begin the process.
- Clients with a dependent personality structure fear being engulfed and

thus virtually destroyed by therapists, who appear to have the power to engulf, to suck them back into the womb, to absorb them, and thus to annihilate them (Chasseguet-Smirgel, 1984). Clients want to avoid merging with one who not only loves them (Eickhoff, 1998) but also has the power to destroy them. They want to gain control over the one whose love is threatening to them. It is not that they do not want to be loved, especially in the sense of having bodily contact, but they do not want to merge with the one who loves. They want to control the therapist rather than engage in mutually modulated love (Kernberg, 1994).

- Clients with a strong need to appease therapists and keep them "sweet" want to seduce them. They desire to form a mutual admiration society wherein therapists are unable to confront them (Roth, 2001). After both parties make exaggerated transference love a means of idealization, idealization and erotic feelings will be linked (Slochower, 1999).
- Clients with a narcissistic personality structure want to prove how powerless therapists really are, how their help is not going to be fruitful, and how they are really not superior to their clients. At the same time, narcissistic clients are vulnerable to lustful feelings that make them feel at first anxious, aroused, disgusted, tormented, angry, and infatuated and then coerced into acting-out sexually rather than feeling.
- Clients with masochistic features and a long history of unhappy love affairs want to express their feelings of sexual inferiority to their therapist. They are frustrated, disappointed, or angry. They unconsciously believe that they will relieve their pain if they pursue what is forbidden with their therapists: the expression of eroticized transference love. Their transference love develops into intense, rigid, and stubborn persistence (Kernberg, 1994). "I want to be loved no matter how much it will hurt," the client unconsciously determines. "Even if it is forbidden, I will pursue my therapist's love for me."
- Clients who have great difficulty with uncertainty want to eliminate traces of a complex therapeutic relationship (Britton, 1985). Rather than deal with the ambiguities of transference love that cannot be realized as such, they want to transform it into a clear, simple expression of sexualized love. This condition is exacerbated when therapists appear strong and centered. Clients want to fuse with them in order take on their core sense of self (Dalenberg, 2000).
- Overstimulated clients with painful feelings of being excluded want to seize control of the situation. If their therapist is overly reflective or introspective, they experience a primal scene in which they are aroused by another's activity but unable to respond in return. Unable to participate in a dialogue with their therapist, they project erotic meaning into the therapist's monologue (Schafer, 1997).
- Clients with experiences of feeling attacked, suffocated, or deadened by apparently caring parental communication want to eroticize and idealize their parental-figure therapist. Instead of facing the pain re-

> lated to their biological parent's passive-aggressive expression of hostility, clients eroticize and idealize their therapist's involvement. Ultimately, sensual desire becomes a camouflage for a condensation of painfully charged non-erotic experiences along with sensual and erotic wishes (Slochower, 1999).

Space permits only one vignette as an example of a client with such serious psychopathology, including a dissociative identity disorder, that she sexualizes her relationship with her therapist in multiple and complicated ways.

*One of the first things the therapist noted was how her adult client spoke like a young girl and fidgeted in her seat like a child. She had attempted suicide many times, switched drugs for booze, ran away in her teens, began stripping, and found men that pimped her out.*

*At the same time, the therapist found her client strangely sweet, smart, and desirous of crossing the invisible line that separated her from the world she wanted, a world of higher education and employment. In short order, the therapist began functioning as a social worker, helping her client fill out college entrance forms, locating suitable jobs, and even asking friends to watch the client's daughter.*

*The client responded to these sincere but misguided efforts on the part of her therapist with revealing her sex life in detail. She began speaking graphically about her experiences with men even though her therapist gave evidence of being uncomfortable and she knew it. Finally the client described in detail her fantasy of climbing in bed with her therapist where she would be safe and warm and expressing her love in the only way she knew. The following session, the client forced an impassioned kiss on the lips of her therapist, pressing her to the desk behind her and trying to tear off her blouse.*

## Non-Erotic Countertransference Love

As a general rule, countertransference love begins non-erotically. It develops from simple empathy as therapists resonate with persons whose pain is real, whose life is adverse, and whose efforts to correct a situation have failed. Subsequently, both male and female therapists fall quickly and naturally into taking on expected maternal roles and performing nurturing and nursing functions (Greenacre, 1954). They feel positive about their clients. To simple empathy they add caring and loving responses to their clients, who act intuitively in accordance with an observation attributed to Ferenczi: "It is the physician's love that heals the patient" (Gerrard, 1999, 29). They, as therapists, unconsciously follow a similar dictum of Freud (1905): "Essentially, one might say, the cure is effected by love" (Freud & Jung, 1974, 8-9).

Thus the core of therapists' response to most of their clients is non-erotic countertransference love (Fox, 1998).

## Erotic Countertransference

However, with or without transferential stimulation, countertransference love can be sexualized from the very beginning. Indeed, "the therapist's desire [can ignite] the transference" (Schaverien, 1997, 6) in that the therapist brings to the therapeutic endeavor an erotic unconscious and an erotic subjectivity (Mann, 1999).

In addition, non-erotic countertransference can become sexualized during the therapeutic process simply because therapists and clients are involved in a frequently occurring intimate exchange. Clients speak to their therapist about their most intimate thoughts and feelings behind closed doors. Week after week therapists receive private and highly personal revelations that remind them and their clients of the early mother-child relationship and the sexualized oedipal relationship.

Yet another phenomenon—and one that seems unlikely at first—helps to explain the development of erotic countertransference: the need for therapists to manage, even dominate, their purely positive feelings for their clients for the sake of therapeutic progress. Besides being caring and empathic, therapists must challenge their clients to do the hard personal work upon which insight into dysfunctional patterns and change of those patterns depends (Stein, 1981). In order for their clients to develop more mature attitudes and act more independently, therapists must permit their basic maternal non-erotic love to evolve into a more egalitarian non-erotic love (Freud, 1909). (4)

If clients want to move from dependence to interdependence, all is well. Non-erotic countertransference love, which becomes a blend of maternal and collegial love, remains a positive force. It provides a substructure that strengthens the therapeutic alliance.

However, if clients do not want to move from dependence to independence, therapists must make difficult choices that, in turn, affect the nature of their countertransferential love. While there are other possible developments, the following two scenarios are relatively common.

If therapists choose to do the work *for* clients, infantalizing elements make non-erotic countertransferential love erotic. Therapists engage in fantasies of a mother-baby fusion that keeps clients psychologically dependent. Unconsciously wanting to meet their needs for bodily contact (Lester, 1985), therapists want to avoid separateness at all costs. Then, as in the case of transference, images of bodily contact that are at first non-erotic become erotic (Welles & Wrye, 1991).

In the second scenario, if therapists choose to expect clients to do their own serious work, anxiety or fear infuse their non-erotic maternal countertransferential love. As therapists await the cooperation of their clients, they tend to create erotic fantasies in an effort to quiet their distressful feelings. By this time, of course, it is likely that clients' transference love has also become erotic, and, consequently, has been providing additional stimuli for sexualized countertransference. Indeed, clients' tendency to discuss sexual material in therapy is the third most common characteristic of clients to whom therapists are attracted

(Pope et al., 1994). Sexualized transference love easily becomes a trigger for sexual countertransference in therapists, Dalenberg (2000) concludes.

## Eroticized Countertransference and Perversion Countertransference

Although one would hope that eroticized countertransference and even more so perversion countertransference are exceedingly rare, under certain circumstances they do arise. As therapists begin to feel the burden of the therapeutic work, angry feelings and aggressive urges can begin to taint maternal erotic love. Countertransferential love can even disappear in the face of growing dislike or actual hate.

In contrast with erotic countertransference, which is an ego-syntonic and energizing human reaction to feeling loved and wanting to love in return, eroticized countertransference and perversion countertransference are ego-dystonic. They are pathological responses to highly exaggerated needs, impulses, or compulsions to love or be loved at any cost. They are very similar, if not identical, to eroticised transference and perversion transference. Their gratification leads to a blatant disregard for reality outside of therapy and professional ethics and to a total denial of responsibility to non-therapeutic others as well as clients.

However, therapists who act-out their eroticized or perversion countertransference somehow believe that they can discharge their disguised archaic instincts with impunity (Bachant & Adler, 1997). They hold the delusion that one can give sexual expression to hatred and hostility without causing harm.

## Conditions under which Eroticized and Perversion Countertransference May Arise

Countertransference tends to become pathological under the following moderating conditions. Like transferential moderating conditions, the following descriptions of pathology characteristic of certain therapists are representative rather than all-inclusive.

- Therapists with significant guilt feelings want to be punished for their transgressions (Kernberg, 1994). They give their countertransferential love a sexual nature, knowing that pursuing what is forbidden will bring them well-deserved punishment.
- Therapists with narcissistic tendencies want to enact their powerful rescue fantasies (Kernberg, 1994). They will save clients craving sexual expressions of love from those strong desires by being sexual with them—in fantasy if not in fact. Especially prone to do so are therapists who are narcissistically imbalanced or extremely needy because of grief-inducing life experiences like unwanted divorce or debilitating

illness.

- Female therapists with strong masochistic tendencies treating highly seductive narcissistic male clients want to make up for the inadequacies of other people in their clients' past (Jacobs, 1986). They feel coerced into becoming persons who meet the needs of demanding, self-entitled clients (Kernberg, 1994).
- Therapists with characterological impatience want their clients to achieve a fuller sense of relatedness. They are irritated by the distance their clients keep from them (Smith, 2000). They may even feel dismissed by their clients and hence wish to use sexual closeness to avoid that painful feeling.
- Therapists with proclivities toward envy want to side for or against clients, usually adolescents, with relative sexual freedom. When they take the side of their clients, they lose objectivity, which can lead to boundary violations (Kernberg, 1998).
- Therapists with omnipotent healer strivings or a strong savior complex want to overcome the resistance of clients who try to thwart them. They throw their sexuality onto the balance in an effort to fulfill their mission (Searles, 1975).

Again, there is space for only one example of how non-pathological erotic transference can become pathological. It is the same case as the one in the section on transference.

*The therapist found her client strangely sweet, not as rough around the edges as so many of the women she knew with similar backgrounds. The therapist liked the fact that her client was motivated to earn a degree and find gainful employment. "What would be wrong with helping her in practical ways?" she asked herself.*

*The therapist herself had major health problems that limited her energy. She knew what a difference it made when others helped her and when they didn't.*

*So she began to assist her client in the practical steps she needed to take, taking less time for engaging in cultural and intellectual pursuits with friends and frequently evaluating how well she was functioning in her extended therapeutic tasks. It wasn't easy, but she would not let her client down, especially when she seemed unable to accomplish her goal-related tasks.*

*Indeed, the therapist felt responsible for her client—as she had for her mentally challenged mother—and guilty when things failed to work out for her. On one occasion, she even left her office to go settle down her client's child alters so that the adults could study, after which she went to a bar in order to ease her stress.*

*Though the therapist never made it a practice of hugging her other clients, she began to feel that an occasional hug of encouragement would go a long way with this particular client. She, at least her child alters, needed physical contact, the therapist reasoned, in order to feel loved. She, a therapist, could easily set limits as to how long the hug lasted. It would definitely be brief.*

*She could not prevent sexual fantasies from occurring in her own mind, however, fantasies which at first involved a simple, loving gesture and then evolved into acts of domination and control. She could only decide never to share these pictures with her client. They would do her client no good. No, she would just offer an occasional hug to comfort her client.*

*Her client, in turn, seemed to respond positively to this physical contact. Indeed, she simply thanked her therapist for being so kind, which made her sexual advance a total surprise.*

One final point is crucial for understanding the issue of pathological countertransference love. No matter what the psychological condition of the therapist, denial of its presence is a greater danger than any pathological condition in and of itself. It is when realities are denied that they are most likely to be acted out.

# Appropriate Responses of Therapists to Sexualized Transference and Countertransference Love

The following guidelines are intended to provide therapists with the rudiments of dealing with sexualized transference love and countertransference love, including preventing them from developing into pathological forms.

## Abstinence

Denying gratification of sexualized transferential and countertransferential love is the first rule of therapy. Without exception, enactment of this kind of love must be frustrated. Understanding the role of transferential and countertransferential sexualized love must replace acting out one's desire of loving and being loved.

Beginning with Freud (1915), both theorists and practitioners have emphasized the untold harm done by therapists' failure to abstain from sexualized transference and countertransference love. They have warned clearly and forcefully of the danger that results from supposing that clients and therapists are free to express their love in physical ways. Therapists who assume that they can avail themselves of that freedom with impunity—believe that they can meet each their clients' and their own sexual needs and yet continue to work together productively as therapist and client—create a seriously impaired therapeutic environment. They harm their clients profoundly.

Thus therapists must be convinced that when clients' "advances [are] returned it [may be] a great triumph for [them] but a complete defeat for the treatment" (Freud, 1915, 164). An actualized love relationship destroys clients' susceptibility to be influenced through therapy. Once they have achieved sexual gratification, they will experience deep remorse and once again repress the pain connected with it. "It is, therefore, just as disastrous for the [treatment] if the [client's] craving for love is gratified as if it is suppressed" (Freud, 1915, 164.) Put succinctly, "the treatment must be carried out in abstinence" (Freud, 1915, 163). Clients and therapists are strictly obligated to refrain from any form of physical expression of their cravings for love and affection.

It is therapists who bear primary responsibility for the maintenance of abstinence. It is they who must set limits for themselves. They must replace their desire for therapist-client sexual gratification with the "counterweight" of a greater love, either the love of truth and one's obligations to self and non-therapeutic others or the passion for healing others (Freud, 1937).

With certain clients therapists must also set firm boundaries. They must refuse to be invaded, lapped up, or consumed by their clients' invasive wishes. Therapists must even go so far as to tell clients who are inclined to act out their sexual fantasies, especially those with highly erotised transference that is charged with violence (Kernberg, 1998), that therapy will be terminated if they do not cease and desist.

## Tolerance

On the other hand, abstinence should not be interpreted as "deprivation of everything that the [client] desires" (Freud, 1915, 163). Abstinence does not mean steering away from sexualized transference love in and of itself, becoming cold and aloof, silent and distant— reactions implying that sexualized transference love is unacceptable, even disgusting. For these responses reinforce clients' pathological sense of being unlovable (Gerrard, 1999) and the low self-regard they already have. Besides inducing guilt, these responses discourage clients from trying to understand their intrinsically human desire to develop mature sexual relationships.

To begin with, abstinence does not automatically lead to terminating or transferring clients who disclose transference love, for such referrals cause disturbance in a significant proportion of clients for years afterwards (Dalenberg, 2000). Instead, therapists need to treat sexualized transference love the same way that they treat all other forms of transference: acknowledge its existence and allow it to develop to the point of revealing its potential force, underpinnings, accompanying affects, and the developmental forms it could take. Therapists then need to decode sexualized transference love, hypothesize about it, and test their hypotheses through observation or interpretation and subsequent dialogue with clients. Therapists may even need to help clients explore appropriate ways of gratifying their sexual desires outside of therapy, for clients may not be able to apply newly acquired knowledge about their therapeutic relationship to other relationships (Westen & Gabbard, 2002).

Without question, therapists also need to experience and process their own sexualized countertransferential feelings, thoughts, fantasies and somatic states (Davies, 1994). They need to hold, observe, and decode sexualized countertransference love and the problematic feelings that often accompany it: dislike, hatred, anger, and fear due to a sense of enmeshment, disgust, or repulsion.

In order to accomplish this work, therapists need to hold—and help clients hold—the belief that simple forms of sexualized transference and countertransference love are neither immature nor pathological. They are respected, respectable, normal human responses to others. Sexualized transference naturally echoes in therapists' countertransferential sensations and desires (Davies, 1994) just as sexualized countertransference naturally echoes in clients' transference.

Furthermore, therapists need to hold the belief that their countertransferential sexual fantasies may reveal the presence of conflictual sexuality in the history of clients who have been abused and still need to process that abuse (Solomon, 1997). In an effort to obtain important information about clients' subjective experience of abuse (Slochower, 1999), therapists may even need to let their fantasies develop into a narrative of an imaginary sexual relationship (Kernberg, 1994). The narrative may portray them as being humiliated, for example, which reveals that their client is expressing love in ways that humiliate or demean the one who is supposedly being loved. Conversely, the narrative may reveal that, as an object of their client's love, therapists feel both cherished and possessed, which suggests that their client is unable to value the object of his or her love without becoming possessive.

*Her client complained of feeling sexually unattractive, claimed that his girlfriend found him so unattractive that she wanted to leave him. As much as this hurt him, what hurt him more was imagining her with another man who would satisfy her sexually in ways he couldn't. Some "onlooker" would compare him to her new lover and find him strikingly inferior. He would experience extreme humiliation, the client imagined.*

*Strangely, the therapist began to experience a strong sexual attraction to her client—strangely because he felt just the opposite. At first the therapist was tempted to attribute her sexual fantasies to mere male-female dynamics, to think she was simply bringing her own issues to the therapy session, and to dismiss what was happening as therapeutically meaningless to her client.*

*She chose to wait with this dismissal, however, and to allow a narrative to begin. At first the "story" was simple: her client was sexually attractive. But then she notices that she felt used. He cancelled sessions at the last minute, then suggested he should not have to pay his late notice fee. The therapist came to realize that her client was thinking of her as a possession to which he had a right.* (5) *She began to wonder if this may also have been his girlfriend's experience.*

To summarize, even though therapists are usually more comfortable in the role of idealized mother than sexual partner (Slochower, 1999), they must tolerate the full range of their loving feelings toward their clients (Coen, 1996). They must prepare themselves to understand their clients' unconscious sexual conflicts by admitting their own sexuality. (6)

They must allow their feelings to unfold while resisting the impulsive urge either to act out or to interpret prematurely. They must be open to "sinking into" sexual fantasies without "drowning" in them (Gabbard, 1994). Or as Welles and Wrye (1991) phrase it, they must be able to tolerate the "heat" without fanning the flames. They must become comfortable with viewing themselves as erotic, both in a maternal sense and an adult sense.

## Working toward Understanding

Understanding sexualized transferential love and the feelings accompanying it begins with talking about it. Thus clients must overcome—and be helped to overcome—their fear of being considered inappropriate, even dangerous, because of their natural impulses and desires. This is especially important if these impulses and desires have acquired sexually degrading overtones, as when clients unconsciously want to feel in control by overpowering and humiliating their therapist (Guttman, 1985).

Understanding sexual transference then moves to considering the possibility that this form of transference love is based in early-life conflictual experiences still needing to be resolved (Gabbard, 1994). Indeed, therapists must introduce most clients to the fact that some elements of very early relationships may be remembered only in erotic fantasies. Clients may "recall" their parents' hostility, for instance, which was hidden behind apparently caring communications, only through their erotic urges toward their parent-substitute, their therapist. They may long not as much for sexual experiences as for unconditional positive regard that will erase memories of their parents' negative feelings toward them. In other cases, clients' sexualized transference love may be a "camouflage for a condensation of painfully charged non-erotic experience along with sensual and erotic wishes" (Slochower, 1999, 1127). Displaced desires may be largely adult feelings or move in and out of adult and pre-adult stages (Schaverien, 1997). Thus exploring sexualized transference love, far focusing exclusively on its erotic aspects, can lead to the resolution of conflicts resultant from exceedingly important earlier experiences (Slochower, 1999).

It is also helpful for therapists to categorize sexualized transference, including its perverse aspects, as both real and unreal. Erotic feelings are certainly real, therapists can explain to clients. Though they may be partly displaced from an earlier time in life, they can be—and often are—as real as non-therapeutic erotic love feelings.

In another sense, however, erotic feelings may be unreal in the sense that they are largely substituting for other problematic feelings, as noted earlier. Love may be defending against anger, for example. Or sex may be defending against genuine, self-sacrificing love or against the grief associated with loss or termination (Gabbard, 1996). Love may be a defense against memories of abuse and neglect, just as indifference may be a defense against memories of being "attacked, suffocated or deadened by apparently caring parental communications" (Slochower, 1999, 1127). Lust may be defending against other troubling feelings of love (Jacobs, 1986). Transference love may be defending against the fear of loving maturely outside of therapy. It may be a resistance to completing therapeutic work, learning to love others, and thus preparing for real life, where love can find a proper place (Freud, 1915).

Along the same lines, therapists must help clients realize that though they may experience their therapist's refusal to act out sexually as a "rejection" of *them*, that response is actually an effort to place deep longings for love in a realistic light. Rather than being a confirmation of prohibitions against their sexual longings or a confirmation of their sexual inferiority, that response respects sexuality *within* personhood (Kernberg, 1994).

Therapists must also help their clients realize that even complex, perverse forms of sexualized transference love can be understood and worked through. If correctly understood, transference love can become a vehicle for discovering how to defend oneself against painful self-realizations and avoid being ruled by unproductive fantasies (Arcaya & Gerber, 1990). It can become a valuable means of learning to distinguish between what is appropriate to pursue and what is not. It can serve as a guide to relating in satisfying ways outside of therapy.

Of course, at the same time that therapists recognize sexualized transference love when it surfaces in therapy, they must not "find" it where it does not exist. Therapists must be careful not to attribute their own arousal to the seduction of their clients (Gabbard, 1996). Male therapists, in particular, must be careful to distinguish genuine transference love from their own sexual arousal, which they may be projecting onto their clients.

Equally important to helping clients understand their sexualized transference love is therapists' responsibility to explore how their own countertransference love may be affecting or being affected by transferential dynamics. Therapists may need to focus, for example, on how clients' transference projections are placing them in a powerful, idealized position and, consequently, how they may be want to act out a corresponding role. Or therapists may need to concentrate on retaining or quickly regaining solid boundaries around their own countertransferential desires so that their clients remain safe (Solomon, 1997).

*She was not particularly handsome, but her fun-loving, optimistic attitude proved charismatic. In time, her therapist noticed her attraction to her client and how much he looked forward to her sessions. He also recognized his pleasure in dwelling on thoughts about her, considerably more so than other clients. Finally, he became aware of sexual feelings toward her.*

*Instead of interpreting his countertransference, however, the therapist dealt with his feelings by assuring her client that he was making enough progress to schedule less frequently.*

*Fortunately, the therapist realized through consultation what he was actually doing. He was avoiding dealing with her own problematic countertransferential love by convincing himself that his client was close to finishing. This gave him the opportunity to revise his plan. He would acknowledge his countertransference and link it with a transference interpretation that reflected the client's behavior.*

*"I find myself attracted to you," he said at the beginning of the next session, "and wanting to avoid potential problems by requesting that you come less fre-*

*quently. I wonder if you have noticed something sexual in your behavior toward me."*

*"No," she said. "But I am extremely attracted to many men. I told you about my two marriages but not about the half-dozen affairs I've had. I just can't feel good if a man isn't in my life in a sexual way—actually more than one man—because I have affairs when I am married as well as divorced."*

*With this disclosure, client and therapist were able to increase the client's understanding of her problematic behavior. Eventually they even dealt with the sexual abuse she had experienced during adolescence and the pleasurable aspects of it.*

## Benefiting from Love in the Transference and Countertransference

If clients are helped to understand their sexualized transference, they can establish symbolic links where, previously, they were mobilizing mindless action (Freud, 1915). They can discover a desire for true self-experience that lies beneath their idealizing and sexualizing of their therapists. If they work to understand what is happening rather than act on it, far from regressing, they can experience a generative shift leading to deeper levels of self-experience (Slochower, 1999). They can experience themselves and others as profoundly good, genuinely desirable, and actually desired.

Clients who understand their sexualized transference can then meet some of their deepest, most intimate desires with words (Covington, 1996). By understanding and dealing with this displaced material, clients can transform immature love into mature love. They can move from "I love you because I am loved" and "I love you because I need you" to "I am loved because I love" and "I need you because I love you" (Fromm, 1976).

Clients can also realize that with their erotic, eroticized, and even perversion transference comes the opportunity to mourn, perhaps for the first time, the loss of early parental figures whose expression of love was so combined with aggression and fear that it was ineffectual, even harmful (Baker, 1993; Slochower, 1999). Their grief is appropriate because what they always wanted from parental figures was and still is unattainable (Maroda, 2000). They must actively provide love for themselves rather than passively yearn for it from others.

Moreover, through appropriate self-love, clients can renounce dysfunctional, limiting boundaries of the self and acquire—if not confirm—their basic sense of goodness (Kernberg, 1994). They can free themselves to enter into unselfish, mutually satisfying relationships.

In sum, clients whose therapists bring into consciousness their unconscious transferential love are able to control their desires and needs (Freud, 1915). They can use powerful psychic forces rather than be used by them. They can then actively re-create life rather than passively repeat it (Bachant & Adler, 1997). They can fashion their lives in a wholesome, purposeful way instead of relying on dysfunctional coping mechanisms learned during early life (Rioch, 1943). They can then use their newly acquired skills to develop loving relationships in the future.

For transference love that is accepted, understood, and processed deepens clients' capacity for relatedness (Schaverien, 1997). It enables them to enjoy an integration of self through loving communication with another. It lets them "experience the human environment as part of the wholeness of their own self" (Rosiello, 2000, 65).

With regard to interpreting sexualized countertransference love to clients, theorists have taken two positions. Some believe that, since this work is more often than not dictated by therapists'—not clients'—needs, it can easily lead to negative outcomes (Dalenberg, 2000). It can unnecessarily distract clients from focusing on their own work.

Others believe, however, that clients who understand the sexualized countertransference at work in their therapy are empowered to apply that knowledge to situations outside of therapy. If client and therapist are conflicted over boundaries, for instance, an interpretation that acknowledges the normalcy of the therapist's sexual attraction and sets clear boundaries can both contribute significantly to successful therapy and serve as a model for wholesome non-therapy relationships. Indeed, clients who clearly recall their therapists' disclosure of countertransference love regard their therapy as successful. In contrast, if therapists choose not to disclose their sexualized countertransference love but instead transfer clients to other therapists or otherwise distance from them, clients tend to feel punished (Dalenberg, 2000).

## Seeking Consultation

When therapists experience sexual arousal in their work with clients or find themselves the object of their clients' intense sexual desires, they must seriously consider consulting with an experienced colleague (Gabbard, 1996). Rather than risking either acting-out or feeling dead, dull, or silent through efforts to defend against acting-out (Welles & Wrye, 1991), therapists do well to process their sexualized countertransference love with knowledgeable consultants. Therapists thereby not only discover their own potential for erotisation and perversions but also become skillful in helping clients address their love-based desires and tendencies.

It is not uncommon, of course, for therapists seeking consultation regarding their sexualized countertransference love to have to overcome their anxiety, embarrassment, and feelings of guilt. Not seeking consultation for this sensitive matter, however, can result in even greater difficulties like Grievance Boards complaints, lawsuits, and debilitating guilt.

# Summary

To say that transference and countertransference love are powerful forces both for good and for evil is an understatement. Displaced love handled poorly can make clients resolve never to return to therapy, for their experience has been diminishing and hurtful, if not outright harmful. What they thought was good, perhaps even holy, becomes regrettable, even horrifying. Poorly handled transference and countertransference love has led to continued conflict over immature expressions of love and mature thoughts and behavior that were originally designed to meet their needs to love and be loved.

By contrast, transference love and countertransference love that are handled well can make therapy an extremely rewarding experience. Their therapeutic relationship has been empowering, strengthening, nourishing, and life-giving. They have felt both cherished and respected as their therapists channeled their countertransference love into unconditional acceptance, profound respect, and willingness to explore fundamental human desires for love. They have learned how to deal with equally difficult situations outside of therapy. Having learned to tolerate passions of love and hate, they have undergone a maturation that would have not otherwise occurred (Coen, 1996). By processing transference and countertransference, they have learned the deepest lessons of the heart (Bachant & Adler, 1997).

It is no wonder that Mann (1999) can write so eloquently:

> In the psychic life [and, consequently, a therapeutic encounter] it is often the erotic that offers the most transformational opportunities in the life of the individual. The erotic in therapy may be thought of as incorporating regressive transference [and countertransference] elements alongside the search for a new transformational [experience] that will lead the individual into a new kind of relationship (80).

# Endnotes

(1) Klein (1937) explains that clients need to arouse their therapist's love in order to discover their own capacities to love and feel lovable, much as infants find their love feelings in response to, not prior to, being loved and cared for. However, some clients are unable to do so because for them love implies a dependence marked by humiliation or inferiority too painful for them to experience again (Kernberg, 1994). Rather than once again risk depending on another for love or even affection, they must insist on being in total control. Thus they approach bonding with an unconscious sadomasochistic intent to inflict or accept pain in the place of love, a narcissistic intent to receive the love to which they are entitled and to punish the giver for even slight infractions, or both. If their activity can in any way be thought of as transference love, it is a perversion.

(2) Although eroticised transference is sometimes thought of as a form of erotic transference (Gabbard, 1996) because of their similarities, eroticised transference is more accurately conceptualized as a defense *against* erotic transference (Slochower, 1999). It is a means of avoiding the pain of mature, erotic love. Because of its intense and frenzied

characteristics, eroticised transference has also been considered a hypersexualized variant of the manic defense.

(3) In a non-therapeutic setting, when perversion transference is acted out, the pervert is touching another's body inappropriately as well as selfishly intruding against the other's will into both his or her mind and body. This should not be surprising, for the unconscious desire to degrade or hurt others is at the center of erotic excitement for one engaged in perversion transference (Solomon, 1997).

(4) In tolerating their own erotic maternal countertransference, therapists do not give into an impulse to rebirth their clients. They do not set out to remake them. If rebirth or remaking is to occur, effective therapists know, clients will accomplish it themselves in their own good time. Therapists must simply experience, contain, and make accessible to clients their erotic issues (Welles & Wrye, 1991).

(5) After projecting their erotic feelings into their therapist, some clients attempt to control the therapist in order to avoid a feared sexual attack from him or her (Kernberg, 1994). In so doing, clients attempt to be a parent to their therapist (Doctor, 1999), protecting him or her from a painful experience.

(6) It is more acceptable to therapists to think of themselves as maternal figures than potential lovers. It is correspondingly more acceptable to clients to think of themselves as non-sexual children than sexual adults. But erotic fantasies, impulses, and desires do occur, and therapists are prone to defend against them.

# REFERENCES


Adler, G., & Rhine, M. W. (1992). The selfobject function of projective identification. In N.G. Hamilton (Ed.), *From inner sources: New directions in object relations psychotherapy* (pp.139-162). Northvale, NJ: Jason Aronson.

Alpert, M. C. (1992). Accelerated empathic therapy: A new short-term dynamic psychotherapy. *International Journal of Short-Term Psychotherapy, 7*, 133-156.

Alpert, M. C., Cohen, N. L., Martz, M., & Robinson, C. (1980). Electroencephalographic analysis: A methodology for evaluating psychotherapeutic process. *Psychiatry Research, 2*, 323-329.

Ambady, N., & Gray, H. (2002). On being sad and mistaken: mood effects on the accuracy of thin slice judgments. *Journal of Personality and Social Psychology, 83*, 947-961.

Anchin, J. C., & Keisler, D.J. (Eds.) (1982). *Handbook of interpersonal psychotherapy*. NY: Pergamon.

Andersen, S., Reznik, I., & Manzella, L. (1996). Eliciting facial affect, motivation, and expectancies in transference: Significant-other representations in social relations. *Journal of Personality and Social Psychology, 71*, 1108-1129.

Arcaya, J. M., & Gerber, G. L. (1990). An object relations approach to the treatment of child abuse. *Psychotherapy, 27*, 619-626.

Arlow, J. (1985). Some technical problems of countertransference. *Psychoanalytic Quarterly, 54*, 164-174.

Atwood, G. E., Stolorow, R. D., & Trop, J. L. (1989). Impasses in psychoanalytic therapy: A royal road. *Contemporary Psychoanalysis, 25*, 554-573.

Bacal, H. A. (1990) Optimal responsiveness and the specificity of self object experience. In H.A. Bacal (Ed.), *Optimal responsiveness: How therapists heal their patients* (pp. 141-170). Northvale, NJ: Jason Aronson.

Bachant, J., & Adler, D. (1997). Transference: Co-constructed or brought to the interaction? *Journal of the American Psychoanalytic Association, 45*, 1097-1120.

Baker, R. (1993). The patient's discovery of the psychoanalyst as a new object. *International Journal of Psycho-Analysis, 74*, 1223-1233.

Balamuth, R. (1998).e-membering the body; A psychoanalytic study of presence and absence of the lived body. In L. Aron & F.S. Anderson (Eds.), *Relational perspectives on the body* (pp. 263-286). Hillsdale, NJ: The Analytic Press, Inc.

Balint, M. (1968). *The basic fault: Therapeutic aspects of regression*. London: Tavistock

Pub.
Banon, E., Evan-Grenier, M., & Bond, M. (2001). Early transference interventions with male patients in psychotherapy. *Journal of Psychotherapy Practice and Research, 10,* 79-92.
Basham, K. (2004). Book Review of J. Mishne's *Multiculturalism and the therapeutic process. Smith College Studies in Social Work, 74,* 457-462.
Bauer, G. P., & Mills, J. A. (1989). Use of transference in the here and how: Patient and therapist resistance. *Psychotherapy, 26,* 112-119.
Beard, D. K. (1992). Somatic knowing with the psychosomatic patient: An answer in kind. *Unpublished doctoral dissertation.* California School of Professional Psychology, Los Angeles.
Benatar, M., Chapman, K. M., & Rutkove, S. B. (2004). Repetitive nerve stimulation for the evaluation of peripheral nerve hyperexcitability. *Journal of the Neurological Sciences. 221,* 47-52.
Benedek, T. (1953). Dynamics of the countertransference. *Bulletin of the Menninger Clinic, 17,* 201-208.
Bernstein, J. (1992). The research method in the making of a psychoanalyst. *Modern Psychoanalysis, 17,* 183-195.
Beutler, L.E. (2000). David and Goliath: When empirical and clinical standards of practice meet. *American Psychologist, 55(9),* 997-2007.
Bezoari, M., Ferro, A., & Politi, P. (1994). Listening, interpreting and psychic change in the analytic dialogue. *International Forum of Psychoanalysis, 3,* 35-41.
Bigras, J. (1979). The interminable analysis of countertransference. *Psychoanalytic Review, 66,* 311-322.
Binder, J. L. (1996). Research findings on short-term psychodynamic therapy techniques. In F. Flack (Ed.), *The Hatherleigh guide to psychotherapy* (pp. 79-97). NY: Hatherleigh Press.
Bion, W. R. (1961). *Experiences in groups.* London: Tavistock.
Bion, W. R. (1967). Notes on memory and desires. *Psychoanalytic Forum, 2,* 272-273 and 279-280.
Bird, B. (1922). Notes on transference: Universal phenomenon and the hardest part of analysis. *Journal of the American Psychoanalytic Association, 20,* 267-301.
Blum, H. P. (1986a). Countertransference and the theory of technique: Discussion. *Journal of the American Psychoanalytic Association, 34,* 309-328.
Blum, H. P. (1986b). Countertransference and technique: Discussion. *Journal of the American Psychoanalytic Association, 34,* 329.
Blum, H. P. (1997). Clinical and developmental dimensions of hate. *Journal of the American Psychoanalytic Association, 45(2),* 359-375.
Boesky, D. (1982). Acting out: A reconsideration of the concept. *International Journal of Psycho-Analysis, 63,* 39-55.
Boesky, D. (1990). The psychoanalytic process and its components. *Psychoanalytic Quarterly, 59,* 550-594.
Bohart, A. C. (1993). Experiencing: The basis of psychotherapy. *Journal of Psychotherapy Integration, 3,* 51-68.
Bollas, C. (1983). Expressive use of the countertransference. *Contemporary Psychoanalysis, 19,* 1-34.
Bollas, C. (1987). *The shadow of the object: Psychoanalysis of the unthought known.* London: Free Association Books.
Bonasia, E. (2001). The countertransference: Erotic, erotised and perverse. *The International Journal of Psychoanalysis, 82,* 249-262.

Bond, M., Banon, E., & Grenier, M. (1998). Differential effects of interventions on the therapeutic alliance with patients with personality disorders. *Journal of Psychotherapy Practice and Research, 7*, 301-318.

Bonnet, G. (1991). *Le transfert dans la clinique psychanalytique.* Paris: Presses University France.

Bornstein, R. F. (1993). Implicit perception, implicit memory, and the recovery of unconscious material in psychotherapy. *Journal of Nervous and Mental Disease, 181*, 337-344.

Bostanov V., & Kotchoubey B. (2004). Recognition of affective prosody: Continuous wavelet of event-related brain potentials to emotional exclamations. *Psychophysiology, 41*, 259-268.

Bowlby, J. (1980). *Attachment and loss:* Loss, sadness and depression (Vol. 3). London: Hogarth Press.

Boyer, L. B. (1961). Provisional evaluation of psycho-analysis with few parameters in the treatment of schizophrenia. *International Journal of Psycho-Analysis, 42*, 389-403.

Boyer, L. B. (1997). The verbal squiggle game in treating the seriously disturbed patient. In V.D. Volken and S. Akhtar (Eds.), *The seed of madness* (pp. 155-176). Madison, CN: International Universities Press.

Brabennder, V. M. (1987). Vicissitudes of countertransference in inpatient group psychotherapy. *International Journal of Group Psychotherapy, 37*, 549-567.

Bremner, J. D., Scott, T. M., & Delaney, R. C. (1993). Deficits in short-term memory in posttraumatic stress disorder. *American Journal of Psychiatry, 150*, 1015-1019.

Brenner, C. (1976). *Psychoanalytic technique and psychic conflict.* NY: International Universities Press.

Brenner, C. (1982). *The mind in conflict.* New York: International University Press.

Briere, J. (1996). *Therapy for adults molested as children: Beyond survival* (2nd ed.). NY: Springer.

Britton, R. (1985). The missing link: Parental sexuality in the Oedipus couples. In J. Steiner (Ed.), *The Oedipus complex today: Clinical implications* (pp. 83-101). London: Karnac.

Brodbeck, H. (1995). The psychoanalyst as participant and observer in the psychoanalytic process: Some thoughts on countertransference from a constructionist perspective. *Psychoanalysis and Contemporary Thought, 18*, 531-558.

Bromberg, P. M. (1991). On knowing one's patient inside out: The aesthetics of unconscious communion. *Psychoanalytic Dialogues, 5*, 55-71.

Bromberg, P. M. (1996). Standing in the spaces: The multiplicity of self and the psychoanalytic relationship. *Contemporary Psychoanalysis, 32*, 509-535.

Buckley, P., Conte, H. R., & Plutchik, R. (1994). Psychodynamic variables as predictors of psychotherapy. *American Journal of Psychiatry, 141*, 742-747.

Butler, J. M., & Rice, L. N. (1963). Adience, self-actualization and drive theory. In J. Wepman & R. Heine (Eds.), *Concepts of personality* (pp. 79-112). Chicago: Aldine.

Cantor, N., Mischel, W., & Schwartz, J. (1982). A prototype analysis of psychological situations. *Cognitive Psychology, 14*, 45-77.

Casement, P. (1991). *Learning from the patient.* New York: The Guilford Press.

Chasseguet-Smirgel, J. (1984). *Creativity and perversion.* London: Free Association Books.

Chodorow, N. (1978). *The reproduction of mothering: Psychoanalysis and the sociology of gender.* Berkeley: University of California Press.

Chodorow, N. (1996). Reflections on the authority of the past in psychoanalytic thinking. *Psychoanalytic Quarterly, 65*, 32-51.

Chused, J. (1992). The patient's perception of the analyst: The hidden transference. *Psycho-*

*analytic Quarterly, 61,* 161-184.
Chused J., & Raphling, C. (1992). The analyst's mistakes. *Journal of the American Psychoanalytic Association, 40,* 137-149.
Coen, S. (1996). Love between therapist and patient: A review. *American Journal of Psychotherapy, 50,* 14-27.
Cohen, M. B. (1952). Countertransference and anxiety. *Psychiatry, 15,* 231-243.
Comas-Diaz, L., & Greene, B. (1994) Overview: An ethnocultural mosaic. In L. Comas-Diaz & B. Greene (Eds.), *Women of color: Integrating ethnic and gender identities in psychotherapy* (pp. 3-9). New York: Guilford Press.
Comas-Diaz, L., & Jacobsen, F.M. (1991). Ethnocultural transference and countertransference in the therapeutic dyad. *American Journal of Orthopsychiatry, 61,* 392-402.
Connolly, M. B., Shappell, S., Barber, J. P., Luborsky, L., Shaffer, C., & Crits-Christoph, P. (1999). The relation of transference interpretations to outcome in the early sessions of brief supportive-expressive psychotherapy. *Psychotherapy Research, 9(4),* 485-495.
Cooper, A. M. (1987). Changes in psychoanalytical ideas: Transference interpretation. *Journal of the American Psychoanalytical Association,* 35, 77-98.
Cooper, S. (1993). Interpretive fallibility and the psychoanalytic dialogue. *Journal of the American Psychoanalytic Association, 41(1),* 95-123.
Covington, C. (1996). Purposive aspects of the erotic transference. *Journal of Analytical Psychology 41,* 339-352.
Crits-Christoph, P., & Barber, J. P. (Eds.). (1991). *Handbook of short-term dynamic psychotherapy.* New York: Basic Books.
Crits-Christoph, P., Barber, J. P., & Kurcias, J. S. (1993). The accuracy of therapists' interpretations and the development of the therapeutic alliance. *Psychotherapy Research, 3 (1),*25-35.
Crits-Christoph, P., Cooper, A., & Luborsky, L. (1988). The accuracy of therapists' interpretations and the outcome of dynamic psychotherapy. *Journal of Clinical and Consulting Psychology,56,* 490-495.
Crowley, R. M. (1988). Human reactions of analysts to patients. In B. Wolstein (Ed.), *Essential papers on countertransference* (pp.84-90). New York: New York University Press.
Cushman, P., & Gilford, P. (2000). Will managed care change our way of being? *American Psychologist, 55(9),* 985-996.
Dalenberg, C. (2000). *Countertransference and the treatment of trauma.* Washington, DC: American Psychological Association.
Damasio, A. R. (1994). *Descartes' error.* New York: Putnam.
Davanloo, H. (1978). *Principles and techniques of short-term dynamic psychotherapy.* New York: Spectrum.
Davanloo, H. (1990). *Unlocking the unconscious.* Chichester, England: Wiley.
Davies, J. M. (1994). Love in the afternoon: A relational reconsideration of desire and dread in the countertransference. *Psychoanalytic Dialogues, 4(2),* 153-170.
Davies, J. M., & Frawley, M. G. (1994). *Treating the adult survivor of childhood sexual abuse: A Psychoanalytic perspective.* New York: Basic Books.
DeLaCour, E. P. (1985). Aspects of transference interpretation. *Smith College Studies in Social Work, 56,* 1-14.
Deutsch, H. (1926). Occult processes during psychoanalysis. In G. Devereux (Ed.), *Psychoanalysis and the occult* (pp.133-146). New York: International Universities Press.
Dewald, P. A. (1994). *The supportive and active psychotherapies.* Northvale, NJ: Jason Aronson, Inc.

Deutsch, H. (1926). Occult processes during psychoanalysis. In G. Devereux (Ed.), *Psychoanalysis and the occult* (pp.133-146). New York: International Universities Press.

Dewald, P. A. (1994). *The supportive and active psychotherapies.* Northvale, NJ: Jason Aronson, Inc.

Diamond, M. J. (1989). Stagnation, chaos, and severe character neuroses. *Psychoanalytic Psychology, 6*, 455-473.

Dieckmann, H. (1976). Transference and countertransference: Results of a Berlin research group. *Journal of Analytical Psychology, 21,* 25-36.

DiPellegrino, G., Fadiga, L., Fogassi, L., & Rizzolatti, G. (1992). Understanding motor events: A neurophysiological study. *Experimental Brain Research, 91,* 176-180.

Doctor, R. (1999). Understanding the erotic and erotised transference and countertransference. In D. Mann (Ed.), *Erotic transference and countertransference: Clinical practice in psychotherapy* (pp. 89-98). New York: Routledge.

Dosamantes, I. (1992). The intersubjective relationship between therapist and patient: A key to understanding denied and denigrated aspects of the patient's self. *The Arts & Psychotherapy, 19,* 359-365.

Dreher, M., Mengele, U., Rainer, K., & Kammerer, A. (2001). Affective indicators of the psychotherapeutic process: An empirical case study. *Psychotherapy Research 11(1),* 99-117.

Edelson, M. (1984). *Hypothesis and evidence in psychoanalysis.* Chicago: University of Chicago Press.

Ehrenreich, J. H. 1989. Transference: Once concept or many? *Psychoanalytical Review, 76,* 37-65.

Eickhoff, F. W. (1979). Panel reports: Technical management of highly erotic transference. *International Journal of Psycho-Analysis, 78*, 587-591.

Elkind, S. N. (1992). *Resolving impasses in therapeutic relationships.* New York: Guilford Press.

Elliott, R. (1991). Five dimensions of therapy process. *Psychotherapy Research, 1*, 92-103.

Emde, R. (1988). Development terminable and interminable: Innate and motivational factors from infancy. *International Journal of Psycho-analysis, 69,* 23-42.

Epstein, L. (1977). The therapeutic function of hate in the countertransference. *Contemporary Psychoanalysis,* 13, 442-461.

Etchegoyen, R. H. (1978). Some thoughts on transference perversion. *International Journal of Psycho-Analysis, 59,* 45-53.

Fadiga, L., Fogassi, L., Pavesi, G., & Rizzolatti, G. Motor facilitation during action observation: A magnetic stimulation study. *Journal of Neurophysiology, 73,* 2608-2611.

Fast, I. (1992). Developments in gender identity: Gender differentiation in girls. *International Journal of Psycho-Analysis, 60,* 443-453.

Federmeier, K. D., & Kutas, M. (1999). Right words and left words: Electrophysiological evidence for hemispheric differences in meaning processes. *Cognitive Brain Research, 8,* 373-392.

Federmeier, K. D., & Kutas, M. (2002). Picture the difference: Electrophysiological investigations of picture processing in the two cerebral hemispheres. *Neuropsychologica, 40,* 730-747.

Feldman, M. (1997). Projective identification: The analyst's involvement. *International Journal of Psycho-Analysis, 78,* 227-241.

Ferenczi, S. (1909). *Sex in psychoanalysis.* New York: Basic Books.

Field, N. (1989). Listening with the body: An exploration in the countertransference. *British*

*Psychoanalytic Review, 73,* 103-120.
Foreman, S. A., & Marmar, C. R. (1985). Therapist actions that address initially poor therapeutic alliances in psychotherapy. *American Journal of Psychiatry, 142,* 922-926.
Fox, R. (1998). The "unobjectionable" positive countertransference. *Journal of the American Psychoanalytic Association, 46,* 1067-1087.
Frances, A., & Perry, S. (1983). Transference interpretations in focal therapy. *American Journal of Psychiatry, 140,* 405-409.
Franch, N. (1996). Transference and countertransference in the analysis of a child with autistic nuclei. *International Journal of Psycho-Analysis, 77,* 773-786.
Freeman, R. D. (2003). Cortical columns: A multi-parameter examination. *Cerebral Cortex, 13,* 70-72.
Fretter, P. B., Bucci, W., Broitman, J.,Silberschatz, G., & Curtin, J. T. (1994). How the patients' plan relates to the concept of transference. *Psychotherapy Research, 4(1),* 58-72.
Freud, S. (1900). The interpretation of dreams. *Standard Edition,* 5. London: Hogarth Press.
Freud, S. (1905). Fragment of an analysis of a case of hysteria. *Standard Edition,* 7: 1-122. London: Hogarth Press.
Freud, S. (1909). Notes upon a case of obsessional neurosis. *Standard Edition,* 10: 151-320. London: Hogarth Press.
Freud, S. (1910a). The future prospects of psychoanalytic therapy. *Standard Edition,* 11: 141-151. London: Hogarth Press.
Freud, S. (1910b). Five lectures on psycho-analysis. *Standard Edition,* 11:9-55. London: Hogarth Press.
Freud, S. (1912). The dynamics of transference. *Standard Edition,* 12: 99-108. London: Hogarth Press.
Freud, S. (1915). Observations on transference-love. *Standard Edition,* 12: 157-171. London: Hogarth Press.
Freud, S. (1917). Introductory lectures on psychoanalysis. *Standard Edition, 16:* 317-326.
Freud, S. (1919). The "uncanny." *Standard Edition, 17: 219-256.*
Freud, S. (1925). Negation. *Standard Edition,* 19: 233-239. London: Hogarth Press.
Freud, S. (1926). Inhibitions, symptoms, and anxiety. In J. Strachey (Ed. & Trans.), *Standard Edition, 20:* 87-151. London: Hogarth Press.
Freud, S. (1937). Analysis terminable and interminable. *Standard Edition,* 23: 209-253. London: Hogarth Press.
Freud, S. (1940). An outline of psychoanalysis. *Standard Edition,* 23: 139-207. London: Hogarth Press.
Freud, S., & Jung, C. G. (1974). *The Freud/Jung letters.* W. McGuire (Ed.) and R. Manheim and R. Hull (Trans.). Princeton, NJ: Princeton University Press.
Friedman, N., & Lavender, J. (1997). On receiving the patient's transference: The symbolizing and desymbolizing countertransference. *Journal of the American Psychoanalytic Association, 45,* 79-103.
Fromm, E. (1976). *The art of loving.* London: Unwin.
Gabbard, G. O. (Ed.). (1989). *Sexual exploitation in professional relationship.* Washington, DC: American Psychiatric Press.
Gabbard, G. O. (1994). Sexual excitement and countertransference love in the analyst. *Journal of the American Psychoanalytic Association, 42,* 1083-1106.
Gabbard, G. O. (1996). Therapeutic approaches to erotic transference. In F. Flack (Ed.), *The Hatherleigh guide to psychotherapy* (pp. 231-247). New York: Hatherleigh Press.
Gabbard, G. O. (2001) What can neuroscience teach us about transference? *Canadian Journal*

*of Psychoanalysis, 9 (1),* 1-18.

Gans, J. E. (1989). Hostility in group psychotherapy. *International Journal of Group Psychotherapy, 39,* 499-516.

Gardner, F. (1999). A sense of all conditions. In D. Mann (Ed.), *Erotic transference and countertransference: Clinical practice in psychotherapy* (pp. 139-149). New York: Routledge.

Garrett, T. (1994). Sexual contact between psychotherapists and their patients. In P. Clarkson and M. Pokorny (Eds.). *The handbook of psychotherapy* (pp. 260-281). London: Routledge.

Gassner, S., Sampson, H., Weiss, J., & Brumer, S. (1982). The emergence of warded-off contents. *Psychoanalysis and Contemporary Thought, 5(1),* 55-75.

Gazzaniga, M. (Ed.) (1995). *The cognitive neurosciences.* Cambridge, MA: The MIT Press.

Gedo, P. M., & Schaffer, N. (1989). An empirical approach to studying psychoanalytic process. *Psychoanalytic Psychology, 6,* 277-291.

Geller, J. D., Cooley, R. S., & Hartley, D. (1981-1982). Images of the psychotherapist: A theoretical and methodological perspective. *Imagination, Cognition and Personality, 1,* 123-146.

Gelso, C. J., & Hayes, J. A. (1998). *The psychotherapy relationship.* New York: John Wiley & Sons, Inc.

Gelso, C. J., Hill, C. E., & Kivlighan, D. M. (1991). Transference, insight, and the counselor's intentions during a counseling hour. *Journal of Counseling and Development, 69,* 428-433.

Gelso, C. J., Kivlighan, D. M., Wine, B., Jones, A., & Friedman, S. C. (1997). Transference, insight, and the course of time-limited therapy. *Journal of Counseling Psychology, 44,* 209-217.

Gerrard, J. (1999). Love in the time of psychotherapy. In D. Mann (Ed.), *Erotic transference and countertransference: Clinical practice in psychotherapy* (pp. 29-41). New York: Routledge.

Gilboa, E., & Revelle, W. (1994). Personality and the structure of affective responses. In S. H. M.. Van Goozen, N. E. Van de Poll, & J.A. Sergeant (Eds.), *Emotions: Essays on emotion Theory* (pp. 135-159). Hillsdale, HJ: Erlbaum.

Gill, M. M. (1982). *Analysis of transference* (Vol.1). New York: International Universities Press.

Giovacchini, P. L. (1960). On scientific creativity. *Journal of the American Psychoanalytic Association,8,*407-426.

Giovacchini, P. L. (1967). Frustration and externalization. *Psychoanalytic Quarterly, 36,* 571-583.

Giovacchini, P. L. (1974). Characterological factors and the creative personality. *Journal of the American Psychoanalytic Association, 19,* 524-542.

Giovaccini, P. (1979). *Treatment of primitive mental states.* New York: Jason Aronson.

Glover, E. (1927). Lectures on technique in psychoanalysis. *International Journal of Psycho-Analysis, 8,* 311-338.

Glover, E. (1955). *Technique of psycho-analysis.* New York: International Universities Press.

Goldin, V. (1985). Problems of techniques. In A. J. Horner (Ed.), *Treating the oedipal patient in brief psychotherapy* (pp. 55-85). Northvale, NJ: Jason Aronson, Inc.

Gomberoff, M., Noemi, C., & De Gomberoff, L. (1990). The autistic object: its relationship with narcissism in the transference and countertransference of neurotic and borderline patients. *International Journal of Psycho-Analysis, 71,* 249-259.

Gorkin, M. (1996). Countertransference in cross-cultural psychotherapy. In R. Perez-Foster, M. Moskowitz, & R.A. Javier (Eds.), *Reaching across boundaries of culture and class: Widening the scope of psychotherapy* (159-176). Northvale, NJ: Jason Aronson.

Gorney, J. W. (1978). The negative therapeutic reaction. *Contemporary Psychoanalysis, 15,* 288-337.

Graf, P., & Schacter, D. L. (1985). Implicit and explicit memory for new associations in normal subjects and amnesic patients. *Journal of Experimental Psychology, Learning, Memory, and Cognition, 11,* 501-511.

Graff, H., & Luborsky, L. L. (1977). Long-term trends in transference and resistance: A report on a quantitative-analytic method applied to four psychoanalyses. *Journal of the American Psychoanalytic Association, 25,* 471-490.

Grayer, E. D., & Sax, P. R. (1986). A model for the diagnostic and therapeutic use of countertransference. *Clinical Social Work Journal, 14,* 295-309.

Greenacre, P. (1954). The role of transference: Practical considerations in relation to psychoanalytic therapy. *Journal of the American Psychoanalytic Association, 2,* 671-684.

Greenson, R. R., & Wexler, M. (1969). The nontransference relationship in the psychoanalytic situation. *International Journal of Psycho-Analysis, 50,* 27-38.

Grigsby, J., & Stevens, D. (2000). *Neurodynamics of personality.* New York: Guilford.

Grinberg, L. 1997. Is the transference fear by the psychoanalyst? *International Journal Psycho-Analysis, 78,* 1-14.

Grindberg, L. (1962). On a specific aspect of countertransference due to the patients' projective identification. *International Journal of Psycho-Analysis, 43,* 436-440.

Grobstein, P. (1994). Variability in brain function and behavior. In V. S. Ramachandran (Ed.), *The encyclopedia of human behavior* (Vol. 4, pp. 447-458). New York: Academic Press.

Grobstein, P. (2003). Getting it less wrong, the brain's way: Science, pragmatism, and multiplism. In A.D. Ritvoi (Ed.), *Interpretation and its objects* (pp. 153-166). Amsterdam: Rodopi.

Grobstein, P. (2005). Making the unconscious conscious, and *vice versa*: A bi-directional bridge between neuroscience/cognitive science and psychotherapy? *Cortex, 41,* 663-668.

Grunebaum, H. (1986). Harmful psychotherapy experience. *American Journal of Psychotherapy, 40,* 165-176.

Guttman, H. A. (1985). Sexual issues in the transference and countertransference between female therapist and male patient. *Journal of the American Academy of Psychoanalysis, 12,* 187- 197.

Hackmann, A., & Holmes, E. A. (2004). Mental imagery and memory in psychopathology. *Memory, 12 (4),* 1-160.

Haesler, L. (1991). Relationship between extratransference interpretations and transference interpretations: A clinical study. International Journal of Psycho-Analysis, 72, 463-479.

Handley, N. (1995). The concept of transference: A critique. *British Journal of Psychotherapy, 12(1),* 49-59.

Hayes, J. A., Riker, J. R., & Ingram, K. M. (1997). Countertransference behavior and management in brief counseling: A field study. *Psychotherapy Research, 7,* 145-153.

Heath, S. (1991). *Dealing with the therapist's vulnerability to depression.* Northvale, NJ: Jason Aronson.

Heimann, P. (1950). On countertransference. *International Journal of Psycho-Analysis, 31,* 81-84.

Heimann, P. (1960). Countertransference. *British Journal of Medical Psychology, 33,* 9-15.

Henry, W. P. & Strupp, H. H. (1989). The Vanderbilt Center for psychotherapy research:

Aims of the research program. Paper presented in the meeting of the Society for Psychotherapy Research, Toronto.

Herron, W. G., & Rouslin, S. (1982). *Issues in psychotherapy.* Washington, DC: Orgin.

Hill, C. E., Nutt-Williams, E., Heaton, K. J., Thompson, B. J., & Rhodes, R. H. (1996). Therapist retrospective recall of impasses in long-term psychotherapy: A qualitative analysis. *Journal of Counseling Psychology, 43 (2)*, 207-217.

Hinshelwood, R. (1999). Countertransference. *International Journal of Psycho-Analysis, 80,* 797-818.

Hoffman, I. Z., & Gill, M. M. (1988). Critical reflections on a coding scheme. *International Journal of Psycho-Analysis, 69(55)*, 55-64.

Hoglend, P. (1993). Transference interpretations and long-term change after dynamic psychotherapy of brief to moderate length. *American Journal of Psychotherapy, 47,* 494-507.

Hoglend, P. (1996). Analysis of transference in patients with personality disorders. *Journal of Personality Disorders, 10(2),* 122-131.

Holmes, D. E. (1992). Race and transference in psychoanalysis and psychotherapy. *International Journal of Psycho-Analysis, 73, (1),* 1-11.

Holmes, J., & Lindley, R. L. (1991). *The values of psychotherapy.* Oxford: Oxford University Press.

Horowitz, M., Marmar, C., Krupnick, J. Wilner, N., Kaltreider, N., & Wallerstein, R. (1984). *Personality styles and brief psychotherapy.* New York: Basic Books.

Horvath, A., & Symond, D. B. (1991). Relation between working alliance and outcome in psychotherapy. *Journal of Counseling Psychology, 38*, 139-143.

Hsieh, J. C., Belfrage, M., Stone-Elander, S., Hannson, P. L., & Ingvar, M. (1995). Central representation of chronic ongoing neuropathic pain studied by positron emission tomography. *Pain, 64,* 303-314.

Hubble, J. P. (1999). Novel drugs for Parkinson's disease. *The Medical Clinics of North America, 83,* 525-536.

Isakower, O. (1963). Minutes of the New York psychoanalytic institute faculty meeting, October 14 (unpublished).

Issacharoff, A., & Hunt, W. (1978). Beyond countertransference. *Contemporary Psychoanalysis, 14 (2),* 291-310.

Jacobs, T. J. (1986). On countertransference enactments. *Journal of the American Psychoanalytical Association, 34,* 289-307.

Jacobson, J. G. (1993). Developmental observation, multiple models of the mind, and the therapeutic relationship in psychoanalysis. *Psychoanalytic Quarterly, 62*, 523-552.

James, M. (1960). Premature ego development: Some observations on disturbances in the first three months of life." *International Journal of Psycho-Analysis, 41*, 288-94.

Jehu, D. (1994). *Patients as victims.* Chichester, England: John Wiley.

Joseph, B. (1987). Projective identification: Clinical aspects. In J. Sandler (Ed.), *Projection, identification, and projective identification* (pp. 65-76). Madison, CT: International Universities Press.

Joyce, A. S., & Piper, W. E. (1993). The immediate impact of transference interpretation in short-term individual psychotherapy. *American Journal of Psychotherapy, 47,* 508-526.

Joyce, A. S., Duncan, S. C., & Piper, W. E. (1995). Task analysis of "working" responses to dynamic interpretation in short-term individual psychotherapy. *Psychotherapy Research, 5(1)*, 49-62.

Jung, C. G. (1921). Psychological types. *Collected works* (Vol. 20). Princeton, NJ: Bollin-

gen.
Jung, C. G. (1966). The archetypes and the collective unconscious. *Collected works* (Vol. 9, Pt. 1). Princeton, NJ: Bollingen.
Kahn, M. (1979) *Alienation in perversions*. New York: International Universities Press.
Kahn, M. (1997). *Between therapist and client: The new relationship* (Revised edition). New York: W. H. Freeman & Co.
Kalsched, D. (1996). *The inner world of trauma: Archetypal defenses of the personal spirit*. New York: Routledge.
Kampe, K. K., Frith, C.D., Dolan, R. J., & Frith, A. (2001). Reward value of attractiveness and gaze. *Nature, 413*, 589.
Kantrowitz, J. (1997). A different perspective on the therapeutic process: The impact of the patient on the analyst. *Journal of the American Psychoanalytic Association, 45*, 127-153.
Kaplan, L. (1991). *Female perversions: The temptations of Madame Bovary*. New York: Doubleday.
Kernberg, O. F. (1987). An ego psychology-object relations theory approach to the transference. *Psychoanalytic Quarterly, 56*, 97-221.
Kernberg, O. F. (1994). Love in the analytic setting. *Journal of the American Analytic Association, 42*, 1137-57.
Kernberg, O. W. (1975). *Borderline conditions and pathological narcissism*. New York: Jason Aronson.
Kernberg, P. (1998). Panel report: Sexuality in the analysis of adolescents: Its impact on the transference-countertransference. *International Journal of Psycho-Analysis, 78*, 366-367.
Kiesler, D. J. (1982b). Confronting the client-therapist relationship in psychotherapy. In J.C. Anchin & D. J. Kiesler (Eds.), *Handbook of interpersonal psychotherapy* (pp. 280-295). New York: Pergamon Press.
Kiesler, D. J., & Watkins, L. M. (1989). Interpersonal complementarity and the therapeutic alliance study of relationships in psychotherapy. *Psychotherapy, 26*, 183-194.
Klein, M. (1937). Love, guilt and reparation. In M. Klein & J. Riviere (Eds.). *Love, hate and reparation* (pp. 57-112). New York: Norton Library.
Klein, M. (1946). Notes on some schizoid mechanisms. *International Journal of Psycho-Analysis, 27*, 99-110.
Klein, M. (1952). The origins of transference. *International Journal of Psycho-Analysis, 33*, 433-438.
Klein, M . (1957). *Envy and gratitude*. London: Tavistock.
Kohut, H. (1971). *The analysis of the self.* New York: International University Press.
Kokotovic, A. M., & Tracey, T. J. (1990). Working alliance in the early phase of counseling. *Journal of Counseling Psychology, 37(1)*, 16-21.
Knox, J. M. (2001). Memories, fantasies, archetypes: An exploration of some connections between cognitive science and analytical psychology. *Journal of Analytical Psychology, 46 (4)*, 616-635.
Lambert, M. J. (2001). The effectiveness of psychotherapy. *Colorado Psychological Association Bulletin, 34*, 9,11,and 15.
Langs, R. (1979). The interactional dimension of countertransference. In L. Epstein & A. J. Feiner (Eds.), *Countertransference* (pp. 71-103). New York: Jason Aronson.
Larsson, K., & Ahlenius, S. (1999). Brain and sexual behavior. *Annals of the New York Academy f Sciences, 877*, 292-308.
Lasky, R. (1990). Catastrophic illness and the analyst's emotional reactions to it. *Interna-*

*tional Journal of Psycho-Analysis, 71*, 455-473.
Lear, J. (1993). An interpretation of transference. *International Journal of Psycho-Analysis, 74*, 739-755.
LeDoux, J. (1995). Emotion: Clues from the brain. *Annual Review of Psychoanalysis, 46*, 209-235.
LeDoux, J. (1998). The emotional brain: The mysterious underpinnings of emotion. New York: Simon & Schuster.
LeDoux, J. (2002). *Synaptic self: How our brains become who we are*. New York: Viking.
Leites, N. (1977). Transference interpretations *only*? *International Journal of Psycho-Analysis, 58*, 275-287.
Lester, E. 1985. The female analyst and the eroticized transference. *International Journal of Psycho-Analysis, 66*, 283-93.
Levin, F. (1997). Integrating some mind and brain views of transference: The phenomena. *Journal of the American Psychoanalytic Association, 45*, 1121-1151.
Levin, F. (1998). A brief history of analysis and cognitive neuroscience. *The American Psychoanalyst, 32*, 1-5.
Lewis, H. B. (1987). Shame and the narcissistic personality. In D. L. Nathanson (Ed.), *The many faces of shame* (pp. 93-132). New York: Guilford Press.
Lewis, M. (1995). Memory and psychoanalysis: A new look at infantile amnesia and transference. *Journal of the American Academy of Child and Adolescent Psychiatry, 34 (4)*, 405-417.
Lieberman, M. A., Yalom, I. D., & Miles, M. B. (1973). *Encounter groups: First facts*. New York: Basic Books.
Lipton, S. D. (1977). The advantages of Freud's technique as shown in his analysis of the Rat Man. *International Journal of Psycho-Analysis, 58*, 255-273.
Little, M. (1951). Countertransference and the patient's response to it. *International Journal of Psycho-Analysis, 32*,32-40.
Little, M. (1957). 'R'–The analyst's total response to his patient's needs. *International Journal of Psycho-Analysis, 38*, 240-254.
Loewald, H. W. (1986). Transference-countertransference. *Journal of the American Psychoanalytical Association, 34*, 275-289.
Looker, T. (1998). "Mama, why don't your feet touch the ground?: Staying with the body and the healing moment in psychoanalysis." In L. Aron and F.S. Anderson (Eds.), *Relational perspectives on the body* (pp. 237-262). Hillsdale, NJ: The Analytic Press.
Luborsky, L. (1984). *Principles of psychoanalytic psychotherapy: A manual for supportive-expressive treatment*. New York: Basic Books.
Luborsky, L., Crits-Christoph, P., Mintz, J., & Auerbach, A. (1988). *Who will benefit from psychotherapy*. New York: Basic Books.
Lyons-Ruth, K. (2000). I sense that you sense that I sense…: Sander's recognition process and the specificity of relational moves in the psychotherapeutic setting. *Infant Mental Health Journal, 21*, 85-98.
Macalpine, I. (1959). The development of the transference. *Psychoanalytic Quarterly, 19*, 501-539.
MacLean, P. D. (1990). *The triune brain in evolution: Role in palaeocerebral functions*. New York: Plenum Press.
Malan, D. H. (1976a). *The frontier of brief psychotherapy*. New York: Plenum Press.
Malan, D. H. (1976b). *Toward the validation of dynamic psychodynamic psychotherapy*. New York: Plenum Press.
Mandal, M. K., & Ambady, N. (2004). Laterality and universality of facial expressions of

emotions: The interface. *Behavioural Neurology, 15*, 23-34.

Mann, D. (1973). *Time-limited psychotherapy.* Cambridge, MA: Harvard University Press.

Mann, D. (1999). Clinical practice in psychotherapy. In D. Mann (Ed.), *Erotic transference and countertransference* (pp. 1-25). New York: Routledge.

Marmar, C. R., Gaston, L., & Thompson, L. W. (1989). Alliance and outcome in late life depression. *Journal of Nervous Mental Disease, 177*, 464-472.

Marmor, J. (1989). The future of dynamic psychotherapy. *International Journal of Short-Term Psychotherapy, 4(4)*, 259-284.

Maroda, K. (1995). Projective identification and countertransference interventions: Since feeling is first. *Psychoanalytic Review, 82(2)*, 229-247.

Maroda, K. (2000). On homoeroticism, erotic countertransference, and the postmodern view of life: A commentary of papers by Rosiello, Tholfsen, and Meyers. *Journal of Gay and Lesbian Psychotherapy, 4 (2)*, 61-70.

Marziali, E. A. (1984). Prediction of outcome of brief psychotherapy from therapist interpretive interventions. *Archives of General Psychiatry, 41*, 301-304.

Marziali, E. A., & Sullivan, J. M. (1980). Methodological issue in the content analysis of brief psychotherapy. *British Journal of Medical Psychology, 53*,19-27.

Mathew, R. J.; Wilson, W. H.; Turkington, T. G.; & Coleman, R. E. (1998). Cerebellar activity and disturbed time sense after THC. *Brain Research, 792 (2)*, 183-189.

Matte Blanco, I. 1975). *The unconscious as infinite sets: An essay in bi-logic.* London: Duckworth.

McCullough, L., & Winston, A. (1991). The Beth Israel psychotherapy research program. In L. Beutler & M. Crago (Eds.). *Psychotherapy research: An international review of programmatic studies* (pp. 525-533). Washington, DC: American Psychological Association Press.

McCullough, L., Winston, A., Farber, B. A., Porter, F., Pollack, J., Laikin, M., Vingiano, W., & Trujillo, M. (1991). The relationship of patient-therapist interaction to outcome in brief psychotherapy. *Psychotherapy, 28*, 525-533.

McDougall, J. (1978). Primitive communication and the use of countertransference. *Contemporary Psychoanalysis, 14*, 173-209.

McGoldrick, M., Giordano, J., & Pearce, J. (Eds.) (1996). *Ethnicity and family therapy.* New York: Guilford.

McLaughlin, J. T. (1990). Clinical and theoretical aspects of enactment. *Journal of the American Psychoanalytic Association, 18*, 595-614.

Meares, R., Stevenson, J., & Comerford, A. (2005). Distinct pattern of P3a event and related in borderline personality disorders. *NeuroReport, 16*, 289-293.

Meissner, W. (1996). *The therapeutic alliance.* New Haven, CN: Yale University Press.

Menninger, K. (1942). *Love against hate.* New York: Harcourt, Brace.

Mishne, J. (2003). *Multiculturalism and the therapeutic process.* New York: Guilford.

Modell, A. H. (1980). Affects and their non-communication. *International Journal of Psycho-Analysis, 61*, 259-267.

Mohr, D. C. (1995). Negative outcome in psychotherapy: A critical review. *Clinical Psychology: Science and Practice, 2 (1)*, 1-27.

Money-Kyrle, R. (1956). Normal counter-transference and some of its deviations. In D. Meltzer & E. O'Shaughnessey (Eds.), *The collected papers of Roger Money-Kyrle* (pp. 330-342). Strathtay, Perthshire: Clunie Press.

Mordecai, E. M. (1991). A classification of empathic failures for psychotherapists and supervisors. *Psychoanalytic Psychology, 8*, 251-161.

Myerson, P. (1993). Listening for the effects of psychoanalytic interventions. *Contemporary Psychoanalysis, 29*, 397-417.

Nathanson, D. L. (1992). The nature of therapeutic impasse. *Psychoanalytic Annuals, 22*, 509-513.

Nunberg, H. (1951). Transference and reality. *International Journal of Psycho-Analysis, 32*, 1-9. O'Crowley, A. M. (1999). The analysis of the transference: Interpretation and changes in psychotherapy. *Dissertation Abstracts International: Section B: the Sciences & Engineering, 60(4-B)*, 1866.

Ogden, T. H. (1982). *Projective identification and psychotherapeutic technique*. New York: Jason Aronson.

Ogden, T. H. (1994). The concept of interpretive action. *Psychoanalytic Quarterly, 63 (2)*, 219-245.

Olds, D. D. (1994). Connectionism and psychoanalysis. *Journal of the American Psychoanalytic Association, 42*, 581-612.

Olinick, S. (1996). An aspect of transference: The struggle to become an analysand. *Journal of the American Psychoanalytic Association, 44 (2)*, 475-489.

Olnick, S. (1969). On empathy and regression in the service of the other. *British Journal of Medical Psychology, 42*, 41-49.

Oschman, J. L., & Oschman, N. H. (1995) Somatic recall: Part 1–Soft tissue memory. *Massage Therapy Journal, 34(3)*, 60-65.

Oschman, J. L., & Oschman, N. H. (1995) Somatic recall: Part 1–Soft tissue holography. *Massage Therapy Journal, 34(3)*, 66-74.

Pally, R. (1996). Reciprocal responsiveness in psychoanalysis. *Journal of Clinical Psychoanalysis, 5*, 7-23.

Pally, R. (1997). Developments in neuroscience: II How the brain actively constructs perceptions. *International Journal of Psycho-Analysis, 78*, 1021-1030.

Pally, R. (1998). Emotional processing: The mind-body connection. *International Journal of Psycho-Analysis, 79*, 349-362.

Pally, R. (2000). *The mind-brain relationship*. New York: Karnac Books.

Pally, R. (2001). A primary role for nonverbal communication in psychoanalysis. *Psychoanalytic Inquiry, 21*, 71-94.

Pally, R., (2005). Non-conscious prediction and a role for consciousness in correcting prediction errors. *Cortex, 41*, 643-662.

Panksepp, J. (1998). *Affective neuroscience: The foundations of human and animal emotions*. New York: The Oxford Press.

Patton, M. J., Kivlighan, D. M., & Multon, K. D. (1997). The Missouri psychoanalytic counseling research project: Relation of changes in counseling process and outcome. *Journal of Counseling Psychology, 44*, 189-208.

Pavan, L., & Mangini, E. (1992). Brief psychotherapy focused on separation. *International Journal of Short-Term Psychotherapy, 7*, 231-242.

Pearlman, L. A., & Saakvitne, K. W. (1995). *Trauma and the therapist: Countertransference and vicarious traumatization in psychotherapy with incest survivors*. New York: Norton.

Pearson, M. (1995). Problems with transference interpretations in short-term dynamic therapy. *British Journal of Psychotherapy, 12*, 37-48.

Perna, P. A. (1997). Reflections on the therapeutic system as seen from the science of chaos and Complexity: Implications for research and treatment. In F. Masterpasqua & P. A. Perna (Eds.), *The psychological meaning of chaos: Translating theory into practice* (pp. 253-272). Washington, DC: American Psychological Association.

Person, E. S. (1995). The erotic transference in women and in men: Differences and consequences. *Journal of the American Psychoanalytic Association, 43*, 159-180.

Pessier, J., & Stuart, J. (2000). A new approach to the study of therapeutic work in the transference. *Psychotherapy Research, 10*, 169-180.

Piaget, J. (1954). *The construction of reality in the child.* New York: Basic Books.

Piaget, J. (1962). *Play, dreams, and imitation in childhood.* New York: Norton.

Pick, I. B. (1985). Working through the countertransference. *International Journal of Psycho-Analysis, 66*, 157-166.

Pick, I. B. (1997). Working through in the countertransference. In R. Schafer (Ed.), *The contemporary Kleinians of London* (pp. 348-367). Madison, CN: International University Press.

Piper, W. E., Azim, H. F. A., Anthony, J., & McCallum, M. (1991). Transference interpretations, therapeutic alliance, and outcome in short-term individual psychotherapy. *Archives of General Psychiatry, 48*, 946-957.

Piper, W. E., Debbane, E. G., Bienvenu, J. P., de Carufel, F., & Garant, J. (1986). Relationships between the object focus of therapist interventions and outcome in short-term individual psychotherapy. *British Journal of Medical Psychotherapy, 59*, 1-11.

Piper, W. E., McCallum, M., Azim, H. F. A., & Joyce, A. S. (1993). Understanding the relationship between transference interpretation and outcome in the context of other variables. *American Journal of Psychotherapy, 47*, 479-493.

Piper, W. D., Joyce, A.S., Rosie, J. S., Ogrundiczuk, J. S., McCallum, M., O'Kelley, J. G., & Steinberg, R. I. (1999). Prediction of dropping out in time-limited, interpretive individual psychotherapy. *Psychotherapy, 36(2)*, 114-122.

Plakun, E. M. (1998). Enactments and the treatment of abuse survivors. *Harvard Review of Psychiatry(5), 6*, 318-325.

Pollack, J., & Horner, A. (1985). Brief adaptation-oriented psychotherapy. In A. Winston (Ed.).*Clinical and research issues in short-term dynamic psychotherapy* (pp. 58-79). Washington, DC: American Psychiatric Press.

Pope, K. S., Sonne, J. L., & Holroyd, J. (1994). *Sexual feelings in psychotherapy: Explorations for therapists and therapists in training.* Washington, DC: American Psychological Association.

Porges, S. W., Doussard-Roosevelt, J. A., & Maiti, A. K. (1994). Vagal tone and the physiological regulation of emotion. *Monograph of the Society for Research in Child Development, 59,*167-186.

Postner, L. (1994). The nullo protein is a component of the actinmyosin network that mediates cellularization in Drosophila melanogaster embryos. *Journal of Cell Science, 107*, 1863.

Pribam, K. (1971). *The Language of the brain.* Englewood Cliffs, NJ: Prentice-Hall.

Prodan, C., Orbelo, D. M., Testa, J. A., & Ross, E. D. (2001). Hemispheric differences in recognizing upper and lower facial displays of emotion. *Neuropsychiatry, Neuropsychology, and Behavioral Neurology, 14*, 206-213.

Pulver, S. E. (1992). Impasses in psychodynamic psychotherapy. *Psychiatric Annals, 22*, 514-519.

Racker, H. (1953). A contribution to the problem of counter-transference. *International Journal of Psycho-Analysis, 34*, 313-324.

Racker, H. (1953). A contribution to the problem of countertransference. *International Journal of Psycho-Analysis, 34*, 313-324.

Racker, H. (1968). *Transference and countertransference.* New York: International Universities Press.

Racker, H. (1972). The meanings and uses of countertransference. *Psychoanalytic Quarterly, 41*, 487-506.
Rank, O., & Ferenczi, S. (1925). *The development of psychoanalysis* (C. Newton, Trans.). New York: Nervous and Mental Diseases Publishing Company.
Rayner, E. (1995). Is there any logic in feelings? An introduction to Matte Blanco's theory of emotions. *British Journal of Psychotherapy, 12*, 242.
Reik, T. (1937). *Surprise and the psychoanalyst.* New York: E.P. Dutton.
Reich. A. (1951). On counter-transference. *International Journal of Psycho-Analysis, 32*, 25-31.
Renik, O. 1990. The concept of a transference neurosis and psychoanalytic methodology. *International Journal of Psycho-Analysis, 71*, 197-204.
Renik, O. 1993. Analytic interaction: conceptualizing technique in the light of the analyst's irreducible subjectivity. *Psychoanalytic Quarterly, 62*, 518-532.
Renik, O. (1995). The ideal of the anonymous analyst and the problem of self-disclosure. *Psychoanalytic Quarterly, 64*, 585-591.
Reviere, P. L. (1996). *Memory of childhood trauma: A clinician's guide to the literature.* New York: The Guilford Press.
Rioch, J. M. (1943). The transference phenomenon in psychoanalytic therapy. *Psychiatry, 6*, 147-156.
Rizzolatti, G., & Fadiga, L. (1995). "Motor facilitation during action observation: a magneticstimulation study. *Journal of Neurophysiology, 73 (6)*, 2608-2611.
Rizzuto, A. (1993). Respect in clinical practice. *Journal of Psychotherapy–Practice and Research, 2(4)*, 277-279.
Rosiello, F. (2000). *Deepening intimacy in psychotherapy: Using the erotic transference and countertransference.* Northvale, NJ: Jason Aronson.
Rotenburg, V. S. (1994). An integrative psychobiological approach to brain hemisphere functions in schizophrenia. *Neuroscience and Biobehavioral Reviews, 18*, 487-495.
Roth, P. (2001). Mapping the landscape: Levels of transference interpretation. T*he International Journal of Psychoanalysis, 82*, 533-543.
Rothschild, B. (2000). *The body remembers: The psychobiology of trauma and trauma treatment.* New York: Norton.
Ryle, A. (1994). Projective identification: A particular form of reciprocal role procedure. *British Journal of Medical Psychology, 67*, 107-114.
Russell, J. (1993). *Out of bounds: Sexual exploitation in counseling and therapy.* London: Sage.
Sampson, H. (1992). The role of "real" experienced in psychopathology and treatment. *Psychoanalytic Dialogues, 2(4)*, 509-528.
Sandler, J. (1976). Countertransference and role responsiveness. *International Review of Psychoanalysis, 3*, 43-47.
Scaer, R. C. (2001). *Trauma, dissociation, and disease: The body bears the burden.* New York: Haworth.
Scaer, R. C. (2005). *The trauma spectrum: Hidden wounds and human resiliency.* New York: Norton & Co.
Schacter, D., Curran, T., Ballucio, L., Milberg, W. P., & Bates, J. F. (1996). False recognition and the right frontal lobe: A case study. *Neuropsychologica, 34*, 793-808.
Schafer, R. (1959). Generative empathy in the treatment situation. *Psychoanalytic Quarterly, 28*, 342-373.
Schafer, R. (1968). *Aspects of internalization.* New York: International Universities Press.

Schafer, R. (1977). The interpretation of transference and the conditions for loving. *Journal of the American Psychoanalytic Association, 25,* 335-362.

Schafer, R. (1982). The relevance of the "here and now" transference interpretation to the reconstruction of early development. *International Journal of Psycho-Analysis, 63,*77-82.

Schafer, R. (1983). *The analytic attitude.* New York: Basic Books.

Schafer, R. (1986). Discussion of transference and countertransference in brief therapy. In Helen C. Meyers (Ed.), *Between analyst and patient* (pp.143-157). Hillsdale, NJ: Analytic Press.

Schafer, R. (1997). Vicissitudes of remembering in the countertransference: Fervent failure, colonization and remembering otherwise. *International Journal of Psycho-Analysis, 78,* 1151-1163.

Schaverien, J. (1997). Men who leave too soon: Reflections on the erotic transference and countertransference. *British Journal of Psychotherapy 14,* 3-16.

Schnider, A., & Ptak, R. (1999). Spontaneous confabulators fail to suppress currently irrelevant memory trances. *Nature Neuroscience, 2,* 677-681.

Schore, A. N. (1994). *Affect regulation and the origin of the self.* Hillsdale, NJ: Lawrence Erlbaum.

Schore, A. N. (1999). Commentary on emotions: Neuro-psychoanalytic views. *Neuropsychoanalysis, 1,* 49-55.

Schore, A. N. (2001b). Minds in the making: Attachment, the self-organizing brain, and developmentally-oriented psychoanalytic psychotherapy. *British Journal of Psychotherapy, 17,* 299-328.

Schore, A. N. (2001a). The effects of early relational trauma on right brain development, affect regulation, and infant mental health. *Infant Mental Health Journal, 22,* 210-266.

Schore, A. N. (2003a). *Affect dysregulation and disorders of the self.* New York: W.W. Norton & Company.

Schore, A. N. (2003b). *Affect regulation and the repair of the self.* New York: W.W. Norton & Company.

Schwaber, E. (1990). Interpretation and the therapeutic action of psychoanalysis. *Journal of Psycho-Analysis, 71,* 229-240.

Searles, H. (1959). Oedipal love in the countertransference. In *Collected papers on schizophrenia.* (1965). London: Hogarth Press.

Searles, H. (1975). The patient as therapist to his analyst/Nontransference. In P. Giovacchini (Ed.), *Tactics and techniques in psychoanalytic therapy: Countertransference* (Vol. II, pp. 95-151). New York: Jason Aronson.

Searles, H. (1979). *Countertransference and related subjects in selected papers.* New York: International Universities Press.

Seligman, S. (1999). Integrating Kleinian theory and intersubjecvtive research: Observing projective identification. *Psychoanalytic Dialogues, 9,* 129-159.

Shapiro, F. (1995). *Eye movement desensitization and reprocessing: Basic principles, protocols, and procedures.* New York: Guilford

Sharpe, E. (1930). The technique of psychoanalysis. *International Journal of Psycho-Analysis, 2,* 361-386.

Sharpe, E. F. (1947). The psycho-analyst. *International Journal of Psycho-Analysis, 28,* 1-6.

Sheldrake, R. (1988). *The presence of the past.* London: Collins.

Shevrin, H. (1998). Psychoanalytic and neuroscience research. *The American Psychoanalyst, 32,* 40-54.

Shevrin, H., Ghannam, J. & Libet, B. (2002). Response to commentary on "A neural corre-relate of consciousness related to repression. *Consciousness and Cognition, 11(2)*, 345-346.

Shuren, J. E., & Grafman, J. (2002). The neurology of reasoning. *Archives of Neurology, 59*,916-919.

Sifneos, P. E. (1979). *Short term dynamic psychotherapy: Evaluation and technique* (2nd ed.). New York: Plenum Press.

Silberschatz, G., Fretter, P. B., & Curtin, T. (1986). How do interpretations influence the process of psychotherapy? *Journal of Consulting and Clinical Psychology, 54*, 646-652.

Singer, B., & Luborsky, L. (1977). Countertransference: A comparison of what is known from the clinical vs. quantitative research. In A. Gurman & A. Razin (Eds.), *The therapists' contribution to effective psychotherapy: An empirical assessment* (pp. 182-202). New York: Pergamon.

Slap, J. W., & Slap-Shelton, L. (1991) *The schema in clinical psychoanalysis*. Hillsdale, NJ: Analytic Press.

Slochower, J. 1999. Erotic complications. *International Journal of Psycho-Analysis, 80*, 1119-1130.

Smith, H. (1990). Cues: The perceptual edge of the transference. *International Journal of Psycho-Analysis, 71*, 219-228.

Smith, H. (2000). Countertransference, conflictual listening, and the analytic object relationship. *Journal of the American Psychoanalytic Association, 48*, 95-128.

Solomon, M. F. (1997). On love and lust in therapeutic treatment. In M. F. Solomon & J. P. Siegel (Eds.), *Countertransference in couples therapy* (pp. 136-154). New York: W. Norton & Company.

Spence, D. (1987). *The Freudian metaphor*. New York: Norton.

Spence, D., Shapiro, D., & Zaidel, E. (1996). The role of the right hemisphere in the physiological and cognitive components of emotional processing. *Psychophysiology, 33*, 112-122,

Spotnitz, M. (1976). *Psychotherapy of preoedipal conditions*. New York: Jason Aronson.

Springer, A. (1996). Female perversion: Scenes and strategies in analysis and culture. *Journal of Analytic Psychology, 42*, 325-338.

Stacy, S. C. (1998). Exploring the role of psychic conflict and development deficit in erotically charged transferences. *Dissertation Abstracts International: Section B: The Sciences & Engineering, 58(12;B)*, 6828.

Stark, M. (1994). *Primer on working with resistance*. New York: Jason Aronson.

Stein, M. (1981). The unobjectionable part of the transference. *Journal of the American Psychoanalytic Association, 29*, 869-891.

Stein, G. S. (1993). A transference psychosis. *Journal of Clinical Psychoanalysis, 2*, 345-262.

Stein, R. (1974). *Incest and human love*. Baltimore: Penguin.

Sternberg, W. F., Bailin, D., Grant, M., & Gracely, R.H. (1998). Competition alters the perception of noxious stimuli in male and female athletes. *Pain, 76*, 231-238.

Stoller, R. (1975). *Perversion: The erotic form of hatred*. New York: Pantheon.

Stolorow, R. D. (1993). An intersubjective view of the therapeutic process. *Bulletin of Menninger Clinic, 57*, 450-457.

Stone, M. H. (1984). *Transference and its context*. New York: Jason Aronson.

Strachey, J. (1934, 1969). The nature of the therapeutic action of psychoanalysis. *International Journal of Psycho-Analysis, 50*, 275-291.

Straker, M. (1968). Brief psychotherapy in an outpatient clinic: Evolution and evaluation.

*American Journal of Psychiatry, 124,* 1219.
Strean, A. (1983). *The sexual dimension.* New York: The Free Press.
Strean, A. (1993). *Therapists who have sex with their patients.* New York: Brunner/Mazel.
Strupp, H. H. (1980). Success and failure in time-limited psycho-therapy. *Archives of General Psychiatry, 37,* 947-954.
Strupp, H. H. (1989). Can the practitioner learn from the researcher? *American Psychologist, 44,*717-724.
Strupp, H. H., & Binder, J. L. (1984). *Psychotherapy in a new key: A guide to time-limited dynamic psychotherapy.* New York: Basic Books.
Strupp, H. H., & Hadley, S. W. (1979). Specific versus nonspecific factors in psychotherapy: A controlled study of outcome. *Archives of General Psychiatry, 36,* 1125-1136.
Strupp, H. H., Hadley, S. W., & Gomes-Schwartz, R. (1977). *Psychotherapy for better or worse: An analysis of the problem of negative effects.* New York: Jason Aronson.
Sue, D. W., & Sue, D. (1999). *Counseling the culturally different: Theory and practice* (3rd ed.). New York: Wiley.
Sullivan, H. S. (1954). *The psychiatric interview.* New York: Norton.
Swift, W. J. & Wonderlich, S. A. (1990). Interpretation of transference in the psychotherapy of adolescents and young adults. *Journal of the American Academy of Child and Adolescent Psychiatry, 29,* 929-935.
Tansey, M. J. (1994). Sexual attraction and phobic dread in the countertransference. *Psychoanalytic Dialogue, 4,* 139-152.
Tancredi, L. R. (2005). *Hardwired behavior: What neuroscience reveals about morality.* New York: Cambridge University Press.
Tower, L. E. (1956). Countertransference. *Journal of the American Psychoanalytic Association, 4,* 224-255.
Treurniet, N. (1993). What is psychoanalysis now? *International Journal of Psycho-Analysis, 74,* 873-891.
Tucker, D. M. (1992). Developing emotions and cortical networks. In M. R. Gunnar & C. A. Nelson (Eds.), *Minnesota symposium on child psychology: Developmental behavioral neuroscience* (Vol. 24, pp. 75-128). Mahwah, NJ: Erlbaum.
Ulanov, A. (1984). Transference/countertransference: A Jungian perspective. In M. Stein (Ed.), *Jungian analysis* (pp. 68-86). Evanston, IL: Northwestern University Press.
van der Kolk, B. A. (1989). Compulsion to repeat the trauma: Reenactment, revictimization, and masochism. *The Psychiatric Clinics of North America, 12,* 389-411.
van der Kolk, B. A. (1996). The body keeps the score: Approaches to the psychobiology of posttraumatic stress disorder. In B. A. van der Kolk, A. C. McFarlane, & L. Weisaeth (Eds.), *Traumatic stress: The effects of overwhelming experience on mind, body and society* (214-241). New York: The Guilford Press.
Vanaerschot, G. (1997). Empathic resonance as a source of experience-enhancing interventions. In A. C. Bohart & L. Greenberg (Eds.), *Empathy reconsidered: New directions in psychotherapy* (pp. 141-165). Washington, DC: American Psychological Association.
Vaslamatizis, G., & Verveniotis, G. (1985). Early dropouts in brief dynamic psychotherapy. *Psychotherapy Psychosomatics, 44,* 205-210.
Vaughan, S. (1998). The un-remembrance of things past: On the link between implicit memory and transference. *The American Psychoanalyst, 32,* 12-19.
Viederman, S. (1974). Interpretation in the analytic space. *International Review of Psychoanalysis, 1,* 467-480.
Volkan, V. (1995) *Six steps in the treatment of borderline personality organization.*

Northvale, NJ: Jason Aronson, Inc.
Waldron, S., Jr. (1997). How can we study the efficacy of psychoanalysis? *Psychoanalytic Quarterly, 66*, 283-322.
Wallach, M. S., & Strupp, H. H. (1960). Psychotherapists' clinical judgments and attitudes towards patients. *Journal of Consulting Psychology, 24*, 316-323.
Wallerstein, J. (1990). Transference and countertransference in clinical intervention with divorcing families. *American Journal of Orthopsychiatry, 60*, 337-345.
Ware, R. C. (1995). Scylla and Charybdis: Sexual abuse or "false memory syndrome"?: Therapy-induced memories of sexual abuse. *Journal of Analytical Psychology, 40*, 5-22.
Weatherill, R. (2000). The seduction of psychotherapy. *British Journal of Psychotherapy, 16*,339-350.
Weiner, M. F. (1974). The psychotherapeutic impasse. *Diseases of the Nervous System, 35*, 258-261.
Weiss, J., & Sampson, H. (1986). *The psychoanalytic process*. New York: Guilford Press.
Wells, J., & Wrye, H. (1991). The maternal erotic countertransference. *International Journal of Psycho-Analysis, 72*, 93-106.
West, J. J., & Schain-West, J. (1997). Envy in the countertransference. In M. J. Solomon and J. P.Siegel (Eds.), *Countertransference in couples therapy* (pp. 126-135). New York: W. Norton & Company.
Westen, D. (1988). Transference and information processing. *Clinical Psychology Review, 8*, 161-179.
Westen, D., & Gabbard, G. O. (2002). Developments in cognitive neuroscience: II. Implications for theories of transference. *The Journal of the Psychoanalytic Association, 50*, 99-134.
Westen, D. (1998). The scientific legacy of Sigmund Freud: Toward a psychodynamically informed psychological science. *Psychological Bulletin, 124*, 333-371.
Wheeler, M. A., Stuss, D. T., & Tulving, E. (1997). Toward a theory of episodic memory: The frontal lobes and autonoetic consciousness. *Psychological Bulletin, 121*, 331-354.
Wicker, B., Michel, F., Henaff, M. A., & Decety, J. (1998). Brain regions involved in the perception of gaze: A PET study. *Neuroimage, 8*, 221-227.
Wicker, B.; Keysers, C.; Plailly, J.; Royet, J.; Gallese, V.; & Rizzolatti, G. (2003). Both of us disgusted in my insula: The common neural basis of seeing and feeling disgust. *Neuron. 40*, 655-664.
Wilber, K. (1982). *The holographic paradigm and other paradoxes*. Boulder, CO: New Science Library.
Wilkinson, M. (2003). Undoing trauma: contemporary neuroscience. *Journal of Analytical Psychology, 48*, 235-243.
Willick, M. S. (2001). Psychoanalysis and schizophrenia: A cautionary tale. *The Journal of the American Psychoanalytic Association, 49 (1)*, 27-56.
Willingham, D. B., Salidis, J., & Gabrieli, J. (2002). Direct comparison of neural systems mediating conscious and unconscious skill learning. *The Journal of Neurophysiology, 88 (2)*, 1451-1460.
Wilson, A. (1993). Hierarchical concepts in psychoanalysis. In A. Wilson & J. Gedo (Eds.), *Hierarchical concepts in psychoanalysis: Theory, research, and clinical practice* (pp. 311-324). NY: Guilford Press.
Wilson, A., & Weinstein, L. (1996). The transference and the zone of proximal development. *Journal of the American Psychoanalytic Association, 44*, 167-200.
Winnicott, D. W. (1949). Hate in the counter-transference. In *Collected papers*. London:

Tavistock.
Winnicott, D. W. (1956). Primary maternal preoccupation. In J. D. Sutherland (Ed.), *Through pediatrics to psychoanalysis* (pp. 300-305). London: Hogarth [The International Psycho-
Analytical Library].
Winnicott, D. W. (1958). *Collected papers.* New York: Basic Books.
Winnicott, D. W. (1960). Countertransference. *British Journal of Medical Psychiatry, 33,* 17-21.
Winnicott, D. W. (1965). *The maturational processes and the facilitating environment.* New York: International Universities Press.
Winnicott, D. W. (1971). *Playing and reality.* London: Tavistock.
Winnicott, D. W. (1975). *Through paediatrics to psycho-analysis.* New York: Basic Books.
Winnicott, D. W. (1988). *Human nature.* London: Free Association Press.
Winston, A., McCullough, L., & Laikin, M. (1993). Clinical and research implications of patient-therapist interaction in brief psychotherapy. *American Journal of Psychotherapy, 47,* 527-539.
Wittig, R., Nessling, M., Will, R. D., Mollenhauer, J., Salowsky, R., Munstermann, E., Schick, M. Helmbach, H., Gschwendt, B., Kom, B., Kioschis, P., Lichter, P., Schadendorf, D., & Poustka, A. (2002). Candidate genes for cross-resistance against DNA-damaging drugs. *Cancer Research, 62 (22),*
Wolf, E. (1988). *Treating the self.* New York: The Guilford Press.
Wolstein, B. (1996). The analysis of transference as an interpersonal process. *American Journal of Psychotherapy, 50,* 499-509.
Wrye, H. K., & Welles, J. K. (1989). The maternal erotic transference. *International Journal of Psycho-Analysis, 70,* 673-684.
Yehuda, R. (1998). *Psychological trauma.* Washington, DC: American Psychiatric Press.
Zetzel, E. R. (1970). *The capacity for emotional growth.* New York: International Universities

# INDEX

# ABOUT THE AUTHOR

Judith Schaeffer, Ph.D., O.S.F., is a psychologist on the staff of Franciscan Community Counseling in Colorado Springs, Colorado. For the past 25 years she has provided psychotherapy for both insured and uninsured individuals, couples, and families. At the present time, she also supervises doctoral interns and serves on the Sexual Abuse Investigation Team of the Diocese of Colorado Springs.

Dr. Schaeffer earned her doctorate in counseling psychology from Loyola University of Chicago and did her residency at the Children and Youth Center of St. Joseph Hospital in Memphis, Tennessee. She has served on the board of the Colorado Psychological Association and the Psychological Society of the Pikes Peak Region.

Dr. Schaeffer has published in *Human Development, Colorado Psychological Association Bulletin, American Journal of Psychotherapy, and Journal of Post-Traumatic Stress.*

www.ingramcontent.com/pod-product-compliance
Ingram Content Group UK Ltd.
Pitfield, Milton Keynes, MK11 3LW, UK
UKHW041142300926
15471UKWH00011B/100

9 780761 836315